Benjamin Kleidt

The Use of Hybrid Securities

WIRTSCHAFTSWISSENSCHAFT

ebs Forschung
Schriftenreihe der
EUROPEAN BUSINESS SCHOOL
International University Schloß Reichartshausen

Herausgegeben von
Univ.-Prof. Dr. Utz Schäffer

Band 54

Die EUROPEAN BUSINESS SCHOOL (ebs) – gegründet im Jahr 1971 – ist Deutschlands älteste private Wissenschaftliche Hochschule für Betriebswirtschaftslehre im Universitätsrang. Dieser Vorreiterrolle fühlen sich ihre Professoren und Doktoranden in Forschung und Lehre verpflichtet. Mit der Schriftenreihe präsentiert die EUROPEAN BUSINESS SCHOOL (ebs) ausgewählte Ergebnisse ihrer betriebs- und volkswirtschaftlichen Forschung.

Benjamin Kleidt

The Use of Hybrid Securities

Market Timing, Investor Rationing, Signaling and Asset Restructuring

With a Foreword by Prof. Dr. Dirk Schiereck

Deutscher Universitäts-Verlag

Bibliografische Information Der Deutschen Bibliothek
Die Deutsche Bibliothek verzeichnet diese Publikation in der Deutschen Nationalbibliografie; detaillierte bibliografische Daten sind im Internet über <http://dnb.ddb.de> abrufbar.

Dissertation European Business School Oestrich-Winkel, 2005

1. Auflage Januar 2006

Lektorat: Ute Wrasmann / Britta Göhrisch-Radmacher

Der Deutsche Universitäts-Verlag ist ein Unternehmen von Springer Science+Business Media.
www.duv.de

Umschlaggestaltung: Regine Zimmer, Dipl.-Designerin, Frankfurt/Main
Druck und Buchbinder: Rosch-Buch, Scheßlitz
Gedruckt auf säurefreiem und chlorfrei gebleichtem Papier

ISBN 3-8350-0247-3

Abstract

It is the objective of this dissertation to examine the use and performance impact of hybrid security issues conducted by US and Western European firms. In a paper-based format, the dissertation firstly addresses the question why firms issue convertible debt by analyzing and comparing changes in operating and stock price performance around convertible debt and seasoned equity offerings. Using a data set of 437 transactions, the analysis provides strong evidence in favour of a market timing-hypothesis, which argues that managers choose to issue convertible debt as a cheaper substitute for straight debt to benefit from temporary mispricings of their firm's common stock. In addition, an increase in systematic equity risk around convertible debt offerings suggests that some firms, even if they liked to obtain seasoned equity, would be foreclosed from participation in the seasoned equity market due to investor uncertainty about their risk characteristics.

The second research question addressed by the dissertation concerns so-called concurrent offerings, where firms issue convertible securities alongside common stock. To explain the use and valuation impact of concurrent offerings, a signaling-hypothesis, which argues that issuing firms intend to trade off adverse selection against financial distress costs to reduce the mispricing of newly issued securities in the capital market, is tested using a sample of 47 US concurrent offerings accounting for a total issuance volume of 50 billion USD. While the signaling-hypothesis is supported for firms that issue mandatory convertibles alongside common stock, firms using ordinary convertible securities alongside common stock (OCF concurrent offerings) are evaluated by the capital market in a surprising fashion: the announcement return of OCF transactions amounts to –7%. After the offering, one third of OCF firms are delisted and the market value is nearly halved for the survivors. Neither the signaling-, nor a market timing- or a rationing-hypothesis can explain this pricing puzzle, which I lay in the hands of future research.

The third research question is why Western European firms issue exchangeable debt and how capital markets respond to the issue announcement. An analysis of 57 transactions that occurred from 1997 through 2003 shows that exchangeable debt is a divestment strategy, which appears attractive due to lower transaction costs and higher announcement returns in comparison to other forms of secondary distributions that disperse concentrated share blocks. The negative valuation impact can be explained by the offer's potential to reduce the efficacy of the stockholders' ability to monitor the management of the exchange company.

Foreword

How firms choose among competing instruments of external finance has been widely discussed in the finance literature for decades. However, many important questions raised in this discussion remain unanswered today – in particular with regard to a firm's use of hybrid securities. The core market for these financing instruments, which comprise structures such as convertible debt, mandatory convertibles or exchangeable debt, is the US market, which has been characterized by a sharp increase in issuance volumes during recent years.

In his thesis, Mr. Kleidt sets out to answer the question why firms issue hybrid securities. This is not only a remarkable endeavour, because Mr. Kleidt uses US-American data, but in particular because he presents state-of-the-art analyses, which are competitive and meet highest international standards.

The thesis on hand carefully identifies and addresses open research questions related to the use of hybrid securities by corporations. Its primary objective was to identify issuance motives for different types of hybrid securities in the US analyzing stock price and accounting data. Thusly objectifying managerial action allows to derive recommendations for financing practice.

Another focus of the thesis concerns the use of exchangeable debt, a divestment vehicle commonly employed by German corporations to disentangle the 'Deutschland AG'. Updated empirical evidence provides significant value-added for capital market participants, in particular financial managers, in Germany and Western Europe.

Mr. Kleidt fully achieves the objectives of this dissertation. The analysis contains many intriguing and surprising results, which make this thesis an interesting read that I highly recommend to corporate finance researchers and practitioners. I wish for the dissertation its due wide diffusion in corporate finance research.

Professor Dr. Dirk Schiereck

Preface

This thesis is a result of the time I spent as a research assistant to the Endowed Chair for Banking and Finance at the European Business School (**ebs**) in Oestrich-Winkel. It was accepted as dissertation by the Department of Business Administration of **ebs** in October 2005.

If it had not been for the help of many people dear to me, this thesis would not have come about in its present form. Therefore, I would like to thank Prof. Dr. Dirk Schiereck for his supervision, encouragement, and guidance. Without his instantaneous and constructive feedback and many inspiring discussions, it would have been hardly possible to navigate through the data and interpret the results. I owe to Prof. Dr. Lutz Johanning for providing a second opinion on the thesis. I also thank the DAAD and the ‚Stiftung Unternehmensfinanzierung und Kapitalmärkte für den Finanzstandort Deutschland' for financial support and the Joseph M. Katz Graduate School of Business and e-fellows.net for research support.

Another essential success factor for this thesis were numerous discussions with my colleagues at the Endowed Chairs for Banking and Finance and Asset Management. I want to thank Volker Floegel, Christian Funke, Carolin Fuß, Timo Gebken, Philipp Henrich, Gaston Michel, Christof Sigl-Grüb, Christian Voigt, and Sebastian Werner most sincerely. I also thank Trudel Thullen for her great helpfulness during our time at the chair. Without her tight grip on internal politics and her excellent management capabilities, I would have been lost at more than one instance.

I want to point out the commitment of my colleagues and friends Martin Ahnefeld and Markus Mentz. Not only have their suggestions improved the quality of this thesis greatly – having had the opportunity to spend three fun years at the chair with them has made the 'doctoral' experience even more lasting and rewarding.

I am very much indebted to my family and friends who contributed directly and indirectly to this dissertation. I would like to thank my friends for keeping my spirits high; Julia for having me throughout the last phase of the dissertation, during which I was certainly not always easy to get along with, and for being my princess; and finally my parents for their continued support and the love they have given me throughout the past 29 years. To them I dedicate this thesis.

Benjamin Kleidt

Contents

List of abbreviations

A	Austria
AC	Asset composition
ACES	Automatically convertible equity securities
AEX	Amsterdam exchanges-index
AG	Aktiengesellschaft
AMEX	American Stock Exchange
ATX	Austrian Traded Index
AV	Abnormal trading volume
BE/ME	Book-to-market equity
BR	Bankruptcy risk
CAC 40	Cotation Assistée en Continue 40
CBS	Convertible bonds
CD	Convertible debt
CE	Capital expenditures
CEO	Chief executive officer
CFO	Chief financial officer
CH	Switzerland
CONVPROB	Conversion probability
CRSP	Center for Research in Security Prices
DAX 30	Deutscher Aktienindex 30
DECS	Dividend-enhanced convertible securities
DISTRESS	Financial distress costs
DSC	Differential slope coefficient
DUM	Dummy variable
DV	Average trading volume
EBIT	Earnings before interest and taxes
ED	Exchangeable debt
EF	Event firm
EUR	Euro
EW	Equal-weighted
EXPROB	Exchange probability
F	France
FCF	Free cash flow
FTSE 100	Financial Times Stock Exchange 100

List of figures

List of tables

GER	Germany
HML	High minus low
I	Italy
IPO	Initial public offering
ISSUES	Forecasted number of security issues
JB	Jarque-Bera test for normality
KfW	Kreditanstalt für Wiederaufbau
L	Luxembourg
M&A	Mergers and acquisitions
MCF	Mandatory conversion feature
MF	Matching firm
MIB 30	Milano Italia Borsa 30 Index
MILES	Market index-linked equity securities
MKTRF	Market return net of risk-free rate
MTB	Market-to-book ratio
MV	Market value
Nasdaq	National Association of Securities Dealers Automated Quotation
NL	The Netherlands
NPV	Net present value
NYSE	New York Stock Exchange
OCF	Ordinary conversion feature
OIBD	Operating income before depreciation and amortization
OLS	Ordinary least squares
PE	Price-earnings ratio
PEPS	Premium equity participating securities
PERCS	Preferred equity redemption cumulative stock
PM	Pure mandatory convertible offerings
POST-EARNINGS	Operating performance following the issue
PRE-EARNINGS	Operating performance prior to the issue
PRIDES	Preferred redemption increased dividend equity securities
PROF	Profitability
PU	Public utility
RD	Research and development
RE	Retained earnings
RIS	Relative issue size

RISK	Firm risk
ROA	Return on assets
RUNUP	Pre-issue share price runup
SA	Sales
SDC	Security Data Corporation
SEO	Seasoned equity offering
SIC	Standard Industry Classification
SIZE	Firm size
SMB	Small minus big
SPI	Swiss Performance Index
SURPRISE	Inverse Mill's ratio
TA	Total assets
TAX	Tax payments
TD	Total debt
TIMCON	Forecasted number of convertible debt issues
TIMEQU	Forecasted number of equity issues
UK	United Kingdom
UMD	Momentum factor
US	United States
USD	United States Dollar
VW	Value-weighted
WC	Working capital
WLS	Weighted least squares

List of symbols

α	Regression intercept
AAR_t	Average abnormal return in time period *t*
AR_{it}	Abnormal return of security *i* in time period *t*
β	Beta factor
$\overline{BHAR_T}$	Average buy-and-hold abnormal return for time period *T*
$BHAR_{iT}$	Buy-and-hold abnormal return of stock *i* for time period *T*
C_t	Number of convertible debt issues in time period *t*
CAR_i	Cumulative abnormal return of security *i*
$CAAR$	Cumulative average abnormal return
D	Sum of positive ranks
d_i	Difference in accounting ratios for firm *i*
Div	Dividend yield
E_t	Number of equity issues in time period *t*
ε_{it}	Error term of security *i* in time period *t*
$E()$	Expectation operator
γ	Regression coefficient
$\hat{\gamma}$	Estimate of coefficient of skewness
I_t	Number of security issues in time period *t*
N	Number of observations
$N(d_2)$	Conversion probability
r	Interest rate
R_{ft}	Risk-free rate in time period *t*
R_{Mt}	Market return in time period *t*
R_{Pt}	Portfolio return in time period *t*
σ	Standard deviation
σ^2	Volatility
S	Stock price
s	Start date of time period
T	Length of time period
t	Time unit
t_{SA}	Skewness-adjusted t-statistic
X	Strike price
Z	Value of statistic of a median test

I Introduction

1 Problem and objectives

One of the most debated issues in the corporate finance literature is the security issue decision.[1] Against the background of the existence of capital market imperfections, a large number of studies show that different external financing decisions may entail different kinds of costs for an issuing firm.[2] These costs have an impact on firm value and therefore, the security issue decision is not trivial.[3]

A considerable part of existing research ascribes hybrid securities, a form of capital that combines characteristics of debt and equity, a special role in mitigating the costs that arise in external finance.[4] Taken at face value, these theories provide intriguing arguments for the use of hybrid securities.

Yet, there is a problem: the theoretical implications are in harsh contrast to documented empirical patterns. Take the example of convertible debt, the most commonly issued form of hybrid security: according to a number of theoretical models, convertible debt eliminates costs of external equity and debt finance that arise from adverse selection, free cash flow or risk-shifting.[5] In other words, when equity or debt issues entail suboptimal investment policies that arise from a number of incentive conflicts among stakeholders in a firm or from asymmetric information, convertible debt has properties that resolve these conflicts.

The major implication that follows from models of convertible debt issuance is that firms should not perform abnormally poorly, other than equity or debt issuers, after they issued convertible debt. The well-documented fact that issuing firms experience declines in earnings

---

1 See Miller (1988), p. 99 ff.; Modigliani (1988), p. 149 ff.; Harris/Raviv (1991), p. 297 ff.; Myers (2001), p. 81 ff.; Schmid Klein/O'Brien/Peters (2002), p. 317 ff.

2 See Pinegar/Lease (1986), p. 795.

3 The neoclassical finance literature, in particular the work of Modigliani/Miller (1958), p. 261 ff., demonstrates that in a neoclassical world of fully informed investors without taxes and with risk-free debt, the value of a firm is determined without regard to a firm's capital structure. Several theories, which follow a neo-institutionalistic approach, relax the assumption of perfect capital markets. Principal-agent conflicts and asymmetric information are two of the most important forms of capital market imperfections that create costs for firms that want to obtain external capital. For seminal models of principal-agency conflicts see Jensen/Meckling (1976), p. 305 ff. and for asymmetric information see Ross (1977), p. 23 ff., Leland/Pyle (1977), p. 371 ff. and Myers/Majluf (1984), p. 187 ff.

4 See Green (1984), p. 115 ff.; Brennan/Schwartz (1988), p. 55 ff.; Stein (1992), p. 3 ff.; Barber (1993), p. 48 ff.; Chemmanur/Fulghieri (1997), p. 1 ff.; Mayers (1998), p. 83 ff.; Chemmanur/Nandy/Yan (2003), p. 1 ff.

5 Stein (1992), p. 3 ff. addresses adverse selection, Mayers (1998), p. 83 ff. free cash flow and Green (1984), p. 115 ff. risk-shifting.

and stock price levels after the offering is obviously inconsistent with this implication.[6] Hence, managers may issue convertible debt for different reasons than researchers think, which demands for new explanations for its use.

The current state of research hardly provides any explanation. In general, the description of hybrid security issue decisions is far from being complete. Evidence on why and how firms use hybrid securities, how the issue decision affects the firm's performance and the market's evaluation of an issuer's cash flows and cost of capital in the shorter- and longer-run is ambiguous.

It is the purpose of this thesis to provide further evidence on the use of hybrid securities in the US and Western European capital markets. A contribution to existing literature shall be made based on the following three objectives:

Objective 1:

Existing theories for the use of convertible debt imply that this security is issued to signal information and restore optimal and net present value- (NPV) maximizing investment policies. In contrast to the implications of these theories, empirical evidence documents that firms issuing convertible debt are poor long-term performers. In this thesis, two alternative hypotheses, based on market timing and investor rationing, for convertible debt issuance will be put forward and their implications be tested empirically for a sample of convertible debt offerings in the US.

Objective 2:

The scope of the analysis of convertible debt issuance is broadened in an examination of so-called 'concurrent offerings'. This innovative transaction structure, where convertible securities are offered alongside common stock, represents an important source of external finance for US corporations, which have raised well over 70 billion USD during the years 2000 through 2002 alone. Up to now, an explanation for the use of concurrent offerings does not exist and empirical evidence on the market's assessment of such transactions is not available. This thesis will discuss hypotheses to explain the use of concurrent

6 See Lee/Loughran (1998), p. 185 ff.; McLaughlin/Safieddine/Vasudevan (1998), p. 373 ff.; Spiess/Affleck-Graves (1999), p. 45 ff.; Lewis/Rogalski/Seward (2001), p. 447 ff.

offerings and present empirical evidence on issuing firm characteristics and the valuation impact of these offerings.

Objective 3:

Exchangeable debt, which is debt exchangeable into stock of a third company, has been increasingly issued by Western European firms during past years. Research on the exchangeable debt issue decision is principally available for US firms and provides controversial evidence on why this type of hybrid security is issued. Some studies argue that exchangeable debt is used to restructure a firm's assets, while other studies argue that it is used to sell an overvalued stock contained in an issuer's portfolio. This thesis will determine why Western European firms decide to issue exchangeable debt and how capital markets respond to this decision.

2 *Organization of the thesis*

The thesis is organized as follows: Chapter II provides definitions of those hybrid securities that are the subject of the analyses. It also familiarizes the reader with the basic terminology of hybrid securities.

Chapter III and IV provide evidence on the convertible debt issue decision (*objective 1*).[7] In Chapter III, two hypotheses, one based on market timing and the other one on investor rationing, are developed with specific attention as to their potential to explain empirical patterns around convertible debt issues documented by previous research. The implications of these explanations are tested for in a comparison of the post-issue operating and stock price performance of firms issuing convertible debt and common stock. This comparison provides new evidence on the potential of the two hypotheses to explain the use of convertible debt.

Chapter IV concentrates on the investor rationing-hypothesis for convertible debt issuance. An examination of the behaviour of systematic risk estimates around convertible debt offerings is informative about the investors' propensity to ration some firms out of the seasoned equity market into the convertible debt market due to uncertainty about the risk characteristics of an issuing firm.

---

7 The discussion in these chapters is based on Kleidt/Schiereck (2005b), p. 1 ff. and Kleidt/Schiereck (2005a), p. 1 ff.

Chapter V contains an analysis of concurrent offerings of convertible securities and common stock (*objective 2*).[8] It develops and tests a signaling-hypothesis to explain the use and valuation impact of concurrent offerings. Particular implications of this hypothesis are tested for in an analysis of pre-issue firm characteristics, announcement returns and long-run post-issue stock returns.

Chapter VI shifts the focus of the analysis to the Western European capital markets.[9] While hybrid security markets are smaller in Western Europe, exchangeable debt is more prevalent than in the US. Previous literature provides controversial evidence on the use of exchangeable debt for US firms. Chapter VI examines the question why Western European firms may issue exchangeable debt by analyzing the magnitude and cross-section of announcement returns to exchangeable debt issues (*objective 3*).

Chapter VII concludes the thesis and indicates areas for future research.

8 The discussion in this chapter is based on Kleidt/Schiereck/Dziarski (2005), p. 1 ff.
9 The discussion in this chapter is based on Kleidt/Scharmer/Schiereck (2005), p. 1 ff.

II Definitions

1 *Hybrid securities*

Hybrid securities combine characteristics of equity and debt capital.[10] They usually give their holder the right to convert a debt-like instrument into common stock.[11] Sometimes a conversion obligation exists.[12] Figure II.1 illustrates the spectrum of hybrid securities according to their degree of resemblance to common stock and straight debt.

The focus of this thesis is on convertible debt, the most commonly issued form of hybrid security, and mandatory convertibles, a recent innovation of convertible preferred securities. These two types of hybrid financing instruments are described in the following sections in greater detail.

Figure II.1: Spectrum of hybrid securities[13]

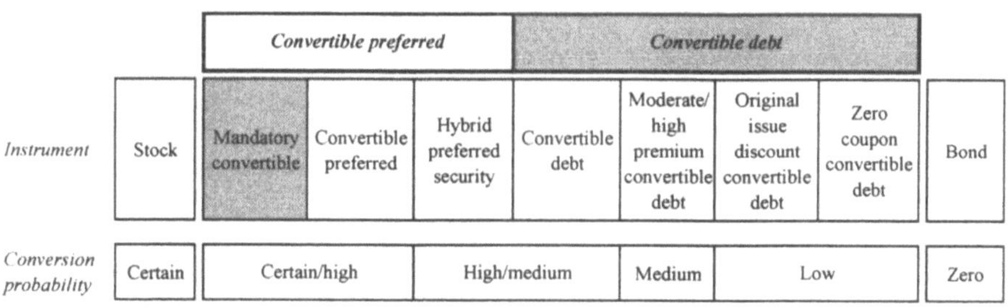

2 *Convertible debt*

Convertible debt is a fixed income financing instrument that increases a firm's leverage before it can be converted into stock of the issuing firm. It is equivalent to a portfolio of two securities: a bond and an equity call option.[14] Apart from the rights that accrue to bondholders, in particular periodic interest payments and repayment of the principal, the holder of a convertible bond receives an option to convert the bond into a pre-specified

---

10 See Calamos (1998), p. 3. Müller-Trimbusch (1999), p. 7 ff. provides a conceptual classification of equity and debt capital and the rights and obligations associated with each of these forms of capital.

11 See Ganshaw/Dillon (2000), p. 24.

12 See Reilly/Brown (2003), p. 1035.

13 Figure II.1 is adapted from Ganshaw/Dillon (2000), p. 27.

14 See Copeland/Weston (1992), p. 475.

number of shares of the issuing firm.[15] Whether it is optimal to exercise this option depends on the price of the issuer's stock: if the stock trades during certain periods throughout the life of the convertible above a pre-agreed conversion price, the conversion option is in-the-money and investors may exercise it to become stockholders of the firm.

Convertible debt, also referred to as convertible bonds or as convertibles throughout this thesis, is the type of hybrid security that is most commonly issued. Figure II.2 shows that it has represented the largest fraction in the US market for hybrid securities during the first years of this millennium.

Figure II.2: Issuance volumes according to type of hybrid security in the US[16]

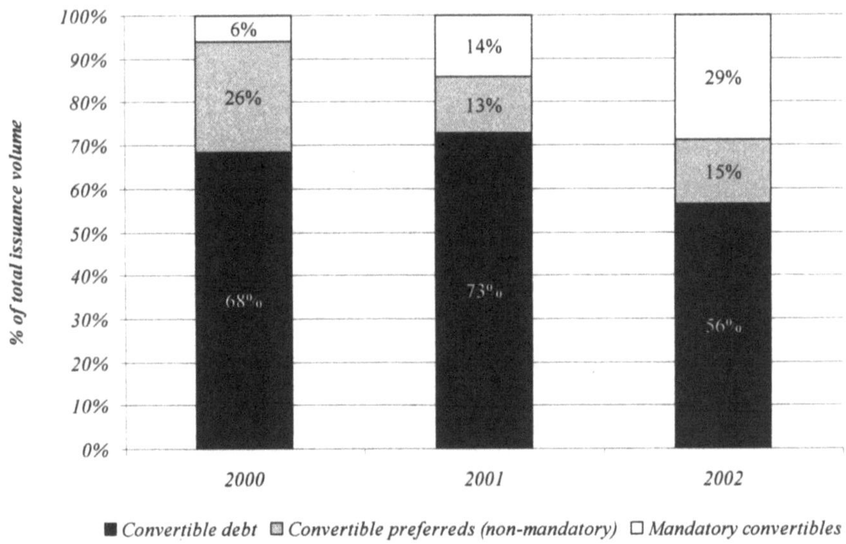

Convertible bonds are characterized by a variety of parameters. An example of terms of typical convertible debt issues is useful to illustrate the mechanics of this financing instrument. It is shown in table II.1.[17]

[15] See Achleitner (2001), p. 521.
[16] Issuance volumes were obtained from Thomson One Banker Deals.
[17] Table II.1 is adapted from Woodson (2002), p. 5.

The debt component of the convertible bond has the following characteristics: it was issued on January 31, 2005 and matures seven years later on January 31, 2012. It pays a coupon of 2.25% per annum. Its face (or nominal) value is 1,000 USD. It is issued and redeemed at par.

Table II.1: Typical terms in convertible debt issues

Debt component	
Coupon	2.25% p.a.
Coupon frequency	Annually
Issue date	January 31, 2005
Maturity	January 31, 2012
Face value	USD 1,000
Issue price	Par (100%)
Redemption price	Par (100%)
Conversion right	
Conversion ratio	10 stocks per convertible bond
Conversion price	USD 100
Conversion period	January 31, 2006 to January 31, 2012
Market data	
Current stock price	USD 80
Parity (conversion value)	USD 800
Conversion premium	25%
Current 5-year risk-free interest rate	3.64%

The equity option gives the convertible bondholder the right to convert one bond into ten shares of the issuer (representing a conversion ratio of ten). The conversion price implied by this conversion ratio and the face value of the bond is 100 USD, as shown in formula II.1.[18] The period during which investors have the right to convert the bond starts one year after issuance and ends at the maturity date.

Formula II.1

$$Conversion\ price = \frac{Face\ value}{Conversion\ ratio} = \frac{USD\ 1{,}000}{10} = USD\ 100$$

[18] See Calamos (1998), p. 25.

The conversion value of the bond, also called parity, is the current stock price multiplied with the conversion ratio, as shown in formula II.2.[19]

Formula II.2 $$Parity = Conversion\ ratio \times Stock\ price = 10 \times USD\ 80 = USD\ 800$$

If the current stock price is 80 USD, the price of the issuer's stock has to rise another 20 USD for the conversion option to be at-the-money. This difference of 25% is called the conversion premium and is calculated according to formula II.3.[20] The conversion premium is a major determinant of the structure of convertible debt, since it largely defines how close the convertible is to common stock or straight debt. The higher the conversion premium, the lower is the conversion probability and the more debt-like is the security, all else equal.[21]

Formula II.3 $$Conversion\ premium = [\frac{Face\ value}{Parity}] - 1 * 100\% = [\frac{USD\ 1{,}000}{USD\ 800}] - 1 * 100\% = 25\%$$

A large number of convertible bonds issued, especially in the US, have provisions that grant the issuer the right to call the bond.[22] An example of a call provision is shown in table II.2.

Table II.2: Call provisions in convertible debt issues

Call protection	Hard call 3 years
Call price	110 USD
Call period	February 1, 2008 to January 31, 2012

19 See Woodson (2002), p. 6.
20 See Woodson (2002), p. 6.
21 In figure II.1, convertible debt encompasses several hybrid security structures that differ principally with regard to their conversion premium. Moderate or high premium convertible debt is mainly used as an alternative to straight debt and commonly features conversion premia ranging from 35% to 70%. It may be a cheaper form of debt for some companies, because it allows an issuer to reduce interest costs compared to straight debt, depending on the exact value of the conversion option. Original issue discount or zero coupon convertible debt is convertible debt with very high conversion premia. It also differs from conventional convertible debt in two further regards: first, it is issued at a discount and does not pay a periodic coupon. Second, put options are often added giving investors the right to sell the convertible in certain circumstances. See Ganshaw/Dillon (2000), p. 25 ff.
22 See Calamos (1998), p. 53.

Call features are commonly included in convertible bonds to enhance an issuer's financial flexibility and to enable it to force conversion, which may eliminate the bondholder's option value.[23] Usually, the call feature is subject to some kind of restriction, a common one being a call protection period of typically three to five years.[24] Call protections may either be 'hard' or 'soft'. In a hard call protection, the bond cannot be called during the protection period at all. Soft call protection means that the bond can be only be called in specific circumstances.[25] Put features give the investor the right to sell the convertible bond back to the issuer. These features, however, are less common.[26]

The payoff profile of convertible debt is illustrated in figure II.3.[27] It shows that investors only participate in share price appreciations above the conversion price. If the underlying stock trades below the conversion price at maturity, the conversion option expires out-of-the-money and investors are repaid the nominal value of the bond. If, in contrast, the conversion option is in-the-money, investors fully participate in any stock price increase.

Figure II.3: Payoff profile of convertible debt

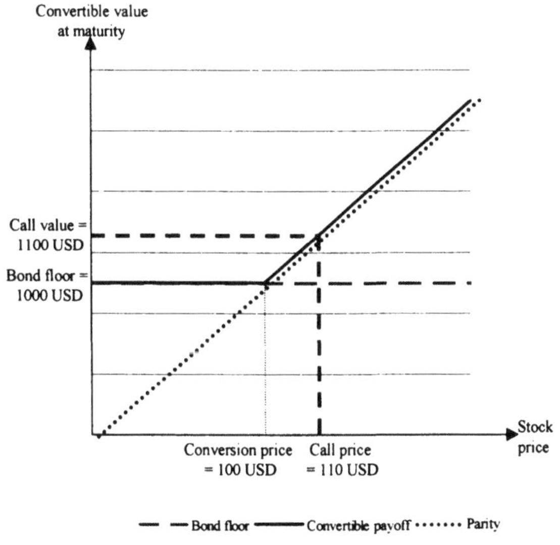

---

[23] See Asquith (1995), p. 1275.

[24] See Brennan/Schwartz (1977), p. 1699. Furthermore, firms that call convertible bonds have to issue a call notice, in which they announce their intention to call the bond. The call notice usually has to be distributed to investors two to four weeks prior to the call date.

[25] An example of a soft call provision is that the price of the underlying stock has to exceed the conversion price by 50% during a particular time period to end the call protection period.

[26] See Ganshaw/Dillon (2000), p. 26. They are mainly used in zero coupon convertible debt issues.

[27] Adapted from Ross/Westerfield/ Jaffe (2002), p. 682 f. The payoff profile assumes a given interest rate and does not consider dividends. See Chemmanur/Nandy/Yan (2003), p. 2.

A firm may also decide to call the convertible: if, for example, the share price in March 2008 was 120 USD and the firm called the convertible, an investor would receive 1,100 USD (10 times the call price of 110 USD) per convertible bond. However, the conversion value at that stock price level would be 1,200 USD. The investor would therefore rather convert the bond than receive the call price and hence, a firm would effectively force conversion.

3 Convertible preferred stock

Convertible preferred stock is similar to convertible debt, since it can be exchanged for common stock as well.[28] Other than convertible debt, it is issued as preferred stock, which is, as convertible debt, commonly classified as a fixed income security, since it shares characteristics of debt securities: preferred dividend payments are contractually pre-specified and paid out before common dividends.[29] However, the payments that accrue to a holder of preferred stock are, in contrast to interest payments specified in debt contracts, not legally binding and not tax-deductible.[30]

4 Mandatory convertibles

Especially during the last couple of years, an innovative form of convertible preferred stock has emerged:[31] mandatory convertibles, which appear in different variations and are marketed under different names by various investment banks.[32] Although product types differ with regard to payoff structures and other provisions, mandatory convertibles share four fundamental characteristics: first, conversion to equity is mandatory. While convertible debt is issued as debt, mandatory convertibles are essentially forward sales of common stock and the investor does not have a conversion right but obligation. Second, the dividend yield on mandatory convertibles usually exceeds the dividend yield on the underlying stock.[33] Third,

---

[28] See Reilly/Brown (2003), p. 1036 f.
[29] See Damodaran (1996), p. 63. Furthermore, preferred stocks usually have restricted or no voting rights.
[30] See Damodaran (1996), p. 63; Reilly/Brown (2003), p. 82.
[31] See White Huckins (1999), p. 89. Hybrid preferred securities mentioned in figure II.1 are combinations of two securities: a trust preferred security and a forward underwriting commitment to issue common stock. These securities are not considered in the analysis. See Ganshaw/Dillon (2000), p. 30 for further information.
[32] Examples are PERCS and PEPS marketed by Morgan Stanley, PRIDES by Merrill Lynch, DECS by Salomon Smith Barney and ACES by Goldman Sachs. See Arzac (1997), p. 54 ff., White Huckins (1999), p. 90 f. and table 5 in Chemmanur/Nandy/Yan (2003) for comprehensive overviews of different types of mandatory convertibles.
[33] See White Huckins (1999), p. 90.

mandatories have either capped or limited upside potential compared to the underlying stock.[34] Fourth, they are mainly issued as preferred stock.[35]

An example, illustrated in figure II.4, of mandatory convertibles are Morgan Stanley's PEPS (premium equity participating securities).[36] A US firm issued 150 million USD PEPS worth 25 USD a unit in June 2000. The firm's share price was 29.125 USD at issuance and hence, one PEPS unit was worth 0.8584 shares. The PEPS paid a dividend of 7.75% per quarter, while the dividend yield on the stock was 2.75%. The PEPS were converted into stock of the firm on August 18, 2003.

Figure II.4: Payoff profile of PEPS

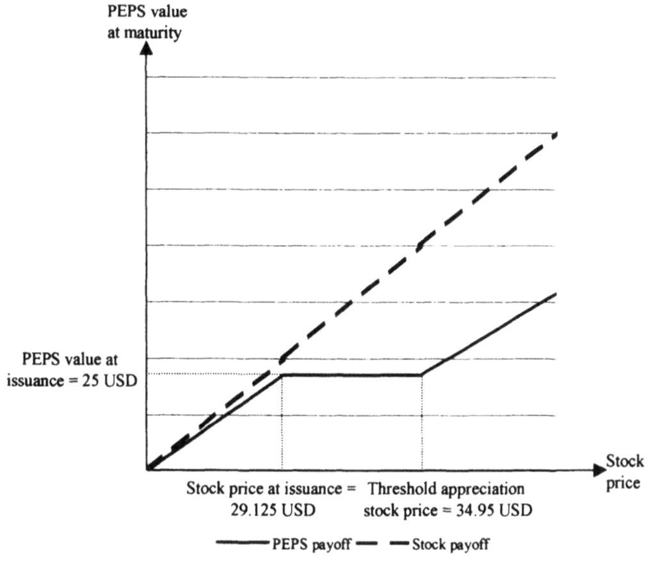

The number of shares a PEPS investor received was dependent on the price of the firm's stock at that date: for a price of 29.125 USD or below, an investor would receive 0.8584 shares per PEPS. If the common stock price was between 29.125 USD and 34.95 USD, the investor would receive a variable fraction of shares giving him a flat payoff of 25 USD. If the stock traded above 34.95 USD, implying a 20% conversion premium, the PEPS investor would

34 See Chemmanur/Nandy/Yan (2003), p. 2.
35 See White Huckins (1999), p. 90.
36 See also Chemmanur/Nandy/Yan (2003), p. 2 f.

receive 0.7153 shares per PEPS, which enabled him to participate in higher share price appreciations during the life of the mandatory.[37]

5 *Exchangeable debt*

A third form of hybrid security that will be examined in this thesis is exchangeable debt.[38] As to its structure, exchangeable debt can be understood as a special form of convertible debt: while convertible debt is converted into stock of the issuing firm, exchangeable debt is exchanged into stock of a third firm, which is also referred to as target or exchange firm throughout this thesis, and in which the issuer has an ownership position.[39] Hence, the holder of a bond has the right to exchange the bond into stocks of an underlying firm, which the issuer has to deliver.

[37] The payoff profile in figure II.4 assumes a given interest rate and does not consider dividends. See Chemmanur/Nandy/ Yan (2003), p. 2.

[38] Throughout this paper, I use the terms 'exchangeable debt' and 'exchangeable bond' interchangeably.

[39] See Ghosh/Varma/Woolridge (1990), p. 251. While it is theoretically possible that an issuing firm does not possess the exchange stock at the time it issues an exchangeable bond, this case is virtually meaningless in practice.

III Why firms issue convertible debt – Market timing and investor rationing

1 *Introduction*

Available theories for the use of convertible debt emphasize the security's useful role in mitigating costs of external debt and equity finance that arise due to capital market imperfections. Green (1984) argues that convertible debt eliminates risk-shifting incentives and aligns the interests of stock- and bondholders.[40] Stein (1992) shows that firms with valuable investment opportunities can use convertible debt to reduce the costs of adverse selection arising in equity issues[41], and Mayers (1998) illustrates that convertible debt can alleviate costs of free cash flow.[42] Empirical tests of the short-term valuation impact of convertible debt offerings support the implications of these theories: convertible debt issues on average entail higher announcement returns than equity issues.[43]

However, research that examines the post-issue operating and stock price performance[44] over longer time horizons cannot confirm that convertible debt restores optimal investment incentives: earnings and stock price levels significantly decline after the offering.[45]

The inconsistency of theoretical arguments with empirical findings raises two questions. First, if convertible debt is issued to mitigate costs of external finance, why does it not work? And second, if convertible debt is issued for other reasons, what are they?

Lewis/Rogalski/Seward (1998, 1999, 2001) address the first question and argue that poor convertible debt design is unlikely to cause convertible debt issuers to underperform.[46] Their evidence leads them to conclude that typical convertible debt issuers do not intend to signal information, mitigate free cash flow or risk-shifting problems. In fact, investors may be unwilling to provide some firms with equity capital and foreclose them from participation in

---

[40] See Green (1984), p. 115 ff.

[41] The terms equity issues and seasoned equity offerings, which are used interchangeably throughout this thesis, refer to issues of new common stock by a company that has previously gone public. See Ross/Westerfield/ Jaffe (2002), p. 537.

[42] See Stein (1992), p. 3 ff.; Mayers (1998), p. 83 ff.

[43] See Eckbo/Masulis (1995), p. 1042 f. for an overview of event studies on financing decisions, which supports this notion.

[44] I use the terms operating and earnings performance as well as the terms stock price and financial performance interchangeably throughout this thesis.

[45] See Lee/Loughran (1998), p. 185 ff.; McLaughlin/Safieddine/Vasudevan (1998), p. 373 ff.; Spiess/Affleck-Graves (1999), p. 45 ff.; Lewis/Rogalski/Seward (2001), p. 447 ff.

[46] Lewis/Rogalski/Seward (1998), p. 32 ff., Lewis/Rogalski/Seward (1999), p. 5 ff. and Lewis/Rogalski/Seward (2001), p. 447 ff. use the same data set in their studies and find that even if convertibles are well-designed, issuers still underperform.

the market for seasoned equity. These firms have no other alternative than raising capital in the convertible debt market, where they are granted access to contingent equity funds depending on their post-issue stock price performance. This rationing-argument appears to be a very good explanation of the 'street view' that convertible debt is often issued as a security of last resort.[47]

On the basis of existing research, it is hard to assess how powerful the rationing-explanation is for the convertible debt issue decision. On the one hand, the reasons why convertible debt issuers should be rationed out of the market for seasoned equity are not well-known. For example, it is yet to determine whether rationing is due to a firm's post-issue earnings characteristics, as argued by Lewis/Rogalski/Seward (2001).[48] On the other hand, post-issue declines in operating and stock price performance are consistent with a market timing-explanation as well.

In this chapter, I provide evidence on why firms use convertible debt by comparing the operating and financial performance of convertible debt and equity issuers. This comparison provides new evidence on the importance of two hypotheses, based on market timing and investor rationing, for the managerial decision to issue convertible debt.

My results for a sample of convertible debt issues occurring from 2000 through 2002 support an explanation that has received little empirical support so far: convertible debt issuers are as concerned about the timing of their security offerings as equity issuers are. I derive this conclusion from several observations. First, convertible debt is issued after large share price appreciations by firms that have unusually high market-to-book ratios. A decline of post-issue earnings levels suggests that capital markets overestimate the value of future cash flows around the time of the issue. Declines in stock prices over the eighteen months following the transaction indicate that investors gradually adjust this assessment of firm value.[49] A cross-sectional analysis reveals that declines in post-issue stock prices are more pronounced for firms with higher pre-issue stock price increases. In sum, these findings suggest that the stock of convertible debt issuers is overvalued at issuance.

If, as I argue, managers intentionally exploit these mispricings, they may intend to use convertible debt as a substitute for straight debt rather than as a substitute for common stock. As long as overvaluation is a transitory phenomenon, as documented by previous research, the

---

47 See Lewis/Rogalski/Seward (2001), p. 449.
48 See Lewis/Rogalski/Seward (2001), p. 472.
49 Loughran/Ritter (1995), p. 23 ff., Spiess/Affleck-Graves (1995), p. 243 ff. and Loughran/Ritter (1997), p. 1823 ff. document similar findings for equity issuers.

likelihood that stock returns will be poor during the years following the offering is high, when investors revise their overoptimistic assessment of a firm's cash flows and sell the stock.[50] From a manager's perspective, this decreases the ex-ante probability of conversion of the bond into common stock.

Around the time of the offering, however, managers who know (or suspect) that their stock is overvalued assign a lower value to the conversion option than outside investors. This disparity allows them to effectively reduce the interest payments of convertible debt below levels payable in straight debt issues.[51] Consistent with the interpretation that convertible debt is used as a cheaper substitute for straight debt, convertible debt issuers have unused debt capacity and may employ convertibles instead of straight debt to adjust their leverage ratio towards a target level.[52]

The analyses also indicate that investor rationing may force some firms to issue convertible debt. However, rationing does apparently not occur on the basis of a convertible debt issuer's earnings characteristics, but due to uncertainty about their risk characteristics. If investors are risk-averse or uncertain whether any adverse changes in systematic risk are adequately compensated with higher returns, they may deny firms the access to direct equity capital. A convertible bond allows investors to screen the firm until conversion can occur. It is attractive as a screening device, because it hedges investors against changes in firm risk.[53]

The remainder of this chapter is organized as follows: section 2 develops three hypotheses for convertible debt issuance. Section 3 describes the data and proxy variables. Section 4 compares the operating performance of convertible debt and equity issuers and analyzes its determinants. Section 5 contains a similar test for the post-issue stock price performance. Section 6 concludes.

---

[50] See Rangan (1998), p. 121.

[51] If managers foresee a post-issue earnings decline, this preservation of cash flow may be of some importance to a firm.

[52] This interpretation explicitly recognizes the market conditions that prevailed during the sample period between 2000 and 2002. However, the market timing-explanation is consistent with a wide array of empirical regularities documented by other studies of convertible debt. For example, it receives support from survey evidence on the convertible issue decision and from evidence that reports an increase of insider selling prior to convertible debt offerings. See Billingsley/Smith (1996), p. 97 and Graham/Harvey (2001), p. 221 for survey evidence, and Karpoff/Lee (1991), p. 18 ff. and Kahle (2000), p. 25 ff. for studies on insider trading.

[53] See Brennan/Schwartz (1988), p. 56. Changes in risk of a firm have opposite effects on the value of the equity option and bond component of a convertible. This makes the value of an appropriately-designed convertible bond largely insensitive to changes in risk.

2 *Existing literature*

Traditional models of convertible debt finance argue that convertible debt mitigates costs of external debt and equity finance.[54] Empirical research, however, documents declines in earnings and stock prices after convertible debt issues that are inconsistent with theoretical considerations.[55] Lewis/Rogalski/ Seward (2001) therefore suggest that convertible debt is issued for demand-side reasons and firms that would like to raise equity capital have no other alternative than issuing convertible debt.[56]

In this section, I will further explore these two arguments for convertible debt issuance. In addition, I include an explanation based on market timing, which has received little attention in the empirical literature up to this point, but has the potential to explain why convertible debt issuers perform poorly after the offering.

2.1 The traditional hypothesis

The traditional hypothesis draws on the models of convertible debt issuance put forward by Green (1984), Stein (1992) and Mayers (1998), which argue that convertible debt mitigates costs of external debt and equity finance.

Green (1984) and Mayers (1998) address agency conflicts described by Jensen/Meckling (1976) and Jensen (1986).[57] These conflicts arise because of diverging interests that exist between stockholders and bondholders, as well as between stockholders and firm managers. Green (1984) addresses the conflict between stock- and bondholders that can arise over investment decisions, where stockholders have an incentive to expropriate wealth from bondholders.[58] Stockholders have the residual claim on firm value that can be interpreted as a call option on a firm's cash flows. They can increase the value of this claim by increasing the risk of a firm's assets (risk-shifting) and may even pursue investment projects with a negative NPV, if these projects are sufficiently risky. Green (1984) shows that convertible debt mitigates the risk-shifting incentive, because it reverses "the convex shape of levered equity

[54] See Green (1984), p. 115 ff.; Stein (1992), p. 3 ff.; Mayers (1998), p. 83 ff.
[55] See Lee/Loughran (1998), p. 185 ff.; McLaughlin/Safieddine/Vasudevan (1998), p. 373 ff.; Lewis/Rogalski/ Seward (2001), p. 447 ff.
[56] See Lewis/Rogalski/Seward (2001), p. 449.
[57] See Jensen/Meckling (1976), p. 305 ff.; Jensen (1986), p. 323 ff.
[58] See Green (1984), p. 115 ff.

over the upper range of the firm's earnings."[59] Hence, convertible debt aligns the interests of bond- and stockholders, which restores NPV-maximizing investment policies.

The free cash flow theory by Jensen (1986) argues that a firm's managers may pursue objectives that are not always consistent with those of stockholders.[60] Managers tend to invest in projects that maximize the amount of resources under their control or increase their wealth, but do not necessarily increase stockholder value. This problem is aggravated in seasoned equity issues: if managers receive funds up-front that are not (contractually) committed to a specific use, they may squander issue proceeds, which results in a suboptimal investment policy.[61]

Mayers (1998) argues that convertible debt mitigates this problem.[62] If a firm has an investment program that requires staged financing, high uncertainty about the value of investment opportunities may translate into a free cash flow problem, when follow-on investment options are not exercised and funds provided up-front remain in the firm without being committed to a specific use. While a firm could use multiple security issues that depend on subsequent funding requirements, this would increase transaction costs significantly.[63] Convertible debt provides a transaction cost-efficient type of sequential financing to a firm that bonds managers to an optimal and value-revealing investment policy: if investment projects pay off, the bond is converted and the funds remain within the firm. If the investment options are not exercised or if managers fail to provide information about the profitability of their investment projects, convertible bond exercise does not occur and a further round of financing is not achieved, since the principal is repaid to the investor at maturity. Managers do not have any surplus funds to squander or allocate to negative NPV projects.

The study of Stein (1992) illustrates that convertible debt can be used to obtain equity capital and simultaneously reduce costs of adverse selection arising in seasoned equity issues described by Myers/Majluf (1984).[64] When managers have private information about the value of a firm's assets and investment opportunities, equity issues can be interpreted as a signal that the issuer considers its securities overvalued, which leads to an adverse valuation effect when the transaction is announced. Stein (1992) shows that firms facing high

59 Green (1984), p. 115.
60 See Jensen (1986), p. 323 ff.
61 See Jensen (1986), p. 323. Corresponding empirical evidence is forwarded by Jung/Kim/Stulz (1996), p. 159 ff. and McLaughlin/Safieddine/Vasudevan (1996), p. 41 ff.
62 See Mayers (1998), p. 83 ff.
63 See Lee/Lochhead/Ritter/Zhao (1996), p. 62.
64 See Myers/Majluf (1984), p. 187 ff.; Stein (1992), p. 3 ff.

incremental costs of financial distress can use convertible debt to send a positive signal about the managements' confidence in the future performance of the firm to investors.

The main implication of the traditional hypothesis is that convertible debt issuers should not underperform financially or with regard to their operating characteristics during the post-issue period: according to Green (1984) and Mayers (1998), convertible debt restores optimal investment policies. Stein's (1992) model implies that convertible debt is issued by firms that have more valuable investment opportunities than equity issuers. As a consequence, it is likely that when these investment projects pay off, the post-issue abnormal performance of convertible debt issuers turns out to be positive.

2.2 The rationing-hypothesis

Lee/Loughran (1998), McLaughlin/Safiedenne/Vasudevan (1998) and Lewis/Rogalski/Seward (2001) provide evidence that convertible debt offerings are followed by significant declines in an issuing firm's earnings and stock prices.[65] This is clearly inconsistent with the theoretical arguments for the superiority of convertible debt described above. It leads Lewis/Rogalski/Seward (2001) to conclude that convertible debt is not able to restore effective investment policies that prominent models of convertible debt finance imply and suggest an alternative explanation for the use of convertible debt: it is issued as a security of last resort, because uncertainty about their post-issue operating performance may force firms to raise capital outside the market for seasoned equity.[66] If investors have difficulties in evaluating a firm's post-issue earnings prospects, they may not be willing to provide a firm with equity funds, because the value of their investment is highly sensitive to the firm's future earnings performance.

However, the firm may obtain capital in the convertible debt market, since convertibles allow investors to screen the issuer until they can convert the bond into stock if the firm performs well and the conversion option is in-the-money. If earnings decline, investors have a downside protection through the bond component of the hybrid security, whose value is less sensitive to earnings deteriorations than the value of the residual claim.

Albeit intriguing and consistent with a 'street view' of convertible debt financing, little evidence exists that supports the rationing-explanation. While it is possible that rationing

---

65 See Lee/Loughran (1998), p. 185 ff.; McLaughlin/Safieddine/Vasudevan (1998), p. 373 ff.; Lewis/Rogalski/Seward (2001), p. 447 ff.

66 See Lewis/Rogalski/Seward (2001), p. 447 and 472.

occurs because investors are uncertain about a firm's future earnings prospects, it is also possible that convertible debt issuers are rationed out of the equity market due to a poor pre-issue operating performance, which investors extrapolate into the future.[67] Finally, rationing might occur because the risk characteristics of convertible debt issuers are difficult to evaluate for investors: if rationing is not due to the level of expected cash flows, it might be uncertainty about the right discount rate that makes the investor's decision difficult. Brennan/Schwartz (1988) argue that convertible debt has attractive properties for investors in this situation, because the value of a convertible is relatively insensitive to changes in firm risk.[68]

One possibility to test the rationing-hypothesis is to compare the operating and financial performance of convertible debt and equity issuers. If rationing occurs on the basis of a firm's post-issue operating performance, one may reason that convertible debt issues are typically followed by larger declines in metrics of operating performance than equity issues. If firms are rationed out of the equity market due to their pre-issue operating performance, one may expect that equity issuers typically have stronger operating characteristics during the period preceding the issue.

2.3 The timing-hypothesis

An apparently powerful explanation for post-issue declines in earnings and stock prices for equity issuers is market timing, which argues that managers issue stock when its valuation level is high and repurchase stock when its valuation level is low.[69] Baker/Wurgler (2002) document that the attempt to time the equity market has persistent effects on firms' capital structures.[70]

Loughran/Ritter (1997) attribute the poor post-issue operating and financial performance of equity issuers to the fact that these firms use windows of opportunity to sell stock when it is overvalued.[71] This allows firms to either invest in what the market (and possibly also

67 Typical convertible debt issuers have a weak earnings performance prior to their offerings. See Lewis/ Rogalski/Seward (2001), p. 454. That investors may extrapolate past earnings patterns into the future is suggested by Rangan (1998), p. 121 for the case of equity issuers.

68 See Brennan/Schwartz (1988), p. 56. Risk changes have opposite effects on the value of the equity option and bond component of a convertible and hence, the value of an appropriately-designed convertible bond is largely unaffected by changes in risk.

69 See Ikenberry/Lakonishok/Vermaelen (1995), p. 181 ff.; Loughran/Ritter (1995), p. 23 ff.; Loughran/Ritter (1997), p. 1823 ff.

70 See Baker/Wurgler (2002), p. 1 ff.

71 See Loughran/Ritter (1997), p. 1848.

managers) perceive as valuable investment projects or increase the amount of financial slack (as emphasized by the pecking order theory).[72]

Teoh/Welch/Wong (1998) and Rangan (1998) show that timing efforts extend to a firm's earnings performance: a higher level of discretionary accruals prior to issuance, potentially to boost earnings, is associated with poorer post-issue performance.[73] If investors extrapolate strong earnings patterns from the past into the future, it is obvious that the transitory nature of pre-issue earnings improvements will become apparent after the issue and stocks will underperform.[74]

Convertible debt issuers may show the same empirical post-issue operating and stock price performance patterns as equity issuers, which would suggest that market timing plays a role in the convertible issue decision as well. Existing evidence consistent with this notion is presented by Lee/Loughran (1998) and Lewis/Rogalski/Seward (2001), who observe that convertible debt issues occur after large increases in the issuer's stock price.[75] Mann/Moore/Ramanlal (1999) examine a timing-explanation for convertible debt issuance and find that more convertible debt issues are conducted in hot issue markets, where a lot of firms choose to issue convertible debt.[76]

The timing-hypothesis predicts that managers use periods, during which they perceive their stock to be overvalued, to issue convertible debt. It implies that issuing firms underperform with regard to operating and financial characteristics during the post-issue period. Moreover, it is likely that the post-issue performance is poorer the more the convertible debt issuer's stock is overvalued prior to the transaction. Hence, an analysis of the determinants of post-issue operating and stock price performance allows to test for the implications of the timing-hypothesis.

3 Data and proxy variables

My data set consists of issues of convertible debt (CD) and seasoned equity offerings (SEO) between January 1, 2000 and December 31, 2002 in the US. The main data source is SDC Platinum provided by Thomson Financial. Since several relevant data items are missing in the SDC database, I use an internal database of Salomon Smith Barney, which contains hand-

72 See Myers/Majluf (1984), p. 220; Hansen/Crutchley (1990), p. 347 ff.
73 See Rangan (1998), p. 101 ff.; Teoh/Welch/Wong (1998), p. 63 ff.
74 See Spiess/Affleck-Graves (1995), p. 265; Spiess/Affleck-Graves (1999), p. 45.
75 See Lee/Loughran (1998), p. 205; Lewis/Rogalski/Seward (2001), p. 459.
76 See Mann/Moore/Ramanlal (1999), p. 101.

collected data to complete the information set on the security offerings.[77] Similar to Loughran/Ritter (1997) and Lewis/Rogalski/Seward (2001), firms in the sample have been chosen on the basis of the following criteria:[78]

1. Issuing firms are listed on the NYSE, AMEX or the Nasdaq.
2. The firm is not a financial institution or a holding company of financial institutions.[79]
3. Stock price and accounting data are available from CRSP and Compustat.[80]
4. The firm has not issued convertible debt or common stock during the five years preceding the issue year.

The samples of convertible debt issues and underwritten equity issues consist of 218 and 219 transactions.

Table III.1 shows the number of issues per year (panel A) and issuer industry affiliation (panel B). Panel A illustrates that most convertible debt issues in the sample occur in year 2001, where the number of equity issues is lowest. In contrast, during the year 2002, the number of equity issues increases while the number of convertible debt issues decreases.

Panel B shows the top seven industries of convertible debt and equity issuers. The industry distribution is similar for the two types of issuers. The only exceptions are the office and computer equipment industry, where more convertible bonds have been issued, and public utilities, where equity transactions prevail.

---

77 The database was generated by the equity-linked securities department of Salomon Smith Barney in New York and contains detailed information on convertible debt offerings.

78 See Loughran/Ritter (1997), p. 1825 f.; Lewis/Rogalski/Seward (2001), p. 451 f. I do not exclude public utilities (SIC codes of 481 and 491 to 494), but repeat the analysis excluding all public utilities. The results remain unchanged.

79 All issuers with a SIC code from 6000 to 6999 are deleted.

80 I require an issuing firm to have Compustat data for the offering year and the year prior to the offering. Stock price data must be available for the year preceding the issue. Stock prices are adjusted for dividend payments and capital actions.

Table III.1: Data summary information

This table shows summary information for the data set. Panel A contains the number of issues per year and panel B the number of issues per industry. Industry classification is based on SIC codes. CD denotes convertible debt and SEO seasoned equity offering.

Panel A: Number of issues per year

	CD		SEO	
Year	***N***	**%**	***N***	**%**
2000	68	31.2%	85	38.8%
2001	103	47.2%	60	27.4%
2002	47	21.6%	74	33.8%
Total	***218***	***100%***	***219***	***100%***

Panel B: Number of issues per industry

		CD		SEO	
Industry	***SIC***	***N***	**%**	***N***	**%**
Oil and gas	13	9	4.1%	12	5.5%
Chemicals and pharmaceuticals	28	35	16.1%	29	13.2%
Office and computer equipment	35	23	10.6%	8	3.7%
Communication and electronic equipment	36	32	14.7%	24	11.0%
Engineering and scientific instruments	38	13	6.0%	9	4.1%
Public utilities	481/491-494	10	4.6%	27	12.3%
Computer and data processing services	73	22	10.1%	25	11.4%
Other	-	74	33.9%	85	38.8%
Total		***218***	***100%***	***219***	***100%***

For the cross-sectional analysis of the post-issue operating and stock price performance, I use several standard proxy variables employed in the finance literature and list them in table III.2.

Table III.2: Description of proxy variables

Variable		Description
SIZE	Firm size	Loughran/Ritter (1997) document that the post-issue deterioration of operating performance is negatively related to firm size.[81] To this end, it is possible that stronger declines in metrics of operating performance for equity than for convertible debt issuers are observable, because the former are smaller firms.[82] *SIZE*, measured as the natural logarithm of the market value of common stock one month prior to the offering announcement, is included to control for a potential size effect.
PU	Public utility	A dummy variable is included to control for the effect of public utilities, which are primarily contained in the equity sample.
RIS	Relative issue size	Hansen/Crutchley (1990) find that the relative issue size is an indicator for the magnitude of the post-issue earnings decline for all types of securities, common stock, convertible and straight debt.[83] *RIS*, calculated as issue proceeds scaled by the market value of common stock, is included to control for expected earnings shortfalls.

---

81 See Loughran/Ritter (1997), p. 1832.

82 The median market value of equity issuers is 717 million USD, while the median market value of convertible debt issuers is 2,811 million USD.

83 See Hansen/Crutchley (1990), p. 349.

Table III.2 continued

Variable		Description
ISSUES	Issuance activity	Spiess/Affleck-Graves (1999) find firms that issue securities in times of high general issuance activity underperform more.[84] I include a timing variable similar to Marsh (1982).[85] **Formula III.1:** $ISSUES_t = \gamma_{0t} + \gamma_{1t}E_{t-1} + \gamma_{2t}R_{M\,t-1} + \gamma_{3t}R_{M\,t-2} + \varepsilon_t$ The equation shows a forecast model of the number of equity issues in the quarter of issue. *E* is the level of new equity issues.[86] R_M is the return on the equity market in quarters *t-1* and *t-2*, which contains information about the general market environment.[87] For convertible bond issuers, I use a similar model, but substitute the number of equity issues by the number of convertible bond issues in the respective quarter. Furthermore, I include the effective yield of a medium-term government security in the two quarters preceding the issue in the analysis, since convertible debt issuers will also take the interest rate environment into account when deciding about a convertible debt issue.
RUNUP	Pre-issue share price runup	The pre-issue share price runup is an important variable in the analysis for different reasons. On the one hand, it might proxy for valuable investment opportunities. For example, Jung/Kim/Stulz (1996) predict that equity issuers with more valuable investment opportunities should have a better performance.[88] Stein's (1992) and Mayers' (1998) models have similar implications for convertible debt issuers.[89] On the other hand, it might capture the degree of overvaluation of a firm's stock. Graham/Harvey (2001) find that managers equate high pre-issue share price runups with high achievable prices for newly issued securities.[90] Bayless/Chaplinski (1991) as well as Jung/Kim/Stulz (1996) find the pre-issue return to be an important determinant of the equity issue decision.[91] According to the traditional hypothesis, firms with higher pre-issue share price runups should have a stronger post-issue operating performance. The timing-hypothesis suggests that the relation should be negative. The pre-issue share price runup is calculated as the cumulative net-of-the-market return during the year preceding the issue announcement.[92]
FCF	Free cash flow	Free cash flow is cash flow in excess of funds required to finance all positive net present value projects.[93] McLaughlin/Safiedinne/Vasudevan (1996) show that equity issuers with higher pre-issue free cash flow have larger declines in post-issue earnings, which is consistent with Jensen (1986).[94] I include the measure of free cash flow as in Lee/Figlewicz (1999).[95]
RISK	Asset risk	The asset beta as a measure for the systematic asset risk a firm faces is included for two reasons. First, risk may lead investors to ration firms out of the equity market. Second, systematic differences in asset risk between convertible debt and equity issuers may have an effect on the post-issue performance. As in Lewis/Rogalski/Seward (2002), I calculate the asset beta by unlevering the equity beta, which is estimated on the basis of stock returns during the year preceding the issue, under the assumption that the debt beta is zero.[96]

84 See Spiess/Affleck-Graves (1999), p. 64 f.
85 See Marsh (1982), p. 133.
86 I obtained issuance volumes from Thomson One Banker deals for the five years preceding the issue to estimate the model.
87 The return on the equity market is measured using an equal-weighted CRSP index.
88 See Jung/Kim/ Stulz (1996), p. 170.
89 See Stein (1992), p. 3 ff.; Mayers (1998), p. 83 ff.
90 See Graham/Harvey (2001), p. 216.
91 See Bayless/Chaplinsky (1991), p. 203; Jung/Kim/Stulz (1996), p. 172.
92 *RUNUP* is calculated for the time frame [-260;-11], where 0 is the announcement day.
93 See Jensen (1986), p. 323.
94 See McLaughlin/Safieddine/Vasudevan (1996), p. 41 ff.
95 See Lee/Figlewicz (1999), p. 551.
96 See Lewis/Rogalski/Seward (2002), p. 72

4 *Operating performance*

The analysis of operating performance is the first test for the implications of the hypotheses described in section 2. I briefly outline the research design in section 4.1. Section 4.2 and 4.3 illustrate the evolution of metrics of operating performance around convertible debt issues and equity issues, respectively. Section 4.4 compares the operating performance of convertible debt and equity issuers, in particular to analyze the implications of the rationing-hypothesis. Finally, section 4.5 tests the implications of the timing-hypothesis in a multivariate analysis of the determinants of the post-issue operating performance.

4.1 Methodology

The analysis of operating performance uses a similar research design as Loughran/Ritter (1997) and Lewis/Rogalski/Seward (2001), who compare six accounting ratios of issuing and matched non-issuing firms.[97] Four ratios of earnings performance (OIBD/assets, return on assets, OIBD/sales and profit margin), which measure the efficient utilization of a firm's asset base and sales, respectively, are examined. Throughout the paper, I refer to these measures as earnings metrics.[98]

In addition, I consider two investment-related performance ratios ((capital expenditures + research and development expenses)/assets and market-to-book ratio). They provide evidence on the current investment intensity and the profitability of future growth opportunities. These ratios are referred to as investment metrics. More information on the six performance metrics is available from the tables in section 4.2.

I examine the operating performance of convertible debt and equity issuers in absolute and relative terms. For the latter, I construct a sample of matched firms that allows the calculation of abnormal operating performance. It also allows controlling for mean reversion in accounting ratios as well as for macroeconomic factors that may have an impact on a firm's operating performance.[99]

---

[97] See Loughran/Ritter (1997), p. 1826 ff.; Lewis/Rogalski/Seward (2001), p. 453.

[98] Operating income before depreciation and amortization (OIBD) is a clean measure of the productivity of a firm's assets, because it excludes special items, tax considerations, minority interests and especially interest expenses. Return on assets and return on sales, in contrast, are based on net income. Hence, OIBD metrics ensure better comparability between convertible debt and equity issues. See Barber/Lyon (1996), p. 364.

[99] Fama/French (1995), p. 136 f. report that accounting ratios are mean-reverting.

An important issue is how this sample of matching firms is selected. I use a propensity score method as in Hillion/Vermaelen (2004).[100] It appears to be superior to the algorithm used by Loughran/Ritter (1997), which I briefly describe in the following for a better understanding.[101] The Loughran/Ritter (1997) method determines matching firms on the basis of size, industry affiliation and the issue-year operating income before depreciation and amortization to assets (OIBD/assets) ratio. Specifically, matching firms have to appear in the Compustat database and have to be listed on the AMEX, NYSE or the Nasdaq. Their last convertible bond or equity issue must date back at least five years prior to the event. From this universe, firms with the same 2-digit-SIC code and with an asset size in the range of 25% to 200% of the issuer's event-year asset size are ranked on the basis of the OIBD/assets ratio. The firm with the ratio of OIBD/assets closest to the issuer's ratio is selected as the matching firm. If no match is found on the basis of these criteria, the non-issuer with an asset size of 90% to 110% of the issuer's asset size, without regard to industry, with the closest but higher ratio of OIBD/assets is chosen.

Two problems can arise with regard to this method to find appropriate matching firms: first, a partial match may not yield the most relevant group for comparison. A match only on OIBD/assets appears arbitrary, and the consideration of further variables of operating performance may improve the quality of the matching firm sample. For example, empirical research shows that convertible debt issuers are investment-intensive firms with higher market-to-book ratios.[102] This finding should be taken into account in the attempt to find the most appropriate matching firm. Second, the requirements imposed on the asset size criterion may not be judicious.[103]

These problems are reflected in the studies of Loughran/Ritter (1997) and Lewis/Rogalski/ Seward (2001) in the fact that several accounting ratios show significant differences for issuing and non-issuing firms in the matching year.[104] These differences do not indicate that the matching algorithm produces relevant groups of comparison for security issuers.

To accommodate these problems, I use a propensity score matching algorithm, which does not impose constraints on the number or value of matching variables and which has performed

[100] See Hillion/Vermaelen (2004), p. 398 ff.
[101] Loughran/Ritter (1997), p. 1826 ff. and Lewis/Rogalski/Seward (2001), p. 453 use this algorithm in their studies.
[102] See Lewis/Rogalski/Seward (2001), p. 454 f.; Essig (1992), p. 39 f.
[103] See Hillion/Vermaelen (2004), p. 398.
[104] See Loughran/Ritter (1997), p. 1829; Lewis/Rogalski/Seward (2001), p. 454 f.

reasonably well in other studies.[105] The nearest-match version of this method works as follows:

1. A logistic regression model is estimated using the same universe of firms (coded as zero) as the Loughran/Ritter (1997) method plus all firms that issued securities (coded as one) to obtain estimated conditional probabilities (propensity scores), both for issuing and non-issuing firms. The explanatory variables in the regression are the natural logarithm of the book value of total assets (Compustat item #6) as well as the six accounting ratios described above in the fiscal year prior to the issue.
2. All issuers are ranked in ascending order according to their propensity score.
3. The non-issuer with the closest score to the respective issuer's score is chosen as the matching firm. I require this firm to have data for the three years preceding the issue year. If a matching firm ceases to be traded independently, I splice in data of a replacement firm on a point-forward basis.
4. The three-step matching procedure is conducted separately for convertible debt and equity issuers for the fiscal year prior to the announcement (1999 to 2001).

The advantage of the propensity score is that it reduces the dimensionality of the matching problem: it chooses the firm as matching firm, which is most comparable to the event firm with regard to all characteristics considered in the analysis, but does not subsequently issue securities.

Due to skewness of accounting ratios, I only report medians and use a Wilcoxon matched-pair signed-rank test (z-statistic), shown in formula III.2, to test for significant differences between medians of issuing and non-issuing firms.[106] The difference in an accounting ratio between issuer *i* and its matching firm is denoted as d_i = *Ratio (issuer*$_i$*)* – *Ratio (non-issuer*$_i$*)*. The absolute values of d_i are ranked from one to N. The positive values of d_i are then summed and denoted as D. Under the null hypothesis that issuer and non-issuer accounting ratios are drawn from the same distribution, the test statistic is unit normally distributed.

Formula III.2: $$Z = \frac{D - E(D)}{\sigma_D} \quad \text{with} \quad E(D) = \frac{N*(N+1)}{4} \quad \text{and} \quad \sigma_D^2 = \frac{N*(N+1)(2N+1)}{24}$$

[105] See for example Villalonga (2004), p. 5 ff.

[106] See Loughran/Ritter (1997), p. 1830. To test for significant differences between metrics for convertible debt and equity issuers, I use ordinary Wilcoxon signed-rank tests.

Table III.3 displays the medians of operating performance metrics for event firms (EF) and matching firms (MF) for the matching year for the Loughran/Ritter (1997) and propensity score algorithm.

Table III.3: A comparison of matching algorithms

This table compares the propensity score and the Loughran/Ritter (1997) algorithm to find appropriate matching firms for convertible debt (panel A) and equity issuers (panel B). Reported are medians of different metrics of operating performance in the matching year, which is year –1 for the propensity score method and year 0 for the Loughran/Ritter (1997) method. The six accounting ratios are OIBD/assets (OIBD plus interest income (item 13 + item 62) divided by total assets (item 6)), OIBD/sales (OIBD plus interest income (item 13 + item 62) divided by sales (item 12)), return on assets (net income including extraordinary items (item 172) divided by total assets (item 6)), profit margin (net income including extraordinary items (item 172) divided by sales (item 12)), (CE+RD)/assets (capital expenditures (item 128) + research and development expenses (item 46) divided by total assets (item 6)) and the market-to-book ratio (shares outstanding (item 54) times price (item 199) divided by book value of common equity (item 60)). Matching firms are drawn from a universe of all firms listed on Compustat and CRSP that have not issued convertible debt or equity during the five years prior to the event. The propensity score matching algorithm chooses benchmark firms as follows: in the year prior to the offering, a logistic regression model is estimated where issuers are coded as one and non-issuers are coded as zero. From this regression, propensity scores are obtained. Issuers are then ranked on their propensity score in ascending order. The non-issuer that has the closest propensity score to the issuer's score is chosen as the matching firm. The Loughran/Ritter (1997) algorithm selects the firm in the same 2-digit SIC industry with assets in the range of 25% to 200% of the event firm that has the closest ratio of OIBD/assets. If no such firm is available, then from all non-issuing firms with an asset size within 90% to 110% of the event firm, the firm with the closest, but higher, OIBD/asset ratio is chosen without regard to industry affiliation. A matching firm is required to have three years of data prior to the event. If it ceases to exist independently in Compustat, data from the next-best firm is spliced in on a point-forward basis. To test for significant differences in performance metrics, I use a Wilcoxon matched-pair signed-rank test (z-statistic) as in Loughran/Ritter (1997). Values of this test statistic are indicated in parentheses. ***, ** and * indicate a significance level of 1%, 5% and 10%, respectively, for a two-sided test. CD denotes the convertible debt sample and SEO is the equity sample. MF is the abbreviation for matching firm.

Panel A: Operating performance of convertible debt issuers and matching firms in matching year

	OIBD/assets	*OIBD/sales*	*ROA*	*Profit margin*	*(CE+RD)/assets*	*Market/book*	*N*
Propensity score							
CD	10.7%	14.5%	2.8%	3.4%	10.5%	3.36	218
MF	11.0%	10.9%	2.6%	2.7%	7.1%	1.92	218
z-statistic	[-1.44] *	[0.53]	[0.45]	[-0.17]	[4.65] ***	[5.92] ***	218
Loughran/Ritter							
CD	9.4%	13.4%	1.7%	1.8%	9.1%	2.61	225
MF	10.0%	10.8%	1.5%	1.3%	7.1%	1.72	225
z-statistic	[-1.78] **	[1.50] *	[1.53] *	[2.05] **	[3.90] ***	[6.29] ***	225

Panel B: Operating performance of equity issuers and matching firms in matching year

	OIBD/assets	*OIBD/sales*	*ROA*	*Profit margin*	*(CE+RD)/assets*	*Market/book*	*N*
Propensity score							
SEO	10.8%	13.0%	2.3%	2.3%	9.6%	2.65	219
MF	11.0%	9.9%	2.5%	2.0%	9.0%	1.67	219
z-statistic	[0.05]	[0.65]	[0.52]	[-0.64]	[0.34]	[4.17] ***	219
Loughran/Ritter							
SEO	10.2%	13.4%	2.7%	3.1%	7.9%	2.13	228
MF	10.6%	11.1%	2.6%	3.1%	7.1%	1.53	228
z-statistic	[-0.13]	[-1.07]	[-0.27]	[-1.71] **	[0.62]	[4.14] ***	228

Panel A shows results for convertible debt issuers. It becomes obvious that the matching procedure is more successful when the propensity score method is used. While it is not possible to find firms that are comparable with regard to the investment metrics, the earnings metrics are not significantly different from each other but OIBD/assets. In contrast, even though the Loughran/Ritter (1997) procedure matches on issue-year OIBD/assets, there are significant differences in this ratio between convertible debt issuers and their matching firms. The other performance metrics are significantly different for issuing and matching firms as well.

Panel B shows results for equity issuers. The Loughran/Ritter (1997) algorithm is much more successful here than for convertible debt issuers, but the set of matching firms produced by the propensity score method still appears to be more appropriate, since here the only significant difference is the market-to-book ratio.

4.2 Operating performance of convertible debt issuers

Metrics of operating performance for convertible debt issuers and their matching firms for year –3 to year +2 around the offering year, year 0, are shown in panel A and B of table III.4. Panel C contains year-by-year z-statistics. A positive (negative) z-statistic indicates that the median operating performance metric for the issuers is higher (lower) than the respective median metric for the non-issuers in the same year.

According to the traditional hypothesis, convertible debt issuers should not underperform. It becomes immediately obvious that this hypothesis has to be rejected, since metrics of operating performance for convertible debt issuers significantly decline. To this end, the evidence is consistent with previous studies of the post-issue operating performance of convertible debt issuers.

In particular, OIBD/assets decline from 9.1% in the issue year to 7.6% two years later. In contrast, the OIBD/assets ratio for matching firms is stable over this time period. The OIBD/sales ratio shows a similar picture, albeit this metric declines less. The profit margin and return on assets decline significantly in the first year following the offering and rebound in year +2. The investment intensity, captured by (CE+RD)/assets, is on a higher level for convertible debt issuers than for matching firms before and after the offering. This is consistent with results from previous studies, which find convertible debt issuers to be more investment-intensive firms.[107]

An important insight into the financing behaviour of firms issuing convertible debt is contained in panel D, where an issuer's pre-issue performance (change from year –3 to year 0) and post-issue performance (change from year 0 to year +2), respectively, is compared with that of its matching firm. The picture is quite clear: during the years preceding the offering, absolute performance declines for convertible debt issuers. However, the positive signs of the test statistics indicate that convertible debt issuers perform stronger than matching firms with regard to the four earnings ratios and hence, the abnormal pre-issue performance is positive.[108]

After the offering, convertible debt issuers perform significantly worse than their matching firms, both in terms of earnings and investment metrics. The market-to-book ratio, which is unusually high prior to the transaction, suggests that investors overestimate the profitability of future investment projects and do not foresee a post-issue earnings decline.[109] This may indicate that a firm is overvalued at issuance. The decline of (CE+RD)/assets suggests that managers do not share the market's overoptimistic assessment of an issuer's future prospects. One would expect this ratio to increase at least in the offering year or the year following the offering, if managers considered investment opportunities to be valuable. This preliminary finding hints to the timing-hypothesis for convertible debt issuance.

[107] See Lewis/Rogalski/Seward (2001), p. 454 f.; Essig (1992), p. 39 f.

[108] To this end, the absolute decline in performance metrics prior to convertible debt issues may also be due to mean reversion or other trends that persist economy-wide.

[109] See Purnanandam/Bhaskaran (2004), p. 813 f. for a similar interpretation for IPOs.

Table III.4: Operating performance of convertible debt issuers

This table reports medians of different metrics of operating performance for a sample of convertible debt issuers in panel A and their matching firms in panel B from year –3 to year +2, where year 0 is the offering year. The six accounting ratios are OIBD/assets (OIBD plus interest income (item 13 + item 62) divided by total assets (item 6)), OIBD/sales (OIBD plus interest income (item 13 + item 62) divided by sales (item 12)), return on assets (net income including extraordinary items (item 172) divided by total assets (item 6)), profit margin (net income including extraordinary items (item 172) divided by sales (item 12)), (CE+RD)/assets (capital expenditures (item 128) + research and development expenses (item 46) divided by total assets (item 6)) and the market-to-book ratio (shares outstanding (item 54) times price (item 199) divided by book value of common equity (item 60)). Due to skewness of accounting ratios, I only report medians and use a Wilcoxon matched-pair signed-rank test as in Loughran/Ritter (1997) to test for significant differences in median performance metrics of event and matching firms. Values of test statistics are indicated in parentheses in panel C. ***, ** and * indicate a significance level of 1%, 5% and 10%, respectively, for a two-sided test. Panel D aggregates the performance for the pre- (changes in medians from year –3 to year 0) and post-issue period (changes in medians from year 0 to year +2). CD denotes the convertible debt sample. MF is the abbreviation for matching firm.

Panel A: Convertible debt issuer median values

Year relative to offering	*OIBD/assets*	*OIBD/sales*	*ROA*	*Profit margin*	*(CE+RD)/assets*	*Market/book*	*N*
-3	11.4%	13.7%	3.2%	3.7%	14.6%	2.90	213
-2	11.5%	14.9%	3.0%	3.2%	12.3%	3.15	218
-1	10.7%	14.5%	2.8%	3.4%	10.5%	3.36	218
0	9.1%	13.4%	1.4%	1.4%	9.1%	2.65	218
1	8.4%	12.5%	1.0%	1.2%	8.6%	2.17	206
2	7.6%	12.5%	1.5%	1.8%	7.7%	2.20	195

Panel B: Matching firm median values

Year relative to offering	*OIBD/assets*	*OIBD/sales*	*ROA*	*Profit margin*	*(CE+RD)/assets*	*Market/book*	*N*
-3	13.7%	12.4%	4.5%	4.0%	8.9%	2.32	213
-2	12.3%	11.2%	3.8%	3.2%	7.3%	1.98	218
-1	11.0%	10.9%	2.6%	2.7%	7.1%	1.92	218
0	10.1%	10.4%	1.8%	1.3%	6.3%	1.76	218
1	9.5%	9.5%	1.7%	1.6%	5.9%	1.64	206
2	10.1%	9.6%	2.5%	1.9%	5.6%	1.80	195

Table III.4 continued

Panel C: Median tests of equality

Year relative to offering	*OIBD/assets*	*OIBD/sales*	*ROA*	*Profit margin*	*(CE+RD)/assets*	*Market/book*	*N*
-3	[-3.35] ***	[0.05]	[-3.30] ***	[-1.59] *	[5.54] ***	[0.10]	213
-2	[-2.14] **	[-0.07]	[-1.97] **	[-1.45] *	[5.39] ***	[4.90] ***	218
-1	[-1.44] *	[0.53]	[0.45]	[-0.17]	[4.65] ***	[5.92] ***	218
0	[-2.42] ***	[2.00] **	[-0.69]	[-1.01]	[3.93] ***	[5.50] ***	218
1	[-2.87] ***	[0.91]	[-1.94] **	[-1.69] **	[4.09] ***	[2.82] ***	206
2	[-3.52] ***	[1.15]	[-2.27] **	[-1.34] *	[4.19] ***	[1.41] *	195

Panel D: Changes in median performance metrics

Year relative to offering	*OIBD/assets*	*OIBD/sales*	*ROA*	*Profit margin*	*(CE+RD)/assets*	*Market/book*	*N*
-3 to 0							
CD	-2.3%	-0.3%	-1.7%	-2.2%	-5.5%	-0.25	213
MF	-3.7%	-2.0%	-2.7%	-2.6%	-2.6%	-0.57	213
z-statistic	[3.07] ***	[3.20] ***	[2.84] ***	[1.44] *	[-3.11] ***	[4.42] ***	
0 to 2							
CD	-1.5%	-0.9%	0.1%	0.4%	-1.4%	-0.45	195
MF	0.0%	-0.7%	0.7%	0.5%	-0.7%	0.04	195
z-statistic	[-2.52] ***	[-3.18] ***	[-1.38] *	[-1.18]	[-0.94]	[-3.43] ***	

4.3 Operating performance of equity issuers

Before I compare operating performance metrics for convertible debt issuers with those of equity issuers to test the rationing-hypothesis, I present them in this section in table III.5.

In panel A, a significant deterioration of all earnings metrics following equity issues can be observed. OIBD/assets drop significantly from year 0 to year +2. So do OIBD/sales, although the decline is less pronounced. The return on assets (profit margin) metric declines from 2.4% (2.7%) in year 0 to 1.9% (2.1%) in year +2.

As for convertible debt issuers, investment expenditures remain on a higher level for equity issuers than those of matching firms. While the median market-to-book ratio is higher, too, for equity issuers from year –3 to year +1, it declines significantly in year +2, where the market revises its evaluation of equity issuers downwards. This pattern is similar to the one detected in table III.4.

When examining changes in operating performance metrics, I find evidence that corresponds to the findings of Loughran/Ritter (1997), Rangan (1998) and Teoh/Wong/Welch (1998):[110] the median change in earnings metrics from year –3 to year 0 is positive and significantly more pronounced for equity issuers than for matching firms, supporting the notion that equity issues are timed with periods of strong operating performance.

However, the changes in performance metrics during the two-year period following the equity issue are negative. Median earnings ratios decline between 0.54% (return on assets) and 2.46% (OIBD/assets).

[110] See Loughran/Ritter (1997), p. 1829; Rangan (1998), p. 101 ff.; Teoh/Welch/Wong (1998), p. 63 ff.

Table III.5: Operating performance of equity issuers

This table reports medians of different metrics of operating performance for a sample of equity issuers in panel A and their matching firms in panel B from year –3 to year +2, where year 0 is the offering year. The six accounting ratios are OIBD/assets (OIBD plus interest income (item 13 + item 62) divided by total assets (item 6)), OIBD/sales (OIBD plus interest income (item 13 + item 62) divided by sales (item 12)), return on assets (net income including extraordinary items (item 172) divided by total assets (item 6)), profit margin (net income including extraordinary items (item 172) divided by sales (item 12)), (CE+RD)/assets (capital expenditures (item 128) + research and development expenses (item 46) divided by total assets (item 6)) and the market-to-book ratio (shares outstanding (item 54) times price (item 199) divided by book value of common equity (item 60)). Due to skewness of accounting ratios, I only report medians and use a Wilcoxon matched-pair signed-rank test as in Loughran/Ritter (1997) to test for significant differences in median performance metrics of event and matching firms. Values of test statistics are indicated in parentheses in panel C. ***, ** and * indicate a significance level of 1%, 5% and 10%, respectively, for a two-sided test. Panel D aggregates the performance for the pre- (changes in medians from year –3 to year 0) and post-issue period (changes in medians from year 0 to year +2). SEO denotes the seasoned equity offerings sample. MF is the abbreviation for matching firm.

Panel A: Equity issuer median values

Year relative to offering	*OIBD/assets*	*OIBD/sales*	*ROA*	*Profit margin*	*(CE+RD)/assets*	*Market/book*	*N*
-3	11.2%	13.7%	2.1%	2.4%	9.5%	1.73	200
-2	10.8%	12.7%	2.1%	2.0%	10.1%	1.60	219
-1	10.8%	13.0%	2.3%	2.3%	9.6%	2.65	219
0	9.9%	13.3%	2.4%	2.7%	7.7%	2.04	219
1	8.5%	12.7%	1.6%	2.3%	7.8%	2.00	205
2	7.4%	12.5%	1.9%	2.1%	6.7%	1.67	187

Panel B: Matching firm median values

Year relative to offering	*OIBD/assets*	*OIBD/sales*	*ROA*	*Profit margin*	*(CE+RD)/assets*	*Market/book*	*N*
-3	14.0%	11.8%	4.3%	3.8%	9.3%	2.08	200
-2	12.5%	11.7%	3.4%	3.6%	8.5%	1.75	219
-1	11.0%	9.9%	2.5%	2.0%	9.0%	1.67	219
0	10.1%	9.1%	0.8%	0.9%	7.3%	1.52	219
1	10.9%	9.3%	1.4%	1.2%	6.8%	1.71	205
2	11.6%	9.6%	3.3%	2.6%	6.6%	1.73	187

Table III.5 continued

Panel C: Median tests of equality

Year relative to offering	*OIBD/assets*	*OIBD/sales*	*ROA*	*Profit margin*	*(CE+RD)/assets*	*Market/book*	*N*
-3	[-2.97] ***	[-0.51]	[-3.53] ***	[-2.45] ***	[1.43] *	[-3.38] ***	200
-2	[-2.78] ***	[-1.36] *	[-3.01] ***	[-2.96] ***	[1.90] **	[-1.04]	219
-1	[0.05]	[0.65]	[0.52]	[-0.64]	[0.34]	[4.17] ***	219
0	[0.49]	[1.17]	[1.03]	[-0.53]	[0.94]	[3.94] ***	219
1	[-1.57] *	[-0.37]	[-1.12]	[-1.21]	[1.68] **	[2.43] ***	205
2	[-2.18] **	[-0.55]	[-1.98] **	[-2.43] ***	[-0.09]	[0.26]	187

Panel D: Changes in median performance metrics

Year relative to offering	*OIBD/assets*	*OIBD/sales*	*ROA*	*Profit margin*	*(CE+RD)/assets*	*Market/book*	*N*
-3 to 0							
SEO	-1.3%	-0.3%	0.3%	0.2%	-1.8%	0.31	200
MF	-3.9%	-2.7%	-3.5%	-3.0%	-2.0%	-0.56	200
z-statistic	[3.39] ***	[2.81] ***	[4.49] ***	[2.33] ***	[-1.24] *	[4.28] ***	
0 to 2							
SEO	-2.5%	-0.9%	-0.5%	-0.6%	-1.0%	-0.37	187
MF	1.5%	0.5%	2.5%	1.8%	-0.8%	0.21	187
z-statistic	[-3.39] ***	[-0.91]	[-4.18] ***	[-2.01] **	[0.57]	[-4.07] ***	

4.4 A comparison of operating performance

The major finding from the previous two sections is that convertible debt and equity issues are followed by declines in operating performance. To this end, convertible debt does not induce optimal investment incentives, which is inconsistent with the traditional hypothesis, but supports the rationing- and timing-hypothesis.

The operating performance of convertible debt and equity issuers has some implications for the rationing-hypothesis. If convertible debt issuers are foreclosed from participation in the equity market, this could be due to the fact that these firms are poorer performers than equity issuers. I compare levels and changes of operating performance metrics of convertible debt and equity issuers in table III.6. Absolute statistics of operating performance are shown in panel A and changes from years –3 to 0 and 0 to +2 in panel B and C.

In panel A, absolute performance metrics are slightly higher for equity issuers, but these differences are not statistically significant. The market-to-book ratio is significantly higher for convertible debt issuers. To this end, if investors use absolute performance metrics to evaluate convertible debt and equity issuers, the rationing-hypothesis does not receive support, since the two types of issuers have comparable issue-year operating characteristics.[111]

In panel B, the pre- and post-issue operating performance is compared. The pre-issue operating performance is generally higher for equity issuers, which shows that these security offerings are timed well with periods of strong operating performance. Differences in performance metrics are significant for the profit margin and return on assets. During the post-issue period, in contrast, convertible debt issuers perform stronger than equity issuers.

A problem with the analysis in panel B is that convertible debt and equity issuers may not be entirely comparable firms. To solve this problem, I calculate the abnormal operating performance for convertible debt and equity issuers as follows: I compute the change in the median of a performance metric from year –3 (0) to year 0 (+2) as in panel B and subtract the change in median of the same metric of the respective matching firm over the same time horizon. I show the results of this analysis in panel C and observe that the main findings from panel B remain unchanged: on the one hand, the abnormal pre-issue operating performance for convertible debt issuers is, albeit positive, weaker than that of equity issuers. On the other hand, the abnormal post-issue operating performance is stronger for convertible debt issuers.

[111] An analysis based on operating characteristics for the year preceding the issue does not yield any different results.

Three metrics, OIBD/assets, OIBD/sales and return on assets, are significantly higher for these firms than for equity issuers in panel C.

Table III.6: A comparison of operating performance

This table compares medians of different metrics of operating performance for a sample of convertible debt issues and equity issues in absolute terms in panel A and absolute changes in medians in panel B. In panel C, I show changes in medians relative to changes in medians of matching firms to construct measures of matching firm-adjusted abnormal performance. The six accounting ratios are OIBD/assets (OIBD plus interest income (item 13 + item 62) divided by total assets (item 6)), OIBD/sales (OIBD plus interest income (item 13 + item 62) divided by sales (item 12)), return on assets (net income including extraordinary items (item 172) divided by total assets (item 6)), profit margin (net income including extraordinary items (item 172) divided by sales (item 12)), (CE+RD)/assets (capital expenditures (item 128) + research and development expenses (item 46) divided by total assets (item 6)) and the market-to-book ratio (shares outstanding (item 54) times price (item 199) divided by book value of common equity (item 60)). To test for significant differences in median performance metrics between convertible debt and equity issuers, I use a one-sided Wilcoxon signed-rank test. Values of test statistics are indicated in parentheses. ***, ** and * indicate a significance level of 1%, 5% and 10%, respectively. CD denotes the convertible debt sample and SEO is the seasoned equity offerings sample.

Panel A: Absolute median values

	OIBD/assets	*OIBD/sales*	*ROA*	*Profit margin*	*(CE+RD)/assets*	*Market/book*
Year 0						
CD	9.1%	13.4%	1.4%	1.4%	9.1%	2.65
SEO	9.9%	13.3%	2.4%	2.7%	7.7%	2.04
z-statistic	[0.36]	[0.55]	[1.22]	[0.62]	[1.21]	[3.05] ***

Panel B: Changes in absolute median performance metrics

Year relative to offering	*OIBD/assets*	*OIBD/sales*	*ROA*	*Profit margin*	*(CE+RD)/assets*	*Market/book*
-3 to 0						
CD	-2.3%	-0.3%	-1.7%	-2.2%	-5.5%	-0.25
SEO	-1.3%	-0.3%	0.3%	0.2%	-1.8%	0.31
z-statistic	[1.25]	[0.36]	[2.69] ***	[1.74] **	[2.56] ***	[0.84]
0 to 2						
CD	-1.5%	-0.9%	0.1%	0.4%	-1.4%	-0.45
SEO	-2.5%	-0.9%	-0.5%	-0.6%	-1.0%	-0.37
z-statistic	[0.30]	[0.62]	[2.22] **	[1.28] *	[1.07]	[0.16]

Panel C: Changes in matching firm-adjusted median performance metrics

Year relative to offering	*OIBD/assets*	*OIBD/sales*	*ROA*	*Profit margin*	*(CE+RD)/assets*	*Market/book*
-3 to 0						
CD	1.4%	1.6%	1.0%	0.4%	-2.8%	0.31
SEO	2.6%	2.4%	3.8%	3.2%	0.2%	0.87
z-statistic	[0.69]	[0.05]	[1.64] **	[0.79]	[1.43] *	[0.16]
0 to 2						
CD	-1.6%	-0.2%	-0.6%	-0.1%	-0.8%	-0.48
SEO	-4.0%	-1.4%	-3.0%	-2.4%	-0.2%	-0.59
z-statistic	[1.36] *	[1.31] *	[2.15] **	[0.60]	[0.64]	[0.69]

My interpretation of these results is that convertible debt issuers are unlikely to be rationed out of the market for seasoned equity on the basis of their operating characteristics. First, differences in the pre-issue operating performance are hardly pronounced. Second, convertible debt issuers perform stronger than their matching firms after the offering. Hence, the market would be systematically wrong in its assessment of convertible debt issuers: if any firm should be foreclosed from participation in the market for seasoned equity due to its post-issue operating performance, it should be the typical equity issuer.

4.5 Determinants of operating performance

Market-to-book ratios for convertible debt and equity issuers are significantly higher than those of matching firms at issuance, although their operating performance after the issue declines abnormally. If the capital market overestimates an issuer's future earnings, firms may time security issues with these transitory mispricings of their stock.

To shed further light on the role of market timing, I analyze the cross-sectional variation in metrics of post-issue operating performance. I employ an OLS-regression framework, where the dependent variables are the abnormal changes of OIBD/assets and return on assets, respectively, from year 0 to year +2.[112] The explanatory variables have been illustrated in table III.2. I estimate the regression model for the complete sample and employ differential coefficients as well as differential slope coefficients to capture differential effects that may exist in the convertible debt sample.[113] Table III.7 documents the regression results for OIBD/assets in panel A and return on assets in panel B.

---

[112] There are two reasons, an economic and a statistical one, why I do not include OIBD/sales and the profit margin in this analysis. The economic reason is that these measures do not provide direct evidence of how efficiently a firm uses its asset base. The statistical reason is that regressions with OIBD/sales and profit margin as dependent variables are misspecified due to significant outliers. This problem is less pronounced for OIBD/assets and return on assets, where it is sufficient to trim the sample and delete issuers below the 2nd or above the 98th percentile to achieve a satisfying model specification.

[113] This approach allows to assess whether statistically significant differences in the convertible debt and equity samples exist. Re-estimation of the regression models for the two samples separately does not qualitively affect my conclusions.

Table III.7: Determinants of operating performance

This table contains an OLS-regression analysis of the determinants of operating performance. The dependent variables are the matching firm-adjusted changes in medians from year 0 to year +2 for OIBD/assets (panel A) and return on assets (panel B). I estimate the regression for the complete sample and include dummy variables as well as differential slope coefficients to capture differential effects that may exist in the convertible debt sample. To reduce the influence of outliers and improve model specification, I trim the sample deleting issuers below the 2nd or above the 98th percentile. The independent variables are: *CD* is a dummy variable that takes the value one for convertible debt issuers. *SIZE* is the natural logarithm of the market value of common stock one month prior to the offering announcement. *PU* is a dummy variable that takes the value one for firms with an SIC code of 481 or 491 to 494. *RISK* is the asset beta of a firm. *RIS* are issue proceeds scaled by the market value of the firm. *FCF* is a variable that measures the amount of free cash flow of a firm. *ISSUES* is a forecast variable for the number of convertible debt and equity issues, respectively, in the quarter of issuance. *RUNUP* is the cumulative net-of-the-market return for a firm during the year preceding the issue. *EARNINGS* is the change in a firm's matching firm-adjusted OIBD/assets ratio (return on assets) in panel A (panel B) from year –3 to year 0. *RUNUP(CD)* is a differential slope coefficient, where I include a dummy variable that takes the value one for convertible debt issuers and multiply it with the value of *RUNUP*. It captures any differential effect in the convertible debt sample. I also include differential slope coefficients for *EARNINGS* and *RISK*. Whenever I find the regression residuals to be heteroskedastic on the basis of a White-test, I use the White (1980) procedure to obtain efficient parameter estimates. ***, ** and * indicate a significance level of 1%, 5% and 10% respectively. CD denotes the convertible bond sample.

Panel A: Regression OIBD/assets

Coefficient	*1*	*2*	*3*	*4*	*5*
CONSTANT	-0.09 **	-0.10	-0.09	-0.10	-0.10
CD	0.04 ***	0.04 **	0.02	0.03 **	0.04
SIZE [a)]	0.08	0.03	0.01	0.03	0.03
PU	0.04 *	0.02	0.01	0.02	0.02
RISK	-0.02 **	-0.02 *	-0.01	-0.02 *	-0.02
RIS [a)]		0.08	0.04	0.07	0.09
FCF [a)]		0.02	0.02	0.03	0.02
ISSUES [a)]		0.01	0.01 *	0.01	0.01
RUNUP		-0.02 ***	-0.05 ***	-0.02 ***	-0.02 ***
EARNINGS		-0.16 ***	-0.16 ***	-0.20 ***	-0.16 ***
RUNUP (CD)			0.04 **		
EARNINGS (CD)				0.10	
RISK (CD)					0.00
Adjusted R^2	3.5%	13.6%	14.6%	14.1%	13.3%
F-test	[3.91] ***	[6.37] ***	[6.26] ***	[6.06] ***	[5.71] ***

Panel B: Regression return on assets

Coefficient	*1*	*2*	*3*	*4*	*5*
CONSTANT	-0.16 **	-0.19 **	-0.18 **	-0.19 **	-0.19 **
CD	0.06 **	0.07 ***	0.05 **	0.06 ***	0.06 **
SIZE [a)]	0.14 *	0.06	0.05	0.06	0.07
PU	0.04 *	0.03	0.03	0.03	0.03
RISK	-0.04 ***	-0.03 **	-0.02 *	-0.03 **	-0.03
RIS		-0.02 **	-0.02 **	-0.02 **	-0.02 **
FCF [a)]		0.03	0.03	0.03	0.03
ISSUES [a)]		0.01 *	0.01 **	0.01 **	0.01 *
RUNUP		-0.02 *	-0.04 *	-0.02 *	-0.02 *
EARNINGS		-0.27 ***	-0.27 ***	-0.28 ***	-0.27 ***
RUNUP (CD)			0.03		
EARNINGS (CD)				0.02	
RISK (CD)					0.00
Adjusted R^2	4.2%	23.2%	23.3%	23.0%	23.0%
F-test	[4.51] ***	[11.18] ***	[10.20] ***	[10.04] ***	[10.03] ***

[a)] The coefficients are multiplied with 10.

The purpose of regression 1 is to assess whether stronger performance for convertible debt than for equity issuers can still be detected when other variables that may influence a firm's operating performance are controlled for. The test variable is a dummy, denominated *CD*, which takes the value one for convertible debt issuers. It is expected to be positive and significant. I find this expectation confirmed in panels A and B of table III.7, which suggests that differences in the post-issue earnings performance of convertible debt and equity issuers cannot be explained by systematic differences in firm size or asset risk.[114]

In regression 2, I include further variables that may have an impact on a firm's operating performance. *FCF*, the free cash flow-measure, is included to examine whether the availability of surplus funds adversely impacts operating performance.[115] *RIS*, the relative issue size, is included to identify whether the volume of the transaction is related to the post-issue operating performance.[116] *ISSUES*, the number of convertible debt and equity offerings in a quarter, controls for the new issue activity in the primary market for convertible debt and equity, respectively. Previous research finds that firms issuing securities in times of higher general issue activity underperform more.[117] However, I do not observe systematic patterns for these variables over panels A and B.

The results provide strong support for the timing-hypothesis, given that variables which capture timing effects, *EARNINGS* and *RUNUP*, have negative and significant coefficients in all regressions.[118] This is intriguing, because I estimate the regression for the complete sample: obviously, changes in operating performance for convertible debt and equity issuers depend on common factors.

Rangan (1998) and Teoh/Welch/Wong (1998) show that equity issuers trim their earnings to overstate issue-year operating performance.[119] This accounts for a certain portion of the post-issue earnings downturn. The negative coefficient of the variable *EARNINGS* suggests that convertible debt issuers in my sample behave similarly.

---

[114] Smaller firms have been found to underperform more. See for example Loughran/Ritter (1997), p. 1832 f. In addition, differences in operating performance might also be due to differences in investment risk, which have to be controlled for. I also use a dummy variable that captures the effect of public utilities.

[115] See McLaughlin/Safieddine/Vasudevan (1996), p. 41 ff.

[116] See Hansen/Crutchley (1990), p. 347 ff.

[117] See Spiess/Affleck-Graves (1999), p. 64 f.

[118] Since regression residuals might be cross-sectionally dependent, I also conduct univariate median tests of equality, where I find corresponding patterns for *RUNUP* and *EARNINGS*.

[119] See Rangan (1998), p. 101 ff.; Teoh/Welch/Wong (1998), p. 63 ff.

The negative coefficient of *RUNUP* provides strong support for the timing-hypothesis.[120] The pre-issue share price runup is on average 39.4% for convertible debt issuers (and 61.8% for equity issuers). It is striking that the post-issue operating performance is negatively related to a financial variable. While one might expect that higher appreciations in a firm's stock price prior to the transaction may result in poorer post-issue stock returns, it is surprising to find a negative relation of *RUNUP* to post-issue earnings.[121] A possible explanation for this finding is that the market has severe difficulties in evaluating the issuing firms' future profitability. The fact that issuers with higher pre-issue share price appreciations have lower post-issue earnings may suggest that investors are 'fooled' by pre-issue increases in earnings. In any case, this result illustrates that investors overestimate the future operating performance of an issuer, which is consistent with an overvaluation-interpretation of the issuers' unusually high market-to-book ratios.

Do firm managers share the investors' overoptimism? If managers, too, overestimate the profitability of available investment opportunities, they may even issue convertible debt to send a signal about their optimistic view of the firm's future profitability to the market.[122] However, what managers, investors (and analysts)[123], perceive as a valuable investment program prior to the transaction is not realized subsequently and results in a poor post-issue operating and stock price performance. If managers do not share the market's overoptimism, the issue decision is not motivated by the availability of investment opportunities, but by the favourable valuation level of the issuer's common stock. Then managers may follow the recommendation of the pecking order and use the opportune moment to increase financial slack.[124]

The results show that this latter interpretation is more likely to apply. On the one hand, the coefficient (not the differential slope coefficient!) of *RUNUP* should be positive, if the first interpretation was correct: even if the value of a firm's investment opportunities is generally overestimated, one should still see that those firms with more valuable investment opportunities perform stronger subsequently. On the other hand, as documented in table III.4, investment activity declines during the post-issue period, which suggests that convertible debt

---

120 In regression 3 of panel A, the differential slope coefficient of *RUNUP* is positive and significant, which suggests that the negative effect of the pre-issue share price runup on the issuer's operating performance is less pronounced for convertible debt issuers, but still negative.

121 McLaughlin/Safieddine/Vasudevan (1998), p. 383 make a similar observation.

122 This would be consistent with Stein (1992), p. 3 ff.

123 Also analysts appear to overestimate an issuing firms' earnings prospects. See for example Ali (1997), p. 1 ff.

124 See Myers/Majluf (1984), p. 220; Loughran/Ritter (1997), p. 1848.

issuers rather increase financial slack. If managers possessed what they perceived as valuable investment opportunities, investment levels should increase.

An important question raised by this interpretation is whether firms issue convertible debt to substitute common stock: if post-issue declines in earnings spill over to a firm's financial performance and managers expect so, they may use convertible debt as a substitute for straight debt, depending on their assessment of the firm's post-issue stock price performance. This notion is further explored in the next section.

Table III.7 also provides evidence on the rationing-hypothesis. I argue above that rationing may occur due to risk rather than earnings characteristics of issuing firms. In my sample, convertible debt issuers have a significantly higher asset risk than equity issuers (the median asset beta is 1.01 as opposed to 0.60 for equity issuers). The negative coefficient of *RISK* in some of the regressions suggests that post-issue performance declines are more pronounced for firms with higher pre-issue asset risk. Risk-averse investors, who are uncertain about the attractiveness of the risk-return profile of an issuing firm or the future risk level of an issuer, may not be willing to provide direct equity funds to a firm. Instead, they use the time until the bond can be converted to screen issuers while being hedged against changes in risk.[125]

5 *Stock price performance*

The results from the previous section suggest that a firm's common stock is overvalued at issuance of convertible debt or seasoned equity and that managers use this window of opportunity to sell these securities at high prices. The analysis of the post-issue stock price performance provides a further test of this timing-interpretation: several studies document that companies, which are temporarily overvalued around the time of their security issue are likely to underperform in the capital market in the years following the offering.[126] Moreover, one may reason that firms that are more overvalued will underperform to a greater extent.

Due to methodological problems, I use a two-pronged approach to the post-issue stock price analysis.[127] First, I employ an event-time characteristics-based approach in order to obtain an

---

125 Brennan/Schwartz (1988), p. 55 ff. emphasize that firms whose risk characteristics are difficult to evaluate may issue convertible debt, because the convertible hedges investors against changes in risk. Consistent with this interpretation, systematic risk increases around convertible debt issues are documented in analyses that are the subject of chapter IV.

126 See Loughran/Ritter (1995), p. 23 ff.; Spiess/Affleck-Graves (1995), p. 265 ff.; Loughran/Ritter (1997), p. 1823 ff.; Spiess/Affleck-Graves (1999), p. 45 ff.

127 A problem emphasized by Fama (1998), p. 283 is that model specification can affect the results of a long-run performance study. Moreover, cross-sectional correlation between firm returns may yield misleading results

estimate of the magnitude of post-issue abnormal returns and analyze their cross-section. Second, I employ a calendar-time method to assess the robustness of my results.

5.1 Buy-and-hold abnormal returns

5.1.1 Methodology

Statistical problems make the analyses of long-run buy-and-hold abnormal returns (*BHARs*) difficult, since their distribution is often severely skewed. To overcome these statistical problems, I use the approach advocated by Lyon/Barber/Tsai (1999), which also eliminates biases arising from new listings and rebalancing of benchmark portfolios.[128] This approach calculates *BHARs* according to formula III.3.

Formula III.3: $$BHAR_{iT} = R_{iT} - E(R_{iT})$$

$BHAR_{iT}$ denotes the buy-and-hold abnormal return for security i over period T (in this analysis eighteen months). R_{iT} is the observed security return for security i over period T after the event and $E(R_{iT})$ is the expected security return for the corresponding period. The latter is proxied using returns of reference portfolios based on size and book-to-market (BE/ME) ratio as well as returns of the CRSP equal- and value-weighted indices.

The Lyon/Barber/Tsai (1999) method recommends the construction of 70 portfolios based on size and book-to-market ratio in the following manner:

1. Monthly returns for all NYSE/AMEX/Nasdaq firms listed on the CRSP file during the years 1999 through 2003 are obtained. Only returns of common stocks are included in the analysis. All event firms, financial institutions as well as firms that have issued convertible bonds or seasoned equity in the five years prior to the event are deleted.
2. Firm size is calculated as the number of shares outstanding multiplied by the share price in June of each year in the sample period.
3. All NYSE firms in the population are ranked to create size decile portfolios. Using the breakpoints from these portfolios, I sort AMEX and Nasdaq firms in the portfolios based on their June market value. To avoid a high concentration of smaller Nasdaq

about the pervasiveness of underperformance in event-time analyses, which are used by most studies. See for example Teoh/Welch/Wong (1998), p. 79; Lee/Loughran (1998), p. 187 f.; McLaughlin/Safieddine/Vasudevan (1998), p. 385.

128 See Barber/Lyon (1997), p. 362 f.; Lyon/Barber/Tsai (1999), p. 165 ff.

firms in the smallest size decile, it is further divided into quintiles based on size rankings. All in all, this procedure yields fourteen size portfolios.

4. The size portfolios are further partitioned into five book-to-market quintiles each without regard to exchange. Book-to-market is calculated as book value of common equity (Compustat data item #60) divided by its market value in the year prior to the offering.[129]

5. The buy-and-hold return of each reference portfolio is calculated according to formula III.4 for each month during the sample period.

Formula III.4: $$E(R_{PsT}) = \sum_{i=1}^{N_s} \frac{[\prod_{t=s}^{s+T}(1+R_{it})]-1}{N_s}$$

$E(R_{PsT})$ denotes the buy-and-hold return for a reference portfolio P consisting of N_s securities calculated in period s for T months and represents an equally-weighted passive investment in all securities contained in the portfolio in the respective period. The portfolio is neither rebalanced, nor adjusted to contain newly-listed firms, and hence does not suffer from the respective biases.[130] In calculating the portfolio returns, I fill missing monthly firm returns, for example for delisted companies, with the corresponding monthly firm returns of a size reference portfolio to mitigate survivor bias. Since the distribution of *BHARs* in some of the samples is skewed, inference is based on a bootstrapped application of a skewness-adjusted t-test, shown in formula III.5, proposed by Lyon/Barber/Tsai (1999), which involves drawing 1000 random resamples of size $N/4$ from the original sample.[131]

Formula III.5: $$t_{SA} = \sqrt{N}(S + \frac{1}{3}\hat{\gamma}S^2 + \frac{1}{6N}\hat{\gamma}) \quad \text{where} \quad S = \frac{\overline{BHAR_T}}{\sigma(BHAR_{iT})} \quad \text{and} \quad \hat{\gamma} = \frac{\sum_{i=1}^{N}(BHAR_{iT} - \overline{BHAR_T})^3}{N\sigma(BHAR_{iT})^3}$$

$\sqrt{N}S$ is a conventional t-statistic, $\overline{BHAR_T}$ is the average buy-and-hold abnormal return for time period T, $\sigma(BHAR_{iT})$ is the cross-sectional standard deviation of buy-and-hold abnormal returns and $\hat{\gamma}$ is an estimate of the coefficient of skewness.

---

[129] I delete all firms that have a negative book value of common equity during the sample period.
[130] See Barber/Lyon (1997), p. 342 f.
[131] See Lyon/Barber/Tsai (1999), p. 173 ff. for a detailed description of this test.

5.1.2 Results

Panel A of table III.8 presents the results of the *BHAR* analysis. Consistent with the rationing- and the timing-hypothesis, significant underperformance for convertible debt and equity issuers for different expected return models is documented. Thereby the results of prior studies are replicated.

The average buy-and-hold raw returns during the 18-month post-issue period are –31.55% for convertible debt and –24.48% for equity issuers. The average buy-and-hold abnormal returns are –23.31% and –21.12% for the Lyon/Barber/Tsai (1999) approach.[132] Hence, abnormal stock price performance is in similar ranges for the two types of issuers, but appears to be more pronounced than in other studies, which document yearly abnormal returns ranging between –6% and –8% for convertible debt and equity issuers on average.[133]

The results indicate that the poor post-issue operating performance has an effect on a firm's stock price performance. While investors appear to be unable to infer post-issue earnings declines from the announcement of the transaction, they gradually adjust their assessment of firm value over a longer time horizon. These results are consistent with those of studies, which conclude that overvaluation causes stock returns to be poor after a firm has issued securities.[134]

A further test of this overvaluation-interpretation consists in the analysis of the cross-section of post-issue stock returns. The assumption of this test is that if the pre-issue share price runup is cross-sectionally correlated with the degree of overvaluation, one should see stronger stock price declines for firms with higher pre-issue share price appreciations.[135] I use an OLS-regression analysis comparable to the one in section 4.5 and show the results in panel B of table III.8.[136]

---

[132] The magnitude of abnormal performance varies considerably. *BHARs* net of CRSP value-weighted returns are highest, since returns of the value-weighted index are dominated by large firms, which tend to have lower returns. See for example Fama/French (1992), p. 427 ff.

[133] See Loughran/Ritter (1995), p. 33; Spiess/Affleck-Graves (1995), p. 254; Loughran/Ritter (1997), p. 1840; Spiess/Affleck-Graves (1999), p. 55; Lewis/Rogalski/Seward (2001), p. 459.

[134] See for example Loughran/Ritter (1995), p. 23 ff.; Loughran/Ritter (1997), p. 1823 ff.

[135] This interpretation corresponds to survey evidence by Graham/Harvey (2001), p. 216 who document that managers equate large pre-issue share price appreciations with high achievable prices.

[136] Since regression residuals might be cross-sectionally dependent, I also conduct univariate median tests of equality, where I find the same patterns for *RUNUP* and *EARNINGS* as documented in table III.8.

Table III.8: Buy-and-hold abnormal returns

This table shows average 18-month raw and buy-and-hold abnormal event-time returns in panel A. *BHARs* are calculated net of Lyon/Barber/Tsai (1999) size/book-to-market portfolio returns and net of CRSP equal- and value-weighted returns. Test statistics are bootstrapped skewness-adjusted t-test (shown in parentheses). Panel B contains an OLS-regression analysis of the determinants of post-issue stock returns. The dependent variables are raw returns and *BHARs* calculated on the basis of reference portfolios as in Lyon/Barber/Tsai (1999). I estimate the regression for the complete sample and include a dummy variable to capture the effect of the convertible debt sample. Differential slope coefficients for the convertible debt sample are omitted in the table, since none of them are significant. The independent variables are: *CD* is a dummy variable that takes the value one for convertible debt issuers. *SIZE* is the natural logarithm of the market value of common stock one month prior to the offering announcement. *PU* is a dummy variable that takes the value one for firms with an SIC code of 481 or 491 to 494. *RISK* is the asset beta of a firm. *RIS* are issue proceeds scaled by the market value of the firm. *FCF* is a variable that measures the amount of free cash flow of a firm. *ISSUES* is a forecast variable for the number of convertible debt and equity issues, respectively. *RUNUP* is the cumulative net-of-the-market return for a firm during the year preceding the issue. *PRE-EARNINGS* is the change in a firm's matching firm-adjusted OIBD/assets and ROA ratio, respectively, from year –3 to year 0. *POST-EARNINGS* is the change in these ratios from year 0 to year +2. Whenever I find the regression residuals to be heteroskedastic on the basis of a White-test, I use the White (1980) procedure to obtain efficient estimates. ***, ** and * indicate a significance level of 1%, 5% and 10%, respectively.

Panel A: 18-month buy-and-hold event-time returns

	Raw returns		*Lyon/Barber/Tsai*		*CRSP VW*		*CRSP EW*	
Complete Sample	-27.82%	[-10.78] ***	-23.17%	[-9.61] ***	-11.76%	[-5.25] ***	-33.57%	[-15.30] ***
Convertible debt sample (CD)	-31.55%	[-9.08] ***	-23.31%	[-7.84] ***	-12.90%	[-4.32] ***	-33.87%	[-11.38] ***
Equity sample (SEO)	-24.48%	[-6.49] ***	-21.12%	[-5.91] ***	-10.63%	[-3.18] ***	-33.28%	[-10.31] ***

Panel B: Multivariate analysis of buy-and-hold raw and abnormal returns

	Buy-and-hold raw returns		**Buy-and-hold abnormal returns**	
Coefficient	***OIBD/assets***	***Return on assets***	***OIBD/assets***	***Return on assets***
CONSTANT	0.65 ***	0.65 ***	0.58 ***	0.56 **
CD	-0.0	0.00	-0.12	-0.10
SIZE	-0.07 ***	-0.07 ***	-0.03	-0.03
PU	-0.22 **	-0.20 *	-0.22 **	-0.20 **
RISK	-0.20 ***	-0.23 ***	-0.13 ***	-0.16 ***
RIS	-0.02	-0.02	-0.01	-0.01
FCF[a)]	0.05	0.08 **	0.03	0.06
ISSUES[a)]	-0.01	0.00	-0.02 *	-0.02 *
RUNUP	-0.14 ***	-0.16 ***	-0.06 **	-0.08 **
PRE-EARNINGS	-0.09	0.06	-0.04	0.09
POST-EARNINGS	0.71 ***	0.18	0.73 ***	0.19
Adjusted R^2	23.6%	21.7%	12.0%	10.1%
F-test	[10.04] ***	[9.19] ***	[4.97] ***	[4.30] ***

[a)] The coefficients are multiplied with 10.

The dependent variables are buy-and-hold raw returns (columns 1 and 2) as well as *BHARs* calculated on the basis of Lyon/Barber/Tsai (1999) benchmark portfolios (columns 3 and 4). The independent variables are the same as in section 4.5 plus *POST-EARNINGS*, defined as the changes in median OIBD/assets and return on assets, respectively, from year 0 to year +2, to control for the post-issue operating performance.[137]

The determinants of post-issue stock returns shown in panel B are similar to the determinants of post-issue operating performance: raw returns as well as *BHARs* are negatively related to *RUNUP* and *RISK*.[138] As argued above, *RUNUP* may capture the degree of overvaluation of a firm. It appears intuitive that firms that are more overvalued around the time of the transaction have lower post-issue stock returns.

The negative and significant coefficient of *RISK* suggests that firms with higher pre-issue asset risk have lower post-issue returns. This result may be due to the fact that the *BHAR* approach fails to control for market risk. It may also indicate that for a lot of high-risk firms in the sample investment projects fail, which causes earnings as well as stock prices to decline during the post-issue period.

An important issue that needs clarification is whether the observed pattern of positive pre- and negative post-issue returns is due to overreaction and mean reversion as in DeBondt/Thaler (1985, 1987).[139] I conduct the same test as Spiess/Affleck-Graves (1999) and reject this explanation for the observed return pattern.[140]

In sum, the magnitude and determinants of raw returns and *BHARs* support the timing-hypothesis for convertible debt issues. All evidence leads to the conclusion that convertible debt issuers (as well as equity issuers) are overvalued when they sell securities. The central implication of this interpretation for convertible debt issues in my sample becomes obvious from the poor raw returns of –31.55% on average (the proportion of positive returns is only

---

137 The negative and significant coefficient of *PU* suggests that public utilities in this sample have poorer 18-month raw returns and *BHARs* than industrial firms. The positive and significant coefficients of *POST-EARNINGS* for the OIBD/assets regressions suggests that firms with a stronger post-issue operating performance have also a stronger post-issue stock price performance. I do not show differential slope coefficients for the convertible debt sample, since none of them are significant.

138 The results in panel B are similar, but adjusted R^2 values are lower and *SIZE* is insignificant for *BHARs*, since it is controlled for in the reference portfolio.

139 See De Bondt/Thaler (1985), p. 793ff; De Bondt/Thaler (1987), p. 557 ff.

140 My test follows Spiess/Affleck-Graves (1999), p. 62 f. I divide my samples into quintiles based on the pre-issue share price runup. If long-term mean reversion is present, I expect to find that 'past winners' are 'future losers' and vice versa. However, underperformance is in similar magnitudes for the first (past losers) and fifth (past winners) quintile, which contradicts mean reversion. This interpretation receives further support by the fact that the relation of *RUNUP* and the post-issue operating performance is also negative.

20%): the probability that the bonds will be converted becomes relatively small.[141] Managers who intentionally take advantage of periods during which the stock is overvalued will expect the transitory nature of the stock's (overly) high valuation to become apparent after the issue and stock prices to revert to a normal level. If they foresee the magnitude of stock price declines their firms experience during the post-issue period, it appears unlikely that they use convertible debt to obtain backdoor equity capital, but to reduce the costs issuing firms would incur in straight debt issues: the information disparity between firm insiders and outsiders prior to the transaction leads to a differential assessment of the value of the conversion option and will effectively reduce the interest payments below the levels payable in straight debt issues. Before entering into a deeper discussion of these ideas, I assess whether the magnitude of post-issue stock returns is robust to variations in computation methods.

5.2 Calendar-time abnormal returns

I use a calendar-time analysis to control for the effects of market timing on long-run returns described by Schultz (2003), who shows that the independence assumption implied in the *BHAR* approach may be problematic, when security issues cluster in calendar-time and managers try to time the market. In these situations, underperformance will most likely be detected in event-time, because there is a high probability that security issues are increasingly conducted immediately before a market downturn can be observed.[142]

That such concerns are of importance in my sample becomes evident from a positive correlation of the number of offerings with offering month returns of the equal-weighted CRSP index. The respective Pearson correlation coefficients are 0.53 for convertible debt and 0.18 for equity issues and suggest that security offerings are increasingly conducted when market returns are high. When recomputing the correlation coefficients for the number of offerings and 18-month buy-and-hold returns of the CRSP index, the correlation becomes significantly negative for convertible debt (-0.24) and remains positive for equity issuers

[141] The median maturity of convertible bonds in my sample is 7 years and the median conversion premium is 27%. From the level that prevails for the typical issuer after eighteen months, the stock price would have to rise almost by 90% in 5.5 years for the conversion option to be at-the-money. However, other studies show that poor returns can be observed up to five years following the offering, which makes conversion unlikely for the typical convertible debt issuer.

[142] See Schultz (2003), p. 483 ff. Moreover, cross-sectional correlation of *BHARs* leads to an inflation of test statistics. This could be the case for firms from the same industry or for firms of similar size. Mitchell/Stafford (2000), p. 305 f. show that test statistics drop below critical values after an adjustment of the sample standard deviation for cross-correlation. Lyon/Barber/Tsai (1999), p. 190 document that an adjustment of the variance-covariance matrix helps to mitigate the impact of cross-sectional dependence, but does not allow for a complete elimination.

(0.17). This indicates that although convertible debt issues are timed with favourable current market conditions, they tend to be followed by periods of poor returns.[143]

5.2.1 Methodology

A calendar-time application of the 3-factor-model (Fama/French 1992, 1993) is potentially useful in capturing systematic patterns in average returns.[144] The dependent variable in the regression is the monthly excess return of an equal-weighted calendar-time portfolio containing all sample firms that participated in an event during the previous eighteen months.[145] Calendar-time portfolios are formed monthly during the period between July 2001 and December 2003 to add companies that have offered securities in the previous eighteen months and drop companies that offered securities more than eighteen months ago. This approach mitigates the cross-sectional dependence problem, because the time-series variation of portfolio returns captures the impact of return correlation across event stocks.[146] The 3-factor-model is shown in formula III.6.

Formula III.6: $$R_{Pt} - R_{ft} = \alpha + \beta \, (R_{Mt} - R_{ft}) + s \, SMB_t + h \, HML_t + \varepsilon_{it}$$

R_{Pt} is the return of the calendar-time portfolio of event stocks and R_{ft} is the risk-free rate in month t. The three factors are the market excess return (*MKTRF*), the return on a zero-investment portfolio measuring the return differential of a portfolio of small and big stocks, *SMB*, and the return of a zero-investment portfolio measuring the return differential of a portfolio of high book-to-market and low book-to-market stocks, *HML*. The variable of interest is the intercept α, which enables a test of the null hypothesis that the average monthly excess return is zero.[147]

---

143 This corresponds to the scenario described by Schultz (2003), p. 492.

144 See Fama (1998), p. 292 f. Prominent applications of the 3-factor-model include Fama/French (1992), p. 427 ff., Fama/French (1993), p. 3 ff., Mitchell/Stafford (2000), p. 287 ff. and Brav/Geczy/Gompers (2000), p. 209 ff.

145 I use equal-weighted returns, since value-weighted returns may underestimate abnormal returns. See Loughran/Ritter (2000), p. 386.

146 See Fama (1998), p. 295.

147 I developed a benchmark to evaluate the long-run performance using the 3-factor-model by testing it with the 25 size-book-to-market equity (BE/ME) portfolios from Fama/French (1992, 1993). Additional calculations that are omitted in the paper show that the model fails to price the complete cross-section of returns correctly, given some intercepts are significantly different from zero. Of particular concern are the size-BE/ME portfolios (1,4), (1,5), (3,1), (4,1) and (5,1). An aggregate of 49% of convertible debt and 34% of equity issuers fall into the categories of these portfolios, which has to be taken into consideration in the interpretation of the results of the calendar-time portfolio regressions. If the calendar-time portfolio returns

5.2.2 Results

I present results for the 3-factor-model (panel B) alongside mean and median monthly calendar-time returns net of returns of the CRSP equal- and value-weighted indices (panel A) in table III.9.

Table III.9: Calendar-time abnormal returns

This table contains mean and median monthly abnormal calendar-time returns in panel A. Panel B shows results for 3-factor-model regressions. The dependent variable, R_{Pt}, is the excess return of a portfolio containing all sample firms that participated in an event in the previous eighteen months and is calculated for every month *t* during the period between July 2001 and December 2003. Portfolios are formed monthly to add companies that have offered securities during the previous eighteen months and to drop companies that offered securities more than eighteen months ago. The three factors are the market excess return, *MKTRF*, the return of a zero-investment portfolio measuring the return differential of a portfolio of small and big stocks, *SMB*, and the return of a zero-investment portfolio measuring the return differential of a portfolio of high BE/ME and low BE/ME stocks, *HML*. I show results for OLS- and WLS-regressions. The weights in the WLS-regressions are based on the square root of the number of firms contained in a portfolio in the respective month. The values of test statistics are shown in parentheses. ***, ** and * indicate a significance level of 1%, 5% and 10%, respectively. CD denotes the convertible bond sample and SEO is the seasoned equity offering sample.

Panel A: Monthly abnormal calendar-time returns

Sample	CD *Mean*	CD *Median*	SEO *Mean*	SEO *Median*
CRSP VW	0.29%	-0.33%	0.05%	0.15%
	[0.30]	[0.00]	[0.06]	[0.06]
CRSP EW	-1.26%	-2.02%	-1.51%	-1.13%
	[-1.65]	[1.85] **	[-2.89] ***	[2.28] **

Panel B: 3-factor model results

Coefficient	CD *OLS*	CD *WLS*	SEO *OLS*	SEO *WLS*
Intercept	0.000	0.003	-0.008	-0.009
	[-0.04]	[-0.58]	[-1.47]	[-1.67]
MKTRF	1.561	1.622	1.113	1.104
	[15.12] ***	[16.51] ***	[10.08] ***	[10.22] ***
SMB	0.646	0.664	0.878	0.951
	[4.25] ***	[4.79] ***	[5.40] ***	[6.03] ***
HML	-0.424	-0.370	0.066	0.065
	[-2.36] **	[-2.23] **	[0.34]	[0.35]
Adjusted R^2	92.5%	93.7%	85.8%	86.9%
F-Test	[119.60] ***	[144.11] ***	[59.52] ***	[65.52] ***

strongly covary with the returns of these portfolios, the display of underperformance may also be due to a model misspecification problem. See Brav/Geczy/Gompers (2000), p. 231.

In panel A, portfolio returns are not significantly different from the monthly returns of the CRSP value-weighted index. However, when the equal-weighted index is used, mean (median) abnormal returns are significant at the 1%-level (5%-level) for equity issuers. For convertible debt issuers, median abnormal monthly returns are negative and significant.

Results for the 3-factor-model are shown in panel B. Since the calendar-time method weights each calendar month equally rather than every offering, there is a chance that the number of offerings are correlated with portfolio returns. This introduces heteroskedasticity in the regression residuals, which I correct by using weighted-least-squares (WLS) regressions, where the weights are based on the square root of the number of firms contained in the portfolio.[148]

The 3-factor-model allows for a correct pricing of the calendar-time portfolio for the convertible debt and equity sample, albeit the intercept for the latter is close to the 10%-level. The inclusion of the momentum factor *UMD* does not change these results.[149]

Hence, it can be stated that the result of the long-run performance analysis is contingent upon methodology. In event-time methods, I find both types of issuers to underperform significantly. Also, median abnormal monthly calendar-time returns net of the CRSP equal-weighted index are significantly negative. The 3-factor-model, in contrast, allows for a correct pricing of calendar-time returns of portfolios containing convertible debt and equity issuers, which is surprising given the low magnitude of *BHARs*.

Whether these latter results are sample-specific is difficult to evaluate, since I use recent data that has not been analyzed before. In related research, Lewis/Rogalski/Seward (2001) and Brav/Geczy/Gompers (2000) detect negative abnormal performance for firms issuing convertible debt and equity using the 3-factor-model in calendar-time analyses.[150]

In order to find out whether the 3-factor-model results are inconsistent with the timing-hypothesis, I calculate announcement returns using a standard short-term event study design.[151] Stock price reactions to the announcement are significantly negative for convertible

[148] See Gompers/Lerner (2003), p. 1387.

[149] See Carhart (1997), p. 57 ff. The momentum factor is the return of a zero-investment portfolio measuring the return differential of portfolios containing stocks with high and low returns during the previous eleven months.

[150] See Brav/Geczy/Gompers (2000), p. 236; Lewis/Rogalski/Seward (2001), p. 462.

[151] To compute cumulative average abnormal returns (*CAARs*), I use a standard market model approach, where the CRSP equal-weighted index is chosen as the market index. The estimation period for the model parameters is [-130;-11], where 0 is the announcement day.

debt and equity issuers, which is consistent with overvaluation.[152] Hence, the calendar-time results may be uncommon, but they are not inconsistent with a timing- or rationing-explanation. Moreover, it has to be taken into consideration that *BHAR* and calendar-time methods are not only different to a statistical end, but also have different economic interpretations:[153] the low magnitude of *BHARs* suggests that firms have earned negative abnormal stock returns during an 18-month post-issue period.[154] Calendar-time abnormal returns, in contrast, are designed to assess whether firms persistently earn abnormal returns. As a consequence, the differences in the results for the two methods may be driven to some extent by the exact structure of post-issue return patterns: if negative stock returns are concentrated in calendar-time, the 3-factor-model may not detect them.

5.3 Discussion

The evidence documented in the previous sections provides strong support for the timing-hypothesis. It also suggests that some firms may be rationed out of the market for seasoned equity. The traditional hypothesis for convertible debt issuance has to be rejected, because it implies that no abnormal operating or stock price performance should be detected. As in previous research, however, earnings and stock prices decline after firms issue convertible debt.[155]

The rationing-hypothesis has the potential to explain why the post-issue performance of convertible debt issuers is poor. However, it appears unlikely that investors foreclose firms from participation in the market for seasoned equity on the basis of their earnings characteristics given that the abnormal pre-issue operating performance is positive and the abnormal post-issue operating performance is stronger for convertible debt than for equity issuers. Even if investors appear to have severe problems to evaluate a firm's earnings prospects, and one cannot completely rule out that rationing occurs on the basis of (potentially biased) earnings expectations, the results favour the interpretation that investors deny convertible debt issuers the direct access to equity capital, because they have difficulties in assessing the risk characteristics of issuing firms. Asset risk, which is negatively related to a firm's post-issue operating and stock price performance, is higher for convertible debt issuers

152 The *CAAR* for the convertible bond sample is –4.44% and the *CAAR* for the equity sample is –3.11%.

153 See Lyon/Barber/Tsai (1999), p. 192.

154 In this analysis, this is an important finding with regard to the propensity of firm managers to use convertible debt as a substitute for straight debt.

155 While this could be due to the inappropriate design of convertible bonds, previous research finds that also issuers of apparently well-designed convertibles underperform. See Lewis/Rogalski/Seward (1998), p. 32 ff.; Lewis/Rogalski/Seward (1999), p. 5 ff.; Lewis/Rogalski/Seward (2001), p. 447 ff.

than for equity issuers.[156] Risk-averse investors, who may be uncertain about the attractiveness of the risk-return profile or about the future risk level of an issuing firm, may not be willing to provide direct equity capital to this firm. A convertible bond gives these investors the possibility to screen issuing firms and simultaneously protects them from adverse consequences changes in firm risk may entail.[157]

Given the results from the cross-sectional analyses of the post-issue operating and stock price performance, the rationing-hypothesis may explain why some firms issue convertible debt, but there is stronger evidence in favour of the timing-hypothesis.

Convertible debt issues as well as equity issues are conducted after large share price appreciations. In my sample, this appreciation amounts to 39.4% during the year preceding the offering for convertible debt and to 61.8% for equity issuers.[158] Market-to-book ratios for both types of issuers are significantly higher than those of matching firms, although post-issue earnings decline. These observations suggest that a firm's stock is overvalued prior to the offering. The analysis of post-issue stock returns further supports this interpretation: buy-and-hold abnormal returns are significantly negative for convertible debt and equity issuers. The negative relation of pre-issue and post-issue stock returns suggests that the degree of overvaluation is a determinant of the magnitude of post-issue stock returns.

Given these observations, an important question is whether managers know that their stock is overvalued when they issue convertible debt, and if so, why they do not sell common stock. My answer to this question is that the typical convertible debt issuer in my sample wants to obtain cheap debt. It appears likely that managers exploit transitory periods of mispricings of their stock to sell convertible debt and economize on coupon payments compared to straight debt issues. While convertible debt issue announcements typically reduce a firm's market valuation more than debt issue announcements, a correction of the level of an issuer's overvalued stock would occur in any case at some point in time.[159] Hence, more negative stock price reactions to convertible debt issues may not be of greater relevance in the decision

---

[156] Moreover, a significant increase in systematic equity risk around convertible debt issues can be detected, which is the subject of the next chapter.

[157] This argument is forwarded by Brennan/Schwartz (1988), p. 56 and receives empirical confirmation in survey evidence by Graham/Harvey (2001), p. 221, who document that risk-insensitivity is a major determinant in the managerial decision to issue convertible debt.

[158] Lewis/Rogalski/Seward (2001), p. 460 report an even larger pre-issue share price increase of 55.8% for a sample of convertible debt issues that covers the years from 1979 through 1990.

[159] See Dann/Mikkelson (1984), p. 165 and 167 for announcement returns of convertible and straight debt issues.

to issue convertible debt.[160] In fact, managers, who anticipate that future returns are poor, and that conversion is unlikely to occur, may decide to increase the operating profit of a firm by selling an overvalued conversion option to investors, which reduces the interest costs of the convertible below the level payable in a straight debt issue. If managers foresee a post-issue earnings decline, this preservation of cash flow may be of some importance to their firm. The following observations support the cheap debt interpretation:

- The advantage of a timing-strategy to issue convertible debt as a (cheaper) alternative for straight debt is the differential assessment of the value of the conversion option between firm insiders and firm outsiders. A firm insider who knows, or at least suspects, that the firm's stock is overvalued will attribute a lower value to the conversion option than a firm outsider who does not have the insider's information. This disparity allows to significantly reduce the level of interest payments. However, if a firm faced other costs in external debt issues, it might not be optimal to pursue a timing-strategy to issue convertible debt. Especially costs of financial distress due to increased leverage may outweigh the reduction of interest costs. Therefore, convertible debt issuers pursuing a timing-strategy in my sample should have the capacity to issue further debt without incurring financial distress costs. To support this notion, I follow Marsh (1982) and Hovakimian/Opler/Titman (2001), who show that target debt levels have lasting effects on the debt-equity choice.[161] I calculate the long-term historical average of a firm's debt ratio as a proxy for its target debt ratio and deduct from it the debt ratio that would prevail, if a firm raised the required funds in the debt market.[162] It becomes obvious from this analysis that the deviation from the historical debt ratio in case of a further debt issue is only marginal for convertible debt issuers (–3%). Equity issuers, in contrast, would deviate on average –27% from their long-term debt ratio if they issued more debt. Hence, this analysis confirms the implication of the timing-hypothesis for convertible debt.[163]

---

[160] Differences in transaction costs are not likely to be material in the convertible debt issue decision either. The study of Lee/Lochhead/Ritter/Zhao (1996), p. 62 shows that differences in transaction costs in convertible and straight debt issues are marginally pronounced for issue sizes of more than 200 million USD. The mean issue size in my sample is 412 million USD.

[161] See Marsh (1982), p. 121 ff.; Hovakimian/Opler/Titman (2001), p. 1 ff.

[162] Further information on this variable is provided in section 3.3 of chapter V.

[163] This notion receives further support from a comparison on market-based debt-asset ratios, which have a median of 8.9% for convertible debt and of 19.6% for their matching firms. Further information on the computation of leverage ratios is provided in the next chapter.

- A firm that wants to obtain delayed equity capital should have valuable investment opportunities according to Stein (1992). If managers possessed what they perceived as valuable investment opportunities, they would most likely increase investment expenses significantly in the issue-year or the year following the issue expecting that these projects increase firm value. However, investment activity (measured by (CE+RD)/assets) declines after the issue.
- Some conclusions may be drawn from the design of convertible bonds. In my sample, the average (median) conversion premium is 28.7% (27%). Even if managers were optimistic about the firm's future prospects (after an average pre-issue runup of almost 40%) they would set a lower conversion premium if they wanted to obtain backdoor equity capital. A more encompassing measure for the design of a convertible, the conversion probability, supports this notion. In my sample, it is 51.3% on average, which would be a very uncommon security structure, if it was intended to substitute common stock.[164]

I find strong support for the timing-hypothesis for a sample of convertible debt offerings that occur during 2000 and 2002. However, during this period market conditions have been specific, which may have had an influence on the use of convertible debt.[165] Hence, a question is what contribution the timing-hypothesis makes to the literature on convertible debt in general.

Put into perspective, market timing appears to be an important part of the explanation for the use of convertible debt: a wide array of previous research on convertible debt is consistent with market timing. First, survey evidence provided by Graham/Harvey (2001) and Billingsley/Smith (1996) shows that the overvaluation argument is considered by 42% and 85.9%, respectively, of managers of issuing firms to be important for the convertible debt issue decision.[166] Second, Karpoff/Lee (1991) and Kahle (2000) show that insiders of firms issuing convertible debt sell their stock significantly more prior to the issue. This is expected according to the timing-hypothesis, because firm insiders may use a transitory period of

[164] See Lewis/Rogalski/Seward (2003), p. 159 f.

[165] For example, it appears likely that market timing can be a strategy to obtain equity capital when market conditions are good. Lewis/Rogalski/Seward (2001), p. 460 report mean annual raw returns of 9% for firms that issued convertible debt during 1979 and 1990, which suggests that even if convertible debt issuers time the market and underperform during the post-issue period, they may still generate returns that are high enough to make conversion of the convertible into common stock attractive for investors.

[166] See Billingsley/Smith (1996), p. 97; Graham/Harvey (2001), p. 221. The data set of Billingsley/Smith (1996) covers the period from 1987 to 1993, which includes economic up- and downturns in the classification from Choe/Masulis/Nanda (1993), p. 16, and which suggests that timing may be important in good and difficult economic conditions.

overvaluation not only to reduce the costs of issuing new securities, but also to maximize their own profit.[167] Third, Danielova/Smart/Boquist (2004) document that other forms of hybrid securities are used to sell overvalued equity as well: firms exploit high valuation levels of stocks in their portfolios to reduce costs in of external debt finance.[168] Finally, market timing is consistent with a salient empirical observation in convertible debt markets: issuance volumes in the convertible debt and equity market are high simultaneously, which suggests that the valuation level of common stock is an important consideration in convertible debt and in seasoned equity offerings.[169]

6 *Conclusion*

In this paper, I examined why firms issue convertible debt by analyzing the post-issue operating and stock price performance of a sample of convertible debt and equity issues that occurred in the US during the period from 2000 to 2002.

A first explanation, referred to as the traditional hypothesis for convertible debt issuance, argues that convertible debt mitigates costs that arise in external debt and equity issues. It has to be rejected on the basis of my analyses, which show that post-issue earnings and stock price levels decline for convertible debt issuers.

The poor post-issue performance is consistent with a rationing-hypothesis, which maintains that convertible debt issuers are foreclosed from the market for seasoned equity. A comparison of the post-issue operating performance of convertible debt and equity issuers reveals that the former have stronger earnings after the offering. Therefore, rationing is unlikely to occur on the basis of post-issue earnings characteristics of convertible debt issuers. The results favour the interpretation that uncertainty about a firm's risk may lead investors to deny some firms the access to direct equity capital. These investors provide external capital to a firm while being hedged against adverse changes in firm risk when they hold the convertible.

---

[167] See Karpoff/Lee (1991), p. 18 ff.; Kahle (2000), p. 25 ff. It has to be taken into account that insider selling could also be triggered by the high share price runup. Hence, one cannot completely rule out that managers are overoptimistic with regard to the value of their investment opportunities. See Lee (1997), p. 23 ff.

[168] See Danielova/Smart/Boquist (2004), p. 1 ff.

[169] See Lewis/Rogalski/Seward (2001), p. 449. For example, the new issue data presented by Choe/Masulis/Nanda (1993) reveals that the correlation between the number of convertible debt and equity issues across the business cycle exceeds 0.90. This suggests that market timing is important in economic up- and downturns for convertible debt and equity issues.

The timing-hypothesis for convertible debt issuance receives strongest support. Convertible debt is issued after large stock price increases, in my sample on average 39.4% during the year preceding the issue, by firms with unusually high market-to-book ratios. After the offering, earnings and stock prices decline abnormally. A cross-sectional analysis shows that these declines are negatively related to an issuer's pre-issue share price runup, which suggests that firms perform worse the more their securities have been overvalued prior to the transaction.

My interpretation of these findings is that managers exploit periods of transitory mispricings of common stock to sell convertible debt. Managers who expect that their firms' post-issue performance will be poor may use convertibles as a cheaper substitute for straight debt. In doing so, they may benefit from the differential assessment regarding the value of the conversion option between themselves and firm outsiders to reduce interest payments below their firms' level in straight debt issues. Consistent with this notion, convertible debt issuers have unused debt capacity and seem to adjust their debt level towards a target ratio.

The timing-hypothesis has received less attention in the empirical literature on convertible debt issuance so far. However, it appears to be an important explanation for the convertible debt issue decision for many firms at least in recent years.

IV A note on systematic risk changes around convertible debt issues

1 *Introduction*

The analysis of the risk characteristics of an issuing firm provides a further test of the rationing-hypothesis for convertible debt issuance. If investors gradually learn about changes in an issuer's systematic risk as they apparently do about a firm's post-issue earnings, this learning process may influence the convertible debt issue decision:[170] it is possible that risk-averse investors deny an issuer the direct access to equity capital, if they have difficulties in evaluating the risk characteristics of an issuing firm or if they anticipate a future increase in systematic risk that may not be compensated with an adequate increase in returns. In these situations, a firm may use convertible debt to enable investors to screen it before the bond can be converted into common stock. During this screening period, uncertainty about the firm's risk (and earnings) may decrease. The advantage of convertible debt is that its value is relatively insensitive to the risk of the issuing firm, which protects investors from adverse consequences of risk uncertainty.[171]

Previous research provides controversial evidence on changes in systematic risk around security offerings. Healy/Palepu (1990) document increases in systematic risk around seasoned equity offerings.[172] Denis/Kadlec (1994), however, attribute increases in beta estimates to changes in trading activity.[173] Lewis/Rogalski/Seward (2002), controlling for this aspect, document declines in systematic equity risk around convertible debt offerings, even though financial risk increases.[174]

This analysis provides new evidence on risk changes around convertible debt offerings: it shows that systematic equity risk significantly increases after a firm has issued convertible debt. The increase is due to an increase in financial risk and persists when effects of thin trading and price adjustment delays are controlled for as in Scholes/Williams (1977) or Dimson (1979) and Fowler/Rorke (1983).[175] No increase in systematic risk can be detected for equity issuers.

---

[170] See Lewis/Rogalski/Seward (2002), p. 67 f.
[171] See Brennan/Schwartz (1988), p. 56.
[172] See Healy/Palepu (1990), p. 25 ff.
[173] See Denis/Kadlec (1994), p. 1787 ff.
[174] See Lewis/Rogalski/Seward (2002), p. 67 ff.
[175] See Scholes/Williams (1977), p. 309 ff.; Dimson (1979), p. 129 ff.; Fowler/Rorke (1983), p. 279 ff.

The results for convertible debt issuers are consistent with the notion that investor uncertainty about their risk characteristics may force some firms to raise capital in the convertible debt market. They also suggest that the poor post-issue stock price performance documented in the previous chapter can be partially explained by updated investor assessments of a firm's cost of capital.[176]

The remainder of this chapter is organized as follows: section 2 presents the data. Section 3 contains an analysis of systematic risk changes around convertible debt and equity offerings. Section 4 concludes the paper.

2 *Data*

The data set used in this analysis is the same as in the previous chapter. For expositional ease, table III.1 is reported again as table IV.1 to provide summary information on the data set.

Table IV.1: Data summary information

This table shows summary information for the data set. Panel A contains the number of issues per year and panel B the number of issues per industry. Industry classification is based on SIC codes. CD denotes convertible debt and SEO seasoned equity offering.

Panel A: Number of issues per year

	CD		SEO	
Year	*N*	%	*N*	%
2000	68	31.2%	85	38.8%
2001	103	47.2%	60	27.4%
2002	47	21.6%	74	33.8%
Total	***218***	***100%***	***219***	***100%***

Panel B: Number of issues per industry

		CD		SEO	
Industry	***SIC***	*N*	%	*N*	%
Oil and gas	13	9	4.1%	12	5.5%
Chemicals and pharmaceuticals	28	35	16.1%	29	13.2%
Office and computer equipment	35	23	10.6%	8	3.7%
Communication and electronic equipment	36	32	14.7%	24	11.0%
Engineering and scientific instruments	38	13	6.0%	9	4.1%
Public utilities	481/491-494	10	4.6%	27	12.3%
Computer and data processing services	73	22	10.1%	25	11.4%
Other	-	74	33.9%	85	38.8%
Total		***218***	***100%***	***219***	***100%***

176 See Lewis/Rogalski/Seward (2002), p. 68.

Since there is no general methodology to match firms on risk attributes, I follow Lewis/Rogalski/Seward (2002) and compare event firms with firms of similar asset size and operating performance.[177] Hence, the sample of matching firms from the previous section is used to find out whether risk changes around convertible debt offerings are firm-specific.

3 *Changes in systematic risk*

Total risk of a firm can be decomposed into a systematic and an idiosyncratic risk component.[178] In this analysis, I focus on the systematic risk component, since I am concerned about the discount rate investors may use to value a firm's cash flows. I measure systematic equity risk using the beta coefficient from a standard two-parameter market model, which I estimate for the year preceding and the two years following the event.[179] Changes in equity beta can arise from changes in asset risk or financial leverage. Financial leverage is measured as a market value-based debt-asset ratio as well as a book value-based debt-asset ratio, as described in table IV.2. Asset risk is estimated by unlevering the equity beta using the market value-based equity-asset ratio.[180]

Table IV.2 documents a significant increase in financial leverage following a convertible debt offering. Since convertible debt is classified as debt until conversion, this result is not unexpected. The median (mean) market value-based debt-asset ratio increases from 16.8% (8.9%) in year –1 to 29.1% (23.9%) in year +2.[181] The median debt-asset ratio based on book values shows a similar increase. Debt-asset ratios for matching firms of convertible debt issuers are on a higher level prior to the offering and do not significantly change during the following years, which indicates that the increase in leverage ratios for convertible debt issuers is firm-specific.

---

177 See Lewis/Rogalski/Seward (2002), p. 71.

178 See Healy/Palepu (1990), p. 29.

179 I use a value-weighted CRSP index in accordance with Lewis/Rogalski/Seward (2002), p. 71. One year has 250 trading days. Year –1 is defined as [-260;-11], year +1 as [+11;+260] and year +2 as [+261;+510], where 0 is the issue day.

180 As in Healy/Palepu (1990), p. 29 and Lewis/Rogalski/Seward (2002), p. 72, the assumption implied here is that the debt beta is zero and is employed due to the lack of market data for outstanding debt. This results in a downward bias of the asset beta, if the debt beta is positive.

181 Leverage ratios are measured at fiscal year-end for the year preceding the offering (year –1), the year following the offering (year +1) and the second year following the offering (year +2).

Table IV.2: Financial risk

Panel A reports debt-asset ratios based on market values for event and matching firms for the year preceding the offering (year –1) and the two years following the offering (year +1 and year +2). Market value-based debt-asset ratios are based on Compustat data and are calculated as long-term debt (item 9)/(long-term debt (item 9) + market value of equity capital (item 25 * item 199)). Panel B reports debt-asset ratios based on book values, which are calculated as (long-term debt (item 9)/(long-term debt (item 9) + total equity capital (item 216)). Matching firms are chosen using the propensity score method. t-statistics are standard t-tests and z-statistics are Wilcoxon signed-rank tests. Values of test statistics are indicated in parentheses. ***, ** and * indicate a significance level of 1%, 5% and 10%, respectively. CD denotes convertible debt and SEO seasoned equity offering.

Panel A: Debt-asset ratios based on market values

	CD			SEO		
	Year -1	***Year +1***	***Year +2***	***Year -1***	***Year +1***	***Year +2***
Event firms						
Mean	0.168	0.292	0.291	0.200	0.205	0.214
Median	0.089	0.243	0.239	0.106	0.142	0.096
Change in mean		0.124	0.123		0.004	0.013
t-statistic		[6.10] ***	[5.59] ***		[0.20]	[0.49]
Change in median		0.153	0.150		0.036	-0.010
z-statistic		[7.72] ***	[6.90] ***		[0.06]	[0.61]
Matching firms						
Mean	0.275	0.314	0.302	0.230	0.245	0.256
Median	0.196	0.246	0.194	0.144	0.166	0.168
Change in mean		0.039	0.026		0.015	0.026
t-statistic		[1.31]	[0.80]		[0.53]	[0.80]
Change in median		0.050	-0.003		0.022	0.024
z-statistic		[1.36]	[0.67]		[0.36]	[0.62]

Panel B: Debt-asset ratios based on book values

	CD			SEO		
	Year -1	***Year +1***	***Year +2***	***Year -1***	***Year +1***	***Year +2***
Event firms						
Mean	0.294	0.427	0.416	0.309	0.284	0.263
Median	0.269	0.411	0.410	0.283	0.265	0.193
Change in mean		0.133	0.122		-0.025	-0.045
t-statistic		[6.16] ***	[5.00] ***		[0.90]	[1.38]
Change in median		0.143	0.141		-0.018	-0.090
z-statistic		[5.64] ***	[4.71] ***		[0.92]	[1.87] *
Matching firms						
Mean	0.304	0.343	0.309	0.273	0.269	0.271
Median	0.293	0.352	0.290	0.243	0.254	0.245
Change in mean		0.039	0.005		-0.005	-0.002
t-statistic		[1.40]	[0.15]		[0.16]	[0.05]
Change in median		0.060	-0.002		0.011	0.002
z-statistic		[1.25]	[0.11]		[0.20]	[0.27]

Leverage ratios for equity issuers do not materially change around the offering. While the median debt-asset ratio based on book values declines from 28.3% to 19.3%, the median market value-based debt-asset ratio remains rather stable. Also the leverage ratios of equity issuers' matching firms are largely unchanged.

Table IV.3 shows beta estimates from a standard two-parameter market model. Panel A shows asset betas and panel B equity betas.

Table IV.3: Systematic asset and equity risk

Equity betas are from a standard two-parameter market model that is estimated for the time frames [-260;-11] for year –1, [+11; +260] for year +1 and [+261; +510] for year +2, where 0 is the issue day. A value-weighted CRSP index is used as the market index. Panel A reports asset betas, which are calculated by unlevering equity betas using the market-based equity-asset ratio under the assumption that the debt beta is zero. Panel B contains equity betas. Matching firms are chosen using the propensity score method. t-statistics are standard t-tests and z-statistics are Wilcoxon signed-rank tests. Values of test statistics are indicated in parentheses. ***, ** and * indicate a significance level of 1%, 5% and 10%, respectively. CD denotes convertible debt and SEO seasoned equity offering.

Panel A: Asset betas

	CD			SEO		
	Year -1	***Year +1***	***Year +2***	***Year -1***	***Year +1***	***Year +2***
Event firms						
Mean	1.158	1.082	1.065	0.771	1.035	1.027
Median	1.005	0.854	0.930	0.602	0.787	0.854
Change in Mean		-0.076	-0.093		0.264	0.257
t-statistic		[0.96]	[1.15]		[3.63] ***	[3.35] ***
Change in Median		-0.151	-0.075		0.185	0.252
z-statistic		[0.42]	[0.02]		[3.39] ***	[3.49] ***
Matching firms						
Mean	0.540	0.594	0.603	0.565	0.546	0.583
Median	0.408	0.502	0.517	0.463	0.483	0.543
Change in Mean		0.054	0.063		-0.019	0.018
t-statistic		[1.01]	[1.00]		[0.30]	[0.25]
Change in Median		0.094	0.109		0.020	0.080
z-statistic		[1.74] *	[1.55]		[0.15]	[0.19]

Panel B: Equity betas

	CD			SEO		
	Year -1	***Year +1***	***Year +2***	***Year -1***	***Year +1***	***Year +2***
Event firms						
Mean	1.326	1.489	1.501	0.932	1.263	1.256
Median	1.192	1.319	1.315	0.799	1.005	1.106
Change in Mean		0.163	0.175		0.331	0.325
t-statistic		[2.00] **	[2.30] **		[4.45] ***	[4.77] ***
Change in Median		0.127	0.122		0.206	0.307
z-statistic		[1.95] **	[2.68] ***		[4.03] ***	[4.83] ***
Matching firms						
Mean	0.746	0.915	0.927	0.720	0.743	0.870
Median	0.649	0.841	0.875	0.665	0.749	0.859
Change in Mean		0.169	0.181		0.023	0.150
t-statistic		[2.58] ***	[2.81] ***		[0.34]	[2.12] **
Change in Median		0.193	0.226		0.084	0.194
z-statistic		[3.52] ***	[4.34] ***		[1.14]	[2.74] ***

It becomes obvious that asset risk for convertible debt issuers declines slightly, although the change is not statistically significant. In contrast, the median asset beta for equity issuers increases significantly from 0.771 in year –1 to 1.027 in year +2. These results are consistent with those of Lewis/Rogalski/Seward (2002) for convertible debt issuers and those of Healy/Palepu (1990) for equity issuers.[182]

Panel B depicts the change in equity betas. Equity betas contain the combined effect of changes in asset and financial risk. For convertible debt issuers, the net effect of increased financial leverage and a slightly decreased asset risk is an increase in systematic equity risk: the median equity beta for convertible debt issuers increases from 1.192 in year –1 to 1.315 in year +2. This contrasts the results reported in Lewis/Rogalski/Seward (2002), who find that systematic equity risk decreases.[183] A possible explanation for the differences in the results may be found in differing market conditions: in my sample, equity betas increase significantly for matching firms, whereas no such increase is documented by Lewis/Rogalski/Seward (2002). This may indicate that increases in systematic equity risk for convertible debt issuers in my sample are (at least partially) driven by an economy-wide trend.[184]

The systematic risk of equity issuers increases significantly as well, driven by the significant increase in asset risk. The change in median of equity betas is 0.307 from year –1 to year +2.

The results in table IV.3 may be biased by effects of infrequent trading and price adjustment delays. Lower trading activity before a corporate event is likely to cause beta estimates to be downward biased. Frictions in the trading process can lead to price adjustment delays that have a similar effect on the risk measure. If trading activity increases after an event, beta estimates are likely to rise as a consequence of inadequate computation methodology and without fundamental economic reason.[185] Hence, if the results in table IV.3 are generated by inaccurate measures of risk, appropriate correction methods should cause the gap between beta estimates before and after the offering to close.

---

182 See Lewis/Rogalski/Seward (2002), p. 74; Healy/Palepu (1990), p. 41.

183 See Lewis/Rogalski/Seward (2002), p. 74.

184 Another possibility is that the increase in financial risk dominates the decrease in asset risk, because the design of convertible debt is different in the data sets used in this study and by Lewis/Rogalski/Seward (2002). Since Lewis/Rogalski/Seward (2002) do not indicate the average conversion probability for their sample, it is hard to confirm this notion. It is also difficult to evaluate the role of firm characteristics. However, an implication from the discussion in the previous chapter is that if convertible bonds are used as substitutes for straight debt, financial risk increases may have a more persistent effect on a firm's risk profile than in the sample used by Lewis/Rogalski/Seward (2002). While no direct evidence is available that confirms this notion, it is interesting to see that those firms that appear more overvalued (i.e. have had higher pre-issue share price runups) have higher increases in systematic equity risk. This, in turn, would suggest that the issue motive has an impact on an issuing firm's cost of capital.

185 See Denis/Kadlec (1994), p. 1777 f.

Table IV.4: Adjusted estimates of systematic equity risk

This table contains beta estimates adjusted for infrequent trading and price adjustment delays. Panel A reports adjusted equity beta estimates for event firms and panel B for matching firms. I follow the methodology of Scholes/Williams (1977) to correct for potential biases. In unreported regressions, I obtain similar results using the approach suggested by Dimson (1979) in the modification of Fowler/Rorke (1983). I only report medians, since these are less vulnerable in the presence of outliers. Matching firms are chosen using the propensity score method. Wilcoxon signed-rank tests are used to assess whether changes in median are statistically significant. ***, ** and * indicate a significance level of 1%, 5% and 10%, respectively. CD denotes convertible debt and SEO seasoned equity offering.

Panel A: Robustness of beta estimates for event firms

		CD			SEO		
Estimatation method		***Year -1***	***Year +1***	***Year +2***	***Year -1***	***Year +1***	***Year +2***
2 lead, 2 lag							
	Median	1.177	1.314	1.430	0.901	1.125	1.170
	Change		0.137 *	0.253 ***		0.224 ***	0.269 ***
5 lead, 5 lag							
	Median	1.135	1.237	1.401	0.913	1.047	1.283
	Change		0.102	0.267 ***		0.134	0.370 ***
10 lead, 10 lag							
	Median	1.210	1.603	1.421	1.215	1.179	1.345
	Change		0.393 **	0.211 *		-0.035	0.130
15 lead, 15 lag							
	Median	1.140	1.409	1.541	1.182	1.340	1.454
	Change		0.269 *	0.401 *		0.158	0.272 *

Panel B: Robustness of beta estimates for matching firms

		CD			SEO		
Estimatation method		***Year -1***	***Year +1***	***Year +2***	***Year -1***	***Year +1***	***Year +2***
2 lead, 2 lag							
	Median	0.571	0.856	0.935	0.705	0.718	0.923
	Change		0.285 ***	0.364 ***		0.013	0.218 **
5 lead, 5 lag							
	Median	0.702	0.858	0.921	0.690	0.757	0.988
	Change		0.156 **	0.220 ***		0.066	0.297 ***
10 lead, 10 lag							
	Median	0.703	1.078	0.995	1.147	0.774	0.957
	Change		0.375 ***	0.292 *		-0.373	-0.191
15 lead, 15 lag							
	Median	0.634	0.996	0.966	0.939	0.786	0.982
	Change		0.362 ***	0.333 **		-0.153	0.042

I use the methodology suggested by Scholes/Williams (1977) to obtain reliable risk estimates.[186] This method regresses security returns on leading, contemporaneous and lagged market returns. Since it is not known a priori how many leads and lags of beta estimates are necessary, I follow the proposition of Denis/Kadlec (1994) and use symmetric lead and lag intervals of up to 31 days (15 lead, one level and 15 lag estimates).[187] Corrected beta estimates are shown in table IV.4, which illustrates that increases in equity risk appear to be caused by fundamental economic risk changes and not by inaccurate estimation methodology for convertible debt issuers and their matching firms. For equity issuers, the difference between equity betas before and after the event ceases to be significant when more leads and lags are included in the regressions. This indicates that frictions in the trading process may have led to a spurious detection of increases in systematic risk.[188]

4 Conclusion

At issuance, risk-averse investors, aware of their inferior access to corporate information in comparison to firm insiders, may be unable to finally evaluate the risk characteristics of some firms that want to raise external capital or may anticipate an increase in systematic risk that is not adequately compensated with higher returns. As a consequence, they may be unwilling to provide a firm with equity funds. However, they may provide external capital via convertible debt, because the value of this investment is relatively insensitive to changes in firm risk. Therefore, firms may use convertible debt to enable investors to screen the firm and protect them from risk changes.[189]

The finding that convertible debt issuers experience increases in systematic risk during the post-issue period as well as earnings declines suggests that most reservations investors may have around the time of the issue are not unfounded. Since increases in systematic equity risk cannot be detected for equity issuers, it is plausible that some firms are rationed out of the market for seasoned equity due to risk considerations.[190]

---

186 See Scholes/Williams (1977), p. 309 ff.

187 See Denis/Kadlec (1994), p. 1789.

188 These results are unchanged when the estimator suggested by Dimson (1979), p. 129 ff. and Fowler/Rorke (1983), p. 279 ff. is used.

189 See Brennan/Schwartz (1988), p. 56.

190 Lewis/Rogalski/Seward (2003), p. 160 argue that firms that want to protect investors from risk changes should assign equal weight to the debt and equity component of the convertible bond, resulting in a conversion probability of around 50%. In my sample, the average conversion probability is 51.3%, which suggests that issuers design convertibles to correspond to investors' needs.

The implication of this observation is that the poor post-issue stock price performance of convertible debt issuers is unlikely to be solely driven by unexpected earnings declines. Post-issue declines in market value of equity are also consistent with updated investor assessments of the cost of capital of an issuer.[191] Hence, a convertible bond issue may signal post-issue earnings declines as well as increases in an issuer's cost of capital.

[191] See Lewis/Rogalski/Seward (2002), p. 68.

V The concurrent offerings puzzle

This chapter aims to explain the use and valuation impact of an interesting and innovative transaction structure: in concurrent offerings, firms issue seasoned equity and convertible securities in combination. Concurrent offerings have neither theoretically nor empirically been examined before. However, a comparable structure exists when firms go public: in unit initial public offerings (IPOs), firms sell bundles of stocks and warrants. Chemmanur/ Fulghieri (1997) present a signaling-model for the use of unit IPOs, which receives empirical support from investigations by How/Howe (2001), Lee/Lee/Taylor (2003) and Byoun/Moore (2003).[192] This model can be adapted for concurrent offerings and is used as a basis for the discussion.

1 Introduction

In recent years, US companies have increasingly used a transaction structure where they have combined the issuance of common stock with an offering of convertible securities in one transaction. For example, a US-based network and solutions provider raised 1.5 billion USD in a concurrent offering of 11 million common shares priced at 83.50 USD alongside convertible bonds due in 2008 that carry a coupon of 3.75% and can be converted at a price of 104.38 USD (implying a 25% conversion premium). The company stated that the funds would be used for investments and other general corporate purposes. A similar structure was employed by a healthcare provider that issued 13 million shares at 28.78 USD alongside mandatory convertibles carrying a 7% coupon and a conversion premium of 24%. The proceeds of the transaction, 1.47 billion USD, were primarily used for balance sheet restructuring and investments. These are two typical examples of concurrent offerings of common stock and convertible securities, which have been used by US firms to raise well over 70 billion USD in the years 2000 through 2002.

Existing theories of security issue decisions do not explain the use of concurrent offerings of common stock and convertible securities: explanations of equity issue decisions include pecking order, managerial discretion problems and market timing.[193] As illustrated in chapter III, theories of convertible debt financing emphasize the security's useful role in obtaining

---

[192] See Chemmanur/Fulghieri (1997), p. 1 ff.; How/Howe (2001), p. 433 ff.; Lee/Lee/Taylor (2003), p. 63 ff. Byoun/Moore (2003), p. 575 ff. study units in seasoned equity offerings.

[193] See Myers/Majluf (1984), p. 187ff; Jensen (1986), p. 323 ff.; Loughran/Ritter (1995), p. 23 ff.; Jung/Kim/ Stulz (1996), p. 159 ff.; Baker/Wurgler (2002), p. 1 ff.

equity capital while simultaneously reducing costs of external equity finance, such as adverse selection costs or costs of free cash flow.[194] Empirical examinations of the convertible issue decision conclude that convertible debt may also be issued for demand-side reasons: investor rationing forecloses some firms from participation in the market for seasoned equity, which have to issue convertible debt as a security of 'last resort'.[195] Finally, convertible debt may be used as a market timing device to reduce interest costs compared to straight debt issues.

To this end, all existing evidence concerning convertible bond issuance postulates that convertibles are used *instead of* and not *concurrent with* common stock. Hence, a natural question is why firms combine the issuance of common stock and convertible securities.

The most promising answer to this question consists in a signaling-hypothesis, which makes use of evidence provided by the literature on unit IPOs and SEOs.[196] I find it to be a powerful explanation for concurrent offerings, where firms combine the issue of common stock with the issue of *mandatory convertibles*, which I refer to as mandatory conversion feature (MCF) concurrent offerings. The signaling-hypothesis argues that MCF concurrent offerings are conducted by firms that want to reduce costs of adverse selection that arise in pure equity issues, as well as costs of incremental financial distress that arise in pure convertible debt offerings. Announcement returns for MCF concurrent offerings amount to –3.46%, and the long-run returns of these firms are not significantly different from those of firms with similar size and book-to-market characteristics. Hence, the transaction announcement is a fully-revealing signal of firm value. All these empirical observations are consistent with the implications that follow from the signaling-hypothesis.

The case is different for concurrent offerings of common stock and *ordinary convertible* securities, which I refer to as ordinary conversion feature (OCF) concurrent offerings, and for which I document puzzling observations: OCF firms have an average stock price runup of 53% during the year preceding the offering and market-to-book ratios that are significantly higher than the industry median (the median industry-adjusted market-to-book ratio is 1.09).

---

[194] See Stein (1992), p. 3 ff.; Mayers (1998), p. 83 ff.

[195] See Lewis/Rogalski/Seward (2001), p. 447 ff.; Lewis/Rogalski/Seward (2002), p. 67 ff.

[196] Units are bundles of common stocks and warrants that may be sold in IPOs or SEOs. Chemmanur/Fulghieri (1997), p. 1 ff. provide a signaling-model for the use of units in IPOs, which may adapted to seasoned equity offerings with minor modifications. Empirical confirmation of this model is provided by How/Howe (2001), p. 433 ff. and Lee/Lee/Taylor (2003), p. 63 ff. for IPOs and Byoun/Moore (2003), p. 575 ff. for SEOs. Another explanation for unit SEOs is provided by Gajewski/Ginglinger/Lasfer (2003), p. 1 ff., who show that units in France are issued to maximize the net issue proceeds of seasoned equity offerings. Because underpricing of French SEOs is restricted, units may be useful to reduce an issuer's flotation costs and the risk of failure of the issue. Since Gajewski/Ginglinger/Lasfer (2003) consider the special institutional setting of the French capital market for their explanation of the use of units, it will not be considered in this analysis.

Hence, OCF firms are evaluated like firms that possess valuable investment opportunities by investors. Yet, when OCF concurrent offerings are announced, there is a highly negative and persistent stock price response of –6.95% on average, although issuers typically intend to use issue proceeds to finance apparently valuable investment projects. Moreover, stock returns after the offering are extremely poor: the market value of OCF firms is nearly halved during the 18-month post-issue period, which indicates that OCF firms have been substantially overvalued prior to the offering. The average buy-and-hold abnormal return is –34% and the median monthly abnormal calendar-time return amounts to –5.89%. In addition, one third of OCF firms do not survive and are delisted during the 18-month period. These observations are inconsistent with the signaling-hypothesis.

Apart from the signaling-hypothesis, I discuss several explanations for these empirical observations, but find it hard to reconcile my results with any of them. The signaling-hypothesis maintains that OCF concurrent offerings are conducted by firms that want to reduce the costs of adverse selection and cannot use pure convertible debt issues due to risk considerations. Hence, OCF firms may consider a concurrent offering a cheaper (and safer) alternative. The signaling-hypothesis is supported by the results from a security choice model based on pre-issue firm characteristics. It can also explain the magnitude and cross-section of announcement returns. However, the poor post-issue stock returns and the high rate of delistings are inconsistent with this hypothesis.

One would expect to make these observations for firms that conduct concurrent offerings as a source of capital of 'last resort', which OCF firms have to fall back on in order to survive. In this case, some investors might not be willing to provide OCF firms with equity capital, because they anticipate that the post-issue performance will be extremely poor. Convertible investors may fund OCF firms, because they have the possibility to screen issuers until the bonds may be converted, which reduces their exposure to asymmetric information, or because they can make some form of arbitrage profit.[197] This hypothesis would explain the negative announcement returns and the poor post-issue performance. However, it is hard to reconcile it with the strong pre-issue performance of OCF firms.

In sum, I document that company characteristics, as well as abnormal stock returns, of firms conducting concurrent offerings differ substantially according to the type of convertible

[197] Some institutional investors, in particular convertible arbitrage hedge funds, may invest in convertible securities, which are often underpriced. This underpricing allows them to make a riskless profit by taking a long position in the convertible and a short position in the stock. See Kang/Lee (1996), p. 231 ff. and Bechmann (2004), p. 421 ff.

issued alongside common stock. The evidence for MCF concurrent offerings is completely in line with a signaling-hypothesis, while OCF concurrent offerings remain a puzzle. A signaling-hypothesis as well as alternative hypotheses always involve inconsistencies that are difficult to solve. Moreover, all explanations imply that either some market participants or firm managers act irrationally.

The remainder of this chapter is organized as follows: section 2 develops the signaling-hypothesis. Section 3 introduces the data and proxy variables. Section 4 contains the first empirical test of the signaling-hypothesis, which compares pre-issue characteristics of firms using concurrent offerings with those of firms issuing only one type of security, common stock or convertible securities, during the same time period. Section 5 examines the magnitude and determinants of announcement returns and section 6 analyzes the post-issue stock price performance over a longer time horizon. Section 7 concludes.

2 *Theoretical background*

In a market characterized by asymmetric information, firms that raise external capital may face an adverse selection problem, where firm insiders know more about the value of the firms' assets and growth opportunities than outside investors. Myers/Majluf (1984) show that a firm's management acting in the best interest of existing shareholders may choose to forego a positive NPV project, if it is restricted to issue underpriced equity to finance the investment.[198] In fact, equity issuance will occur when shares are overpriced, which leads to a price decline when the transaction is announced. This situation is not desirable, since it entails a suboptimal investment policy. Consequently, firms should avoid this financing trap when they are faced with an issue-invest decision.

Myers/Majluf (1984) develop a pecking order of financing instruments where firms should exploit financing sources that are less sensitive to mispricing first. To this end, firms should use internal funds before turning to outside investors, and if they do, they should issue debt.[199] Equity should only be issued when other financing sources have been fully explored and a further debt issue would impose high costs of financial distress on the firm. Although empirical tests of the pecking order theory do not reach a unanimous conclusion, several

---

198 See Myers/Majluf (1984), p. 188.

199 See Myers/Majluf (1984), p. 219.

studies, especially event studies, support its implications.[200] They document a negative relation between announcement returns to equity issues and the degree of adverse selection.[201] To this end, it seems likely that firms can reduce the costs of an equity issue, and hence avoid a suboptimal investment policy, if they efficiently time it with periods of reduced adverse selection.

Another solution to the underinvestment and adverse selection problem consists in the use of convertible securities to signal a firm insiders' private information about the true value of the firm to investors.[202] Stein (1992) presents a signaling-model of convertible debt financing.[203] He argues that firms can use convertible debt to obtain equity capital while simultaneously signaling superior firm quality. The rationale is that a firm facing significant incremental costs of financial distress will choose convertible bonds only if it is optimistic about its future prospects, meaning that the stock price rises sufficiently to make conversion of the bonds into stock attractive for investors. The display of such confidence will allow firms to reduce the extent of adverse stock price reactions to new issue announcements compared to equity issues.[204] A necessary condition for a convertible bond to be a credible signal of superior firm value is that the convertible bond issuer incurs significant costs of financial distress, if it adds debt to its capital structure.[205]

Not only ordinary convertible bonds mitigate costs of external equity finance related to adverse selection: Chemmanur/Nandy/Yan (2003) present a model to explain the use and valuation impact of mandatorily convertible securities.[206] Similar to Stein (1992), they build their model on the notion that firms are concerned about the misvaluation of their securities in

---

200 See Shyam-Sunder/Myers (1999), p. 224 f. and Schmid Klein/O'Brien/Peters (2002), p. 336 ff. for an overview of studies on the pecking order.

201 Korajczyk/Lucas/McDonald (1991), p. 685 ff. provide evidence on time-varying adverse selection costs and suggest that equity issues should follow credible information releases such as earnings announcements. Bayless/Chaplinsky (1996), p. 253 ff. show that timing of an equity issue with favourable market conditions and a high level of general issuance activity also allows to reduce information costs. D'Mello/Ferris (2000), p. 78 ff. use analyst activity and consensus to proxy for the degree of information asymmetry faced by a firm and find a negative relationship between stock price reactions and the degree of information asymmetry.

202 See Brennan/Kraus (1987), p. 1225 ff. and Constantinides/Grundy (1989), p. 445 ff. for prominent examples. Both models show that convertible debt issuance may be a fully-revealing signal about the true value of a firm under certain conditions.

203 See Stein (1992), p. 3 ff.

204 See Eckbo/Masulis (1995), p. 1042 f. for a survey of event study results, which provides corresponding empirical evidence.

205 See Stein (1992), p. 4.

206 See Chemmanur/Nandy/Yan (2003), p. 1 ff. Arzac (1997), p. 55 mentions that mandatory convertibles can reduce costs of asymmetric information compared to equity offerings. White Huckins (1999), p. 89 ff. confirms this notion in a study of mandatorily convertible preferred stock. She finds that mandatory issuers have high debt-ratios, low interest coverage and high bankruptcy risk.

capital markets as well as their probability of being in financial distress and incurring financial distress costs.

Chemmanur/Nandy/Yan (2003) differentiate between three types of firms: good, medium and bad firms that have different probabilities of being in financial distress. These firms can either issue straight or convertible debt, mandatory convertibles or common stock. What type of security a firm chooses will depend on the costs and benefits of doing so. Good firms can distinguish themselves from bad firms by issuing straight debt and medium firms from bad firms by issuing ordinary convertible debt rather than equity. However, this increases the probability of financial distress for good and medium firms, too. When this probability becomes sufficiently high, it may be optimal to issue mandatory convertibles for all types of firms, since the incremental costs of financial distress in straight or convertible debt issues outweigh the reduction of adverse selection costs. Using this rationale, it can be shown that mandatory convertible issuance is optimal in a partially separating equilibrium that is characterized by moderate information asymmetry and a financial distress probability that is larger for medium and bad firms than for good firms.[207] In this situation, especially larger firms that are already substantially levered may choose to issue mandatory convertibles. Since the equilibrium is partially pooling, short- and long-run abnormal returns will be negative for mandatory convertible issuers, but higher than those of equity issuers.[208] In a fully pooling equilibrium, which is characterized by significant financial distress costs for all types of firms, no firm issues debt, but all firms issue mandatory convertibles. Valuation effects will be neutral.[209]

Given the explanations for equity and convertible debt issuance, what could lead firms to combine these two types of securities in a concurrent offering? First and foremost, the existing literature on convertible securities suggests to make a distinction between concurrent offerings according to the nature of the conversion feature attached to the security offered alongside common stock.

---

[207] In this equilibrium, a medium firm could issue straight or convertible debt to separate itself from bad firms, but this would increase the costs of financial distress. If adverse selection costs are low and the benefit derived from a separating strategy is smaller anyway, it will be better for the medium firm to pool with the bad firm. In this case, the costs arising from misvaluation of the securities are lower than the costs of financial distress the firm would incur in the case of a (convertible) debt issue. A good firm may still find it optimal to issue straight debt. Medium and bad firms issue mandatory convertibles rather than equity, because the value of these securities is less sensitive to asymmetric information than the market value of common stock. See Chemmanur/Nandy/Yan (2003), p. 18. In addition, higher coupon payments that investors receive as compensation for the capped or limited upside potential and the missing option right may be a positive signal concerning the firm's cash flow situation itself.

[208] See Chemmanur/Nandy/Yan (2003), p. 5.

[209] See Chemmanur/Nandy/Yan (2003), p. 23.

If this security features mandatory conversion, I expect that firms facing low adverse selection costs and high costs of financial distress rely on this type of offering.[210] If a firm chooses to conduct a concurrent offering rather than a pure mandatory convertible offering, it appears likely that it faces a lower degree of adverse selection and a higher degree of financial distress costs than issuers of pure mandatory convertibles. The implications for the valuation impact are difficult to determine ex-ante. One hypothesis is that in a partially separating as well as in a pooling equilibrium, no distinction can be made between bad and medium firms (and good firms, respectively) and hence, combining equity and mandatory convertibles would not make any difference: valuation effects would be negative or neutral.

If a convertible security with an ordinary conversion feature is used in a concurrent transaction, it may constitute a positive signal about the value of the issuing firm. In related research for unit IPOs, Chemmanur/Fulghieri (1997) show that contingent claims can serve as cost-efficient signals, when issuing firms are very risky.[211] Risk in this context is determined by the uncertainty related to the payoff structure of investment opportunities and by the probability of a firm being in financial distress.

Combining these aspects enables a scenario, where a concurrent offering of common stock and ordinary convertible securities may be plausible from a financial manager's point-of-view: a manager of a firm will issue a convertible bond to distinguish the firm from issuers of common stock, thereby signaling his superior assessment of firm value. The signal is credible if the firm faces high incremental costs of financial distress. However, if these costs are too high, managers may not find it optimal to conduct a pure convertible bond offering. This may be aggravated when the firm faces a high uncertainty as to the reception of a positive payoff from its investment program. In such a situation, a manager may intend to send a positive signal about firm value by a convertible bond offering backed up by an offering of common stock. Consistent with this notion, Byoun/Moore (2003) show that firms using units in SEOs have greater stock price volatility and higher debt levels. These firms are able to reduce announcement returns compared to pure SEOs.[212]

Given these arguments, firms issuing ordinary convertible securities alongside common stock should possess valuable investment opportunities and face a considerable risk of being in financial distress and of receiving a positive payoff from investment projects. Announcement returns should be higher for these firms than for equity issuers.

---

[210] See Chemmanur/Nandy/Yan (2003), p. 4

[211] See Chemmanur/Fulghieri (1997), p. 15; Lee/Lee/Taylor (2003), p. 65.

[212] See Byoun/Moore (2003), p. 578 and 582.

3 *Data and proxy variables*

3.1 Sample selection procedure

The data set consists of three individual samples: concurrent offerings, convertible bond and equity issues. The concurrent offering sample includes issues where common stock is offered alongside with convertible securities that either have an ordinary conversion feature (OCF) or a mandatory conversion feature (MCF). The convertible bond (CBS) and seasoned equity offering (SEO) samples function as control groups.[213]

I use two sources to identify concurrent offerings. The primary source is the SDC Platinum Global New Issues Database provided by Thomson Financial. The second source is an internal database generated by the equity-linked securities department of Salomon Smith Barney containing hand-collected data on concurrent and convertible bond offerings, which I require to complete the information set on the transactions.[214] The final sample of concurrent offerings satisfies the following selection criteria:

1. The transaction is conducted during the period between January 1, 2000 and December 31, 2002 by a US firm listed on the NYSE/AMEX/Nasdaq.
2. The issuer is not a financial institution.[215]
3. The transaction consists of a concurrent offering of common stock and a convertible security. The selection criterion is the data item „Equity & equity-related simultaneous offering“ in the SDC database.[216]
4. The announcement day can be identified relying on the press research engine Factiva.
5. The announcement does not coincide with the announcement of other corporate events, such as dividend or earnings announcements.

---

[213] I have experimented with two alternative convertible bond control samples. The first sample includes, apart from ordinary convertible bonds, a portion of convertible preferred stocks as well as a portion of mandatory convertibles to match the structure of the concurrent offerings sample. The other sample includes only convertible bonds. The results are not affected by the exact composition of the convertible bond control sample. I use the mixed sample for the following analyses and refer to it as the convertible bond sample to avoid confusion with convertible securities in the OCF sample.

[214] The database was generated by the equity-linked securities department of Salomon Smith Barney in New York and contains detailed information on convertible debt offerings.

[215] All issuers with a SIC code from 6000 to 6999 are deleted.

[216] This criterion has only been available since 2000.

6. Stock price and accounting data are available from Thomson Financial Datastream and Thomson Financial Worldscope.[217]

47 transactions satisfy the criteria listed above. 26 of them are concurrent offerings where convertible securities have an ordinary conversion feature (OCF) and 21 have a mandatory conversion feature (MCF). The samples of convertible bond issues and underwritten equity issues are constructed in a similar fashion and consist of 290 and 247 observations.[218]

3.2 Data summary information

Summary statistics for the data set are reported in table V.1. Panel A shows transaction and firm characteristics. The mean issue sizes are 950 (OCF) and 1,011 (MCF) million USD for the two types of concurrent offerings, which are significantly larger than the average issuance volumes of pure convertible bond (429 million USD) and pure equity issues (251 million USD). Similarly, concurrent offerings are conducted by larger firms.

Table V.1: Transaction and firm characteristics

	Ordinary conversion feature (OCF, N=26)		Mandatory conversion feature (MCF, N=21)		Convertible bond sample (CBS, N=290)		Equity sample (SEO, N=247)	
Descriptive Measure	*Mean*	*St. Dev.*	*Mean*	*St. Dev.*	*Mean*	*St. Dev.*	*Mean*	*St. Dev.*
Total proceeds (mio. USD)	950	996	1,011	482	429	475	251	358
Market value (mio. USD)	11,741	18,143	10,046	7,676	8,243	14,694	2,232	4,732
Issue size market value stock	23%	21%	16%	13%	12%	13%	25%	66%
Number of shares (mio.)	12.8	10.5	41.2	117.1	14.2	32.6	7.9	14.2
Maturity (years)	10.0	6.3	3.2	0.4	11.8	8.2	-	-
Coupon	5.3%	1.3%	7.8%	1.0%	4.4%	2.0%	-	-
Conversion premium	25%	4%	22%	4%	28%	9%	-	-
Call protection (years)	3.2	1.0	3.1	0.3	3.5	1.1	-	-

Rating	*% N*	*% N*	*% N*
Investment grade	15.4%	81.0%	33.8%
High yield	57.7%	9.5%	26.2%
No rating	26.9%	9.5%	40.0%

With regard to their structure, it is obvious that convertible securities in the OCF sample have a slightly lower maturity than convertible securities in the CBS sample. For the former, I also

[217] I require issuing firms to have accounting and stock price data for the year preceding the issue. Stock prices are total return index levels, which assume a reinvestment of (cash) dividend payments and are adjusted for capital actions.

[218] Overall, 57 offerings in my sample are conducted by public utilities. From these, three are contained in the OCF sample, seven in the MCF sample, nineteen in the convertible bond sample and 28 in the equity sample. I control for offerings of public utilities in particular when analyzing abnormal returns.

observe higher coupon payments, which may indicate that the credit quality of firms in the OCF concurrent offerings sample is on average lower than that of firms in the pure convertible bond sample, a fact that is supported by the rating distribution in the lower part of panel A. The conversion premia of the convertible securities in the OCF sample are lower than those in the convertible bond sample, indicating a more equity-like character of these securities.

The average maturity of mandatory convertibles in the MCF sample is significantly lower than the maturity of convertible securities in the other samples. So is the average conversion premium. The coupons of the mandatory convertibles are higher, since they represent the compensation for the capped or limited upside potential and the missing option right. Low standard deviations of the maturity, coupon payments and the conversion premium show that although different mandatory convertible product types have been used in concurrent offerings, these securities bear a high degree of structural resemblance.

Table V.2 shows the structure of concurrent offerings. Its purpose is to illustrate that the weightings of equity and equity-linked securities is on average equal in both, the OCF and MCF samples. In no case is the proportion of the convertible security lower than 25.8% or higher than 75.0%.

Table V.2: Structure of concurrent offerings

	Ordinary conversion feature (OCF, N=26)					Mandatory conversion feature (MCF, N=21)				
	T$ Stock	*T$ Conv*	*T$ Total*	*% Stock*	*% Conv*	*T$ Stock*	*T$ Conv*	*T$ Total*	*% Stock*	*% Conv*
Mean	493	457	950	50.3%	49.7%	504	507	1,011	50.7%	49.3%
Median	325	300	675	49.7%	50.3%	466	420	950	53.1%	46.9%
Max	2,158	2,700	4,838	74.2%	74.6%	1,020	1,500	2,001	68.6%	75.0%
Min	60	100	160	25.4%	25.8%	151	150	301	25.0%	31.4%
St. Dev.	526	521	996	11.8%	11.8%	265	332	482	14.2%	14.2%

Table V.3 contains an overview of the use of proceeds. In the case of MCF firms, I find refinancing of debt to be the dominant motive, which is consistent with the notion that these firms are financially distressed and need to reduce leverage. Investment-related motives do not appear to be a driver of the security issue decision. Firms in the OCF sample, in contrast, emphasize investments and general corporate purposes more than debt-refinancing.

Table V.3: Use of proceeds

This table shows the use of proceeds for firms conducting concurrent offerings. Since a lot of firms indicated more than one use of proceeds, multiple entries are possible.

	Ordinary conversion feature (OCF, N=26)		Mandatory conversion feature (MCF, N=21)	
Use of proceeds	*N*	%	*N*	%
Investments	16	62%	5	24%
Refinance debt	10	38%	15	71%
General corporate purposes	15	58%	10	48%
No indication	5	19%	3	14%
Firms indicating 2 uses	8	31%	8	38%
Firms indicating 3 uses	6	23%	2	10%

3.3 Proxy variables

The signaling-hypothesis highlights the role of adverse selection costs, costs of financial distress as well as the value and risk of a firm's investment opportunity set. In this section, I present proxy variables that I use to quantify these dimensions and that will allow for a test of the empirical implications derived from the signaling-hypothesis.[219] For the sake of brevity, I describe proxy variables that are more critical for the analysis here and refer to further control variables in table V.5.

SIZE. The degree of asymmetric information that a company faces influences the security issue decision as well as investor reactions. Following Lewis/Rogalski/Seward (2003), I use *SIZE*, measured as the natural logarithm of the market value of equity of a firm one month prior to the offering announcement, as a proxy for adverse selection costs, since usually more information is available for larger firms.[220]

RISK. The role of risk is emphasized by the signaling-hypothesis for OCF transactions. I measure risk as the standard deviation of a firm's daily stock returns during the year preceding the offering.[221]

---

219 Variables are measured at the fiscal year-end in the year prior to the offering. The corresponding Worldscope data item is indicated in parentheses.

220 See Lewis/Rogalski/Seward (2003), p. 163 and 168.

221 According to Marsh (1982), p. 132 and Jung/Kim/Stulz (1996), p. 170, I consider the total risk of a firm. It is a more appropriate measure of risk, because systematic as well as idiosyncratic risk can affect a firm's

DISTRESS. The signal about a firm's true value sent by a convertible bond is credible, if the firm faces high incremental costs of financial distress. To measure these costs, I follow Marsh (1982) and use a firm's deviation from its target debt ratio. I compute *DISTRESS* as the difference between the target debt ratio, which I compute as the 10-year historical average of the debt ratio, and the debt ratio that would prevail if a firm issued straight debt.[222] The debt ratio is defined as long-term debt (WC03251) plus short-term debt (WC03051) divided by total assets (WC02999). This ratio has several advantages: first, it is a measure for incremental costs of financial distress. Second, it is consistent with the notion that firms adjust their debt ratio towards a target debt ratio that they consider to be optimal.[223] Finally, the ratio explicitly takes into account that a financial distress cost-function may be company-specific. I rely on book values to calculate this variable, as book values have been found to be more suitable for explaining corporate treasurers' decision-making.[224] *DISTRESS* is negatively related to the amount of costs of financial distress a firm faces. As an alternative measure, I compute a firm's industry-adjusted debt ratio (*LEVERAGE*), where industry affiliation is based on the 3-digit SIC code.[225]

MTB. Apart from risk, the role of investment opportunities plays a major role in the signaling-hypothesis for OCF firms. I use the market-to-book ratio (*MTB*) to measure the market's assessment of the value of a firm's growth opportunities. As in Lewis/Rogalski/Seward (2003), it is defined as total assets (WC02999) plus the market value of common stock minus its book value (WC03501) divided by total assets.[226] Lewis/Rogalski/Seward (2003) relate the value of a convertible bond issuer's investment opportunity set to that of an industry composite firm and find significant differences between the two numbers. To account for these findings and to adjust for any industry-specific differences in market-to-book ratios, I use the same approach: *MTB* is measured as the deviation of a firm's market-to-book ratio from the industry median, where industry affiliation is based on the 3-digit SIC code.

---

investment decisions. See for example Lewis/Rogalski/Seward (2002), p. 71. The use of the beta as a measure of systematic risk leaves the results unaltered.

222 See Marsh (1982), p. 130 f. Due to data constraints, not all target debt ratios can be estimated over ten years. The mean number of years to estimate the target debt ratio is 7.36 for the complete sample.

223 Hovakimian/Hovakimian/Theranian (2004), p. 517 ff. underline the importance of target debt ratios using the case of dual debt-equity offerings.

224 See Marsh (1982), p. 131.

225 I rely on the Compustat database in this case, because it provides access to the accounting data for the whole stock market universe in the US.

226 See Lewis/Rogalski/Seward (2003), p. 162 f.

RUNUP. Following Lucas/MacDonald (1990) and Jung/Kim/Stulz (1996), I include the issuer's share price performance (*RUNUP*) prior to the offering, calculated as cumulative abnormal market-adjusted return during the year preceding the issue, as a further measure for the availability of profitable investment opportunities.[227]

RIS. The relative issue size is calculated as total proceeds from the issue scaled by the market capitalization of the issuing firm. The *RIS* variable is included to account for a possible relation of the security issue decision and the amount of financing needed by a firm.[228]

Table V.4 summarizes the empirical implications of the signaling-hypothesis and relates them to the proxy variables described above. Further control variables are contained in table V.5.

Table V.4: Summary of empirical implications of the signaling-hypothesis

Empirical implication	Proxy Variable
I OCF firms...	
(1) ... face high adverse selection costs.	*SIZE*
(2) ... face incremental costs of financial distress that are larger than those of convertible bond issuers.	*DISTRESS*
(3) ... have investment opportunities that are comparable to those of convertible bond issuers.	*MTB, RUNUP*
(4) ... are more risky than convertible bond issuers.	*RISK*
(5) ... have announcement returns that are higher than those of equity issuers and that are positively (negatively) related to the value of a firm's investment opportunities (level of risk).	*CAR*
II MCF firms...	
(1) ... face a lower degree of adverse selection costs than convertible bond issuers.	*SIZE*
(2) ... face higher incremental costs of financial distress and bankruptcy risk than convertible bond issuers.	*DISTRESS, BR*
(3) ... have announcement returns that are higher than those of equity issuers and that are negatively related to financial risk.	*CAR*

[227] See Lucas/McDonald (1990), p. 1019 ff.; Jung/Kim/Stulz (1996), p. 170.
[228] See Jung/Kim/Stulz (1996), p. 173.

Table V.5: Overview of further proxy variables

Variable		Description
FCF	Free cash flow	I control for free cash flow, since it may play an important role in the issue decision of firms in the equity sample. I use the variable as in Lee/Figlewicz (1999), defined as cash flow (WC04860) minus capital expenditures (WC04601), plus common and preferred dividends (WC04551), standardized by the sales level (WC01001), as a proxy for the agency costs of free cash flow.[229]
AC	Asset composition	To account for the fact that historical averages are only approximations of target debt levels, I include asset composition defined as fixed to total assets (the sum of WC02250, WC02501 and WC02649 divided by WC02999). The higher the proportion of assets already in place, the higher the target debt ratio can be expected to be.[230]
TIMEQU/ *TIMCON*	Timing equity/ Timing convertible bond market	I include variables to control for timing efforts. *TIMEQU* and *TIMCON* are derived from Marsh (1982). However, they have been moderately modified for the purpose of this study:[231] **Formula V.1:** $TIMEQU_t = \gamma_{0t} + \gamma_{1t} E_{t-1} + \gamma_{2t} R_{M\,t-1} + \gamma_{3t} R_{M\,t-2} + \varepsilon_t$ **Formula V.2:** $TIMCON_t = \gamma_{0t} + \gamma_{1t} C_{t-1} + \gamma_{2t} R_{M\,t-1} + \gamma_{3t} R_{M\,t-2} + \gamma_{4t} r_{t-1} + \gamma_{5t} r_{t-2} + \varepsilon_t$ The equations show forecast models of the number of equity and convertible bond issues in the quarter of issue. *E* is the level of new equity issues. R_M is the return on the equity market in quarters *t-1* and *t-2*, which contains information about the general market environment.[232] *C* accounts for the number of convertible security issues in the respective quarter.[233] As convertible bond issuers are likely to consider equity market returns as well as the interest rate environment in the issue decision, I include both variables, with *r* being the effective yield of a medium-term government security in the two quarters preceding the issue.
PROF	Profitability	Profitability is measured as net income (WC01751) divided by total assets. More profitable companies are likely to have lower costs of financial distress and less information asymmetry as to the value of their investment opportunities.[234]
TAX	Taxes	I control for a tax-based explanation for the use of a convertible security in a concurrent offering by employing the *TAX* variable as in Jung/Kim/Stulz (1996), defined as tax payments (WC01451) scaled by the book value of total assets.[235] Since the gain from the tax deductibility of interest from debt and convertible debt increases with a firm's tax rate, convertible debt and dual security issuers are likely to display higher tax variable values.
BR	Bankruptcy risk	As an alternative measure of financial distress, I compute the z-score (*BR*), presented by Altman (1968) and also used in Chemmanur/Nandy/Yan (2003):[236] **Formula V.3** $BR = 1.2 * WC / TA + 1.4 * RE / TA + 3.3 * EBIT / TA + 0.6 * MV / TD + 1.0 * SA / TA$ *WC* is working capital (WC03151), *TA* is the book value total assets, *RE* is retained earnings (WC03495), *EBIT* is earnings before interest and tax (WC18191), *MV* is the market value of equity, *TD* is the book value total debt and *SA* is sales. Firms with higher z-scores have a lower probability of bankruptcy.

229 See Lee/Figlewicz (1999), p. 551.

230 See Marsh (1982), p. 132. Asset composition has been found to play a role for the decision to issue convertible debt as well. For example, Essig (1992), p. 32 ff. finds the proportion of tangible to total assets to be negatively related to the propensity of firms to issue convertible debt. In Stein (1992), this has an information interpretation, because the degree of asymmetric information will be higher for companies that have many intangible assets.

231 See Marsh (1982), p. 133.

232 The return on the equity market is measured using an equal-weighted CRSP index.

233 I obtained issuance volumes from Thomson One Banker deals for the five years preceding the issue to estimate the model.

234 See Jung/Kim/Stulz (1996), p. 170; Lewis/Rogalski/Seward (2003), p. 163.

235 See Jung/Kim/Stulz (1996), p. 170.

236 See Altman (1968), p. 594; Chemmanur/Nandy/Yan (2003), p. 26.

4 *Empirical analysis of company characteristics*

4.1 Presentation of pre-issue company characteristics

Before carrying out any multivariate analyses, I report means, medians and standard deviations of the pre-issue characteristics variables for the concurrent offerings sample and the convertible bond and equity control samples in table V.6. I also indicate the results of a univariate analysis, where I conduct a median test of equality across transaction-type samples. The results in table V.6 support the signaling-hypothesis for MCF and OCF concurrent offerings.

The characteristics of OCF firms are shown in column 1. OCF concurrent offerings are conducted by larger firms, which is surprising, since smaller firms whose prospects are more difficult to evaluate for firm outsiders should benefit more from signaling. However, OCF firms have higher total risk (*RISK*), which indicates that asymmetric information may be a problem when managers have private information about firm risk. This corresponds to the unit IPO-scenario discussed by Chemmanur/Fulghieri (1997), where high-risk firms going public package equity with warrants to send a cost-efficient signal to the capital market.[237] Since the financial risk of OCF firms is also high (measured by *DISTRESS*), managers may decide to conduct a concurrent offering, because a pure convertible bond offering may increase the costs of financial distress for their firms too much.

Despite their higher risk, OCF firms are evaluated like firms with valuable investment opportunities by the capital market. The median industry-adjusted market-to-book ratio (*MTB*) is significantly higher than the median value for convertible bond issuers. The pre-issue share price runup shows a corresponding pattern and amounts to 53% on average.

[237] See Chemmanur/Fulghieri (1997), p. 3.

Table V.6: Presentation of pre-issue firm characteristics

This table shows statistics of proxy variable values for the different transaction-type samples. *SIZE* is computed as the natural logarithm of the market value of equity measured one month prior to the offering announcement. *RISK* is the standard deviation of stock returns during the year preceding the issue. *DISTRESS* is defined as the average of long-term debt plus short-term debt divided by total assets minus the value of this ratio that would prevail, if the firm issued debt. *LEVERAGE* is the industry-adjusted leverage ratio, where industry affiliation is based on the 3-digit SIC code. *MTB* is the industry-adjusted market-to-book ratio, defined as total assets plus the market value of common stock minus its book value divided by total assets. *RUNUP* is the market-adjusted cumulative excess return during the year preceding the issue. *FCF* is the free cash flow proxy defined as cash flow minus capital expenditures plus common and preferred dividends standardized by the sales level. *AC* is computed as fixed assets divided by total assets. *TIMEQU* and *TIMCON* are forecast variables for the equity and convertible bond market, respectively, in terms of number of issues. *PROF* is measured as net income scaled by total assets. *TAX* are tax payments scaled by total assets. *RIS* are total proceeds from the issue divided by the market value of the firm. *BR* is Altman's bankruptcy risk measure. *CONVPROB* is defined as the $N(d_2)$ calculated from the Black/Scholes formula.[238] Since some variables are not normally distributed, I test the equality of medians of the different samples against each other using a Wilcoxon signed-rank test. If an equal sign is shown, the null hypothesis of equality of the medians cannot be rejected at the 5%-level. [a)] means that the difference is significant at the 10%-level.

	1			2			3			4			5		
	Ordinary conversion feature (OCF, N=26)			Mandatory conversion feature (MCF, N=21)			Convertible bond sample (CBS, N=290)			Equity sample (SEO, N=247)			Median tests of equality		
Variable	*Mean*	*Median*	*St. Dev.*	*Mean*	*Median*	*St. Dev.*	*Mean*	*Median*	*St. Dev.*	*Mean*	*Median*	*St. Dev.*			
SIZE	8.32	8.44	1.35	8.87	8.90	0.91	8.06	7.94	1.22	6.76	6.58	1.29	CBS = OCF > SEO	CBS < MCF > SEO	MCF[a)] > OCF
RISK	0.05	0.04	0.02	0.02	0.02	0.01	0.04	0.04	0.02	0.04	0.04	0.02	CBS < OCF > SEO[a)]	CBS > MCF < SEO	MCF < OCF
DISTRESS	-0.10	-0.13	0.32	-0.15	-0.11	0.19	-0.04	-0.03	0.18	-0.26	-0.21	0.24	CBS > OCF < SEO	CBS > MCF > SEO	MCF = OCF
LEVERAGE	0.12	0.07	0.24	0.08	0.09	0.19	0.07	0.03	0.16	0.06	0.00	0.21	CBS = OCF = SEO	CBS = MCF = SEO	MCF = OCF
MTB	2.69	1.09	4.51	0.22	0.15	0.39	2.79	0.64	10.95	5.07	0.63	28.67	CBS < OCF = SEO	CBS > MCF < SEO	MCF < OCF
RUNUP	0.53	0.53	0.68	-0.07	0.06	0.48	0.39	0.30	0.97	0.58	0.47	0.72	CBS < OCF = SEO	CBS > MCF < SEO	MCF < OCF
FCF	-0.66	-0.20	1.32	-0.08	-0.01	0.17	-0.65	0.00	4.86	-2.24	-0.01	17.89	CBS > OCF < SEO	CBS = MCF = SEO	MCF > OCF
AC	0.60	0.66	0.26	0.64	0.65	0.17	0.45	0.45	0.24	0.47	0.48	0.27	CBS < OCF > SEO	CBS < MCF > SEO	MCF = OCF
TIMEQU	117	109	16	120	115	18	120	111	20	126	125	25	CBS = OCF < SEO	CBS = MCF = SEO	MCF = OCF
TIMCON	104	104	12	97	100	19	105	108	14	98	102	16	CBS > OCF < SEO[a)]	CBS > MCF = SEO	MCF[a)] < OCF
PROF	-0.04	0.01	0.13	-0.05	0.02	0.30	-0.01	0.04	0.31	-0.06	0.02	0.25	CBS > OCF = SEO	CBS > MCF = SEO	MCF = OCF
TAX	0.02	0.01	0.02	0.00	0.00	0.04	0.02	0.02	0.03	0.02	0.01	0.03	CBS = OCF = SEO	CBS > MCF < SEO	MCF[a)] < OCF
RIS	0.23	0.18	0.21	0.16	0.10	0.13	0.12	0.10	0.13	0.25	0.16	0.66	CBS < OCF = SEO	CBS < MCF < SEO	MCF < OCF
BR	2.82	1.43	5.04	0.23	0.77	2.32	10.67	2.40	65.51	14.06	2.16	79.12	CBS = OCF = SEO	CBS > MCF < SEO[a)]	MCF < OCF
CONVPROB	85%	88%	15%	100%	100%	0%	52%	52%	7%	-	-	-	CBS < OCF -	CBS < MCF -	MCF > OCF

[238] See Black/Scholes (1973), p. 644; Lewis/Rogalski/Seward (2003), p. 160.

The characteristics of firms in the mandatory conversion feature sample are displayed in column 2. Consistent with the signaling-hypothesis, MCF firms are significantly larger than convertible bond and equity issuers, which suggests that they face a lower degree of adverse selection costs (measured by *SIZE*). While these firms appear to have a lower total risk (*RISK*), they have a higher financial risk than convertible bond issuers. A further debt issue would lead to a deviation from the target debt ratio that is higher for MCF firms than for CBS firms. To this end, they are likely to face significant incremental costs of financial distress (measured by *DISTRESS*). The bankruptcy risk measure, *BR*, supports this interpretation and is significantly lower for MCF firms than for all other firms in the sample. In contrast, the market-to-book ratio, *MTB*, and the pre-issue share price runup, *RUNUP*, are lower for MCF firms, which indicates that they possess less valuable investment opportunities. Given these characteristics, it becomes obvious that MCF firms are firms that derive their value mainly from assets-in-place rather than from growth opportunities.

4.2 A regression model of security choice

In this section, I develop a multinomial logistic regression model based on the variables from the previous section.[239] This multivariate analysis represents a test of security choice of my sample firms.[240] The independent variable in the regression model is the security issue decision made by a firm. Equity issues take the value zero and convertible bond issues take the value one. In the first regression set, I include all concurrent offerings featuring ordinary convertibles and code these transactions as two. I re-estimate the regressions, substituting OCF transactions by MCF transactions.

Table V.7 shows regression results in panels A and B. Concurrent offerings are the reference category. Therefore, a negative sign indicates an increased probability that a concurrent offering occurs.

---

[239] I omit *LEVERAGE* and Altman's bankruptcy risk variable (*BR*) in the model and rely solely on *DISTRESS* to capture costs of financial distress. Re-estimation of the model including these variables does not change the conclusions drawn from the analysis, but reduces the pseudo R^2 values.

[240] Previous research using this methodology to model the managerial security issue decision has for example been forwarded by Marsh (1982), p. 121 ff., Billingsley/Lamy/Thompson (1988), p. 43 ff., Bayless/ Chaplinsky (1991), p. 195 ff., Jung/Kim/Stulz (1996), p. 159 ff., Lee/Figlewicz (1999), p. 547 ff. and Hovakimian/Opler/Titman (2001), p. 1 ff.

Table V.7: Results for the regression model of security choice

This table shows results for a multinomial logistic regression model for OCF and MCF concurrent offerings. In panel A (panel B), OCF (MCF) concurrent offerings are compared with pure convertible bond and equity offerings. Note that in these panels, concurrent offerings are the reference category. A negative sign indicates an increased probability that a concurrent offering occurs when the value of a variable increases. In panel C, I show a binary logistic regression model, where MCF firms take the value one and pure mandatory convertible issuers (PM) take the value zero. The explanatory variables are: *SIZE* is computed as the natural logarithm of the market value of equity measured one month prior to the offering announcement. *RISK* is the standard deviation of stock returns during the year preceding the issue. *DISTRESS* is defined as the average of long-term debt plus short-term debt divided by total assets minus the value of this ratio that would prevail, if the firm issued debt. *MTB* is the industry-adjusted market-to-book ratio. *RUNUP* is the market-adjusted cumulative excess return during the year preceding the issue. *FCF* is the free cash flow proxy defined as cash flow minus capital expenditures plus common and preferred dividends standardized by the sales level. *AC* is computed as fixed assets divided by total assets. *TIMEQU* and *TIMCON* are forecast variables for the equity and convertible bond market, respectively, in terms of number of issues. *PROF* is measured as net income scaled by total assets. *TAX* are tax payments scaled by total assets. *RIS* are total proceeds from the issue scaled by the market value of the firm. P-values are calculated from Wald test statistics. ***, ** and * indicate a significance level of 1%, 5% and 10%, respectively. Pseudo R^2 values are as in Nagelkerke (1991).[241] Classification plots indicate the model's ability to categorize a transaction correctly. Concurrent offerings where an ordinary convertible security is issued alongside common stock are denominated as OCF, while concurrent offerings of common stocks and mandatory convertibles are denominated as MCF. CBS is the abbreviation for the convertible bond sample and SEO for the equity sample.

	Panel A: OCF concurrent offerings		**Panel B: MCF concurrent offerings**		**Panel C: MCF versus pure mandatories (PM)**
	1	**2**	**3**	**4**	**5**
	CBS vs. OCF	**SEO vs. OCF**	**CBS vs. MCF**	**SEO vs. MCF**	**MCF vs. PM**
Variable	***Coef***	***Coef***	***Coef***	***Coef***	***Coef***
Constant	7.25 **	16.29 ***	2.44	11.39 ***	-68.56 **
SIZE	-0.37	-1.20 ***	-0.66 **	-1.48 ***	7.97 **
RISK	-45.56 ***	-65.59 ***	111.38 ***	91.20 ***	-190.39
DISTRESS	1.22	-5.65 ***	14.07 ***	6.54 **	-13.32 *
MTB	0.00	0.00	0.52	0.52	0.09
RUNUP	-0.55 **	-0.68 **	1.37 *	1.21 *	1.22
FCF	0.00	-0.01	-0.78	-0.78	0.54
AC	-3.17 ***	-2.02 *	-2.60	-1.22	-5.39
TIMEQU	0.03 **	0.04 **	0.00	0.01	0.06
TIMCON	-0.01	-0.06 ***	0.05 **	0.00	-0.10
PROF	0.33	0.78	0.89	1.54	8.50
TAX	-3.83	0.62	21.17 ***	26.69 ***	-169.81 *
RIS	-1.03	-0.63 *	-0.83	-0.60	83.65 **

		% correct OCF	0.0%		*% correct MCF*	40.0%			
		% correct CBS	86.4%		*% correct CBS*	86.8%		*% correct MCF*	76.5%
		% correct SEO	78.1%		*% correct SEO*	77.2%		*% correct PM*	85.0%
Pseudo R^2	0.54	*Overall*	79.8%	0.62	*Overall*	80.9%	0.77	*Overall*	81.1%

The signs and significant coefficients in table V.7 provide further evidence in favour of the signaling-hypothesis and are consistent with the results from the univariate analysis. Hence,

[241] See Nagelkerke (1991), p. 691 f.

for the OCF sample *RUNUP* and *RISK* have negative signs and are significant. This indicates that OCF firms possess valuable investment opportunities and communicate these to the capital market. This, in turn, seems to lead to a share price appreciation prior to the issue and increases the probability that an OCF concurrent offering occurs. Simultaneously, OCF concurrent offerings are more likely to be conducted by riskier firms. For these firms, the uncertainty of receiving a positive payoff from investing is high, which translates into an increased uncertainty of bond conversion. In this case, the potential increase in financial distress costs may outweigh the reduction of adverse selection costs of a convertible bond issue. Since OCF firms are larger firms (*SIZE* has a negative coefficient in regression 2), for which adverse selection costs are lower per se, managers may consider OCF concurrent offerings to be cheaper alternatives than convertible bond issues.

The *RIS* variable accounts for a possible relation of the security issue decision and the amount of financing needed by a firm.[242] The negative coefficient of *RIS* indicates that the amount of financing required by a firm may play a role in the decision to conduct a concurrent offering of ordinary convertible securities and common stock.

Panel B contains the comparison of the MCF sample with the convertible bond and equity control samples. I find *SIZE* to be significant and negative in columns 3 and 4, which indicates an increased probability that an MCF transaction occurs as *SIZE* increases. Similarly, *DISTRESS* has a significant and positive coefficient, which suggests that firms are more likely to offer mandatory convertibles alongside common stock, when their incremental costs of financial distress are larger (remembering that *DISTRESS* is negatively related to the amount of incremental costs of financial distress a firm faces). For MCF firms, it will be better to issue mandatory convertibles alongside common stock rather than ordinary convertible securities, because the increase in financial distress costs incurred in a convertible bond issue may dominate the decrease of adverse selection costs.

MCF firms do not require investment capital, but need to reduce leverage: the significantly positive coefficient of *RUNUP* indicates that the availability of investment opportunities is not a major determinant in the decision to conduct an MCF concurrent offering. This also underlines that MCF concurrent offerings are no product of market timing, given an average share price runup of –7%.

---

[242] This may introduce a simultaneous equation bias in the model, since it is possible that the type of transaction and the issuance volume are jointly determined. However, when I omit *RIS*, the coefficients of other variables remain qualitively unchanged.

While panel B addresses the question why firms conduct MCF concurrent offerings rather than pure convertible bond or equity issues, it is still to determine why these firms do not offer pure mandatory convertibles. Regarding this second question, I show results of a binary logistic model in panel C, where MCF concurrent offerings take the value one and pure mandatory convertible offerings (PM) take the value zero. The results turn out to be intuitive: larger firms that have higher incremental costs of financial distress and want to obtain more capital are more likely to conduct MCF concurrent offerings. In theory, the combination of common stock and mandatory convertibles should not cause stock price reactions towards the new issue announcement to be more adverse, since mandatory convertibles and common stocks are issued in a pooling equilibrium.[243] Moreover, larger firms are likely to have lower adverse selection costs anyway, and will clearly benefit more from a combined offering, where they reduce financial distress costs more directly.

In sum, the results of the security choice regression model are consistent with the predictions of the signaling-hypothesis for MCF and OCF concurrent offerings. The data indicates that these firms want to trade off adverse selection costs against financial distress costs to achieve a better valuation of newly issued securities in the capital market.

To assess the success of this signaling effort, I examine the valuation impact of the transaction announcements in the next section. In doing so, it is important to control for anticipation: despite high pseudo R^2 values, the classificatory ability of the security choice model is poor and it categorizes all but four OCF concurrent offerings as convertible bond issues. This raises the question to what extent the capital market anticipates that a firm conducts an OCF transaction. If investors expect a firm to issue convertible bonds and it instead issues a combination of convertible securities and common stock, the concurrent offering may actually convey negative information about firm risk rather than positive information about profitable investment projects. This, in turn, would imply more adverse announcement effects, since investors may update their assessment of a firm's cost of capital.

---

[243] Compare the discussion in section 2 of this chapter.

5 *The stock price reaction to the announcement of concurrent offerings*

A straight-forward test for the signaling-hypothesis is to examine the investors' reaction to the transaction announcement. If signaling is successful, one would expect stock price reactions to concurrent offerings to be less adverse than to equity issue announcements.

I calculate cumulative average abnormal returns (*CAARs*) for different event windows around the announcement day for each transaction-type sample in a first step and test whether *CAARs* are different across transaction-type samples on a univariate basis.[244] In a second step, I conduct a more extensive analysis in a multivariate framework to further test the predictions of the signaling-hypothesis.

5.1 The magnitude of cumulative average abnormal returns

CAARs and cumulative median abnormal returns, as well as the level of significance for parametric and non-parametric test statistics, are shown in table V.8.[245]

The results are striking. The *CAAR* for OCF concurrent offerings is –6.95% for the event window [-1;+1], which is significantly more negative than *CAARs* for other samples and also much more negative than stock price reactions generally reported in previous event studies of financing decisions.[246] In particular, it is much lower than the *CAAR* reported by Byoun/Moore (2003) of –1.97% for offerings of common stock in combination with warrants.[247]

---

[244] To compute *CAARs*, I use a standard market model approach, where the CRSP equal-weighted index is chosen as the market index. The estimation period for the model parameters is [-130;-11], where 0 is the announcement day. The parametric test statistic follows Boehmer/Musumeci/Poulsen (1991), p. 253 ff. Wilcoxon signed-rank tests are used to test for statistical significance of the medians.

[245] A surprising finding from table V.8 is that the *CAAR* for the convertible bond sample is –4.46%, while the *CAAR* for the equity sample is only –3.09%. Usually, convertible debt produces less negative valuation effects than common stock. In analyses based on the findings of chapters III and IV, I find cumulative abnormal returns to be unrelated to a firm's pre- and post-issue operating performance or changes in systematic risk. This suggests that other factors, such as hedge fund activity, cause the *CAAR* for the convertible bond sample to be more negative than the *CAAR* for the equity sample. See Bechmann (2004), p. 421 ff. for a related analysis.

[246] See Eckbo/Masulis (1995), p. 1042 f. for an overview of this literature.

[247] See Byoun/Moore (2003), p. 582. They use an event window of [-1;0]. For this event window, the *CAAR* of OCF firms is –5.79%.

Table V.8: The magnitude of cumulative average abnormal returns

This table shows event study results for the event window [-1;+1] in panel A. Panel B and C contain results for the event windows [-5;+5] and [-10;+10]. The event study uses a standard market model approach with an estimation period for the market model coefficients of 120 trading days over the period [-130;-11]. The CRSP equal-weighted index is the benchmark index. I report cumulative average abnormal returns for the different samples in the column denoted as 'Mean' and cumulative median abnormal returns in the column denoted as 'Median'. Mean test statistics follow Boehmer/Musumeci/Poulsen (1991) and median test statistics are Wilcoxon signed-rank tests. JB are Jarque-Bera tests for normality. To test for significant differences in the mean and median cumulative abnormal returns between the different samples, I use a standard t-test as well as a non-parametric Wilcoxon signed-rank test of equality of medians and report the values of the test statistics in parentheses. ***, ** and * indicate a significance level of 1%, 5% and 10%, respectively. Tests of equality are one-sided tests.

Panel A: Event window [-1;+1]

Sample	Mean	Median	JB	Mean test of equality					Median test of equality				
Complete sample	-3.96% ***	-3.73% ***	53.08 ***		MCF	OCF	CBS	SEO		MCF	OCF	CBS	SEO
Ordinary conversion feature (OCF)	-6.95% ***	-7.25% ***	0.37	MCF	0				MCF	0			
Mandatory conversion feature (MCF)	-3.46% ***	-3.05% ***	1.18	OCF	[1.98] **	0			OCF	[1.89] **	0		
Convertible bond sample (CBS)	-4.46% ***	-4.70% ***	0.26	CBS	[0.63]	[1.70] **	0		CBS	[0.92]	[1.66] **	0	
Equity sample (SEO)	-3.09% ***	-2.77% ***	1.55	SEO	[0.24]	[2.61] ***	[2.21] **	0	SEO	[0.27]	[2.40] ***	[2.34] ***	0

Panel B: Event window [-5;+5]

Sample	Mean	Median	JB	Mean test of equality					Median test of equality				
Complete sample	-4.51% ***	-4.21% ***	104.35 ***		MCF	OCF	CBS	SEO		MCF	OCF	CBS	SEO
Ordinary conversion feature (OCF)	-10.48% ***	-11.34% ***	0.49	MCF	0				MCF	0			
Mandatory conversion feature (MCF)	-2.25% **	-2.13% ***	0.38	OCF	[2.42] ***	0			OCF	[2.21] **	0		
Convertible bond sample (CBS)	-4.64% ***	-4.61% ***	57.61 ***	CBS	[0.83]	[2.16] **	0		CBS	[1.17]	[2.10] **	0	
Equity sample (SEO)	-3.92% ***	-3.33% ***	38.20 ***	SEO	[0.57]	[2.39] **	[0.64]	0	SEO	[0.73]	[2.16] **	[0.67]	0

Panel C: Event window [-10;+10]

Sample	Mean	Median	JB	Mean test of equality					Median test of equality				
Complete sample	-1.91% **	-3.80% ***	15066.64 ***		MCF	OCF	CBS	SEO		MCF	OCF	CBS	SEO
Ordinary conversion feature (OCF)	-10.00% ***	-8.72% **	0.10	MCF	0				MCF	0			
Mandatory conversion feature (MCF)	0.17%	-3.57%	3.25	OCF	[2.20] **	0			OCF	[2.15] **	0		
Convertible bond sample (CBS)	-2.21% ***	-3.95% ***	13111.97 ***	CBS	[0.45]	[1.59] *	0		CBS	[1.33] *	[1.82] **	0	
Equity sample (SEO)	-0.90%	-2.98% *	34.67 ***	SEO	[0.22]	[2.04] **	[0.66]	0	SEO	[0.76]	[2.07] **	[1.08]	0

The cumulative median abnormal return is –7.25% and shows that the adverse valuation impact is not driven by a few outliers. The *CAAR* is also significant when longer intervals are examined and even increases to –10.48% (–10.00%) for an event window of [-5;+5] ([-10;+10]). It is also robust to variations in parameters of the event study model, such as the use of value-weighted versus equal-weighted market indices.[248]

The highly adverse announcement effect is in harsh contrast to the results from the previous section, which suggests that OCF firms possess profitable growth opportunities. According to pre-issue firm characteristics, stock price reactions should be more positive than those of equity issuers, but the opposite is true.

A possible explanation for this observation is that firm managers intend to signal superior firm value, but employ an inappropriate transaction structure. If a manager wants to signal superior firm value by issuing convertible bonds, the credibility of the signal depends on how much the firm is hurt if anything goes wrong. Stein (1992) explicitly recognizes that "costly financial distress plays a key role in shaping the informational consequences of a convertible issue."[249] In a concurrent offering, costly financial distress is alleviated by the equity component.

This has important implications for the investor reaction towards the new issue announcement. In choosing a concurrent offering, it is possible that firm insiders even convey negative information about firm value: if firm insiders have private information about the risk of the firm, as outlined in Chemmanur/Fulghieri (1997), investors may infer this from the concurrent offering announcement and indeed, stock price reactions could be highly negative.[250]

Alternatively, it is possible that the signaling-hypothesis is wrong and issuing firms have been overvalued by the market prior to the transaction. I will address these two possibilities further by analyzing (i) the determinants of cumulative abnormal returns and (ii) long-run returns.

Before I turn to the multivariate analysis of announcement returns, it should be noted that the average stock price reaction to MCF concurrent offering announcements is consistent with the signaling-hypothesis. The average *CAAR* for MCF firms (-3.46%) is not significantly

---

[248] To assess the robustness of my results, I also calculated beta estimates as outlined in Dimson (1979), p. 129 ff. and Fowler/Rorke (1983), p. 279 ff. to control for infrequent trading and find my results unchanged. Also, estimating beta for a time period around the offering or using a value-weighted market index leaves the results largely unchanged.

[249] Stein (1992), p. 4.

[250] See Chemmanur/Fulghieri (1997), p. 2.

different from those of convertible bond and equity issuers for the event window [-1;+1].[251] However, when the event window is extended to [-5;+5] and [-10;+10] in panel B and C of table V.8, the negative announcement effect is not persistent. While *CAARs* remain significant for the CBS and OCF sample, they cease to be significant for the MCF sample, which might indicate that valuation effects are temporary. To shed further light on this matter, I compute abnormal returns for the time frames [-10;-1] and [0;+10]. It turns out that announcement effects are neither significant for [-10;-1] nor for [0;+10].[252] For this sample, significantly negative abnormal returns cluster tightly around the announcement day. To this end, the negative valuation effect may to some extent be due to a temporary shock and not solely driven by negative information.

5.2 The cross-section of cumulative abnormal returns

I use an OLS-regression model, where the dependent variable is the cumulative abnormal return and the independent variables are the same as in the multinomial logistic regression. In addition, I include the inverse Mill's ratio (*SURPRISE*) obtained from the conditional probabilities computed in the multinomial logistic regression to control for anticipation.[253] The White (1980) procedure corrects for heteroskedasticity to obtain efficient least-squares estimators.[254] I also add a dummy variable (*PU*) to capture the effect of public utilities (SIC codes 481 and 491 to 494).[255]

A problem that arises in the estimation of the regression is that the number of observations in the concurrent offerings sample, 21 observations in the MCF sample and 26 in the OCF sample, is too low for a comparison of the coefficients obtained in a sample-by-sample

[251] It has to be taken into account at this point that the MCF sample contains a higher proportion of public utilities, which tend to have higher stock price reactions. See for example Eckbo/Masulis (1995), p. 1042 f. I will specifically control for the effect of public utilities in a cross-sectional analysis of cumulative abnormal returns.

[252] Cumulative abnormal returns for equity issuers are on average positive for [-10;-1] and significantly negative for [0;+10]. To this end, the share price increase during the ten days preceding the announcement neutralizes the negative announcement effect that persists during [0;+10]. Hence, the insignificant announcement effect for the SEO sample for [-10;+10] appears to be an effect of market timing.

[253] See Heckman (1979), p. 153 ff.; Lee (1983), p. 507 ff. Initially, the two-step procedure from Heckman (1979) was designed to mitigate selection bias. However, I use it in the sense of Amihud/Li (2004), p. 11, where it serves as a measure for the surprise element contained in the announcement of an event: if a probit model is used to forecast the probability of event occurrence, the regression residual captures the probability of non-occurrence of the event. Since Heckman's procedure is based on probit regressions, I obtain "quasi" probit scores using the inverse cumulative distribution function of the normal distribution. A similar application of the inverse Mill's ratio is used by Byoun/Moore (2003), p. 584.

[254] See White (1980), p. 817 ff.

[255] I also include industry dummy variables in the regression, but omit them in table V.9 for expositional ease. In computing the regressions, it is not necessary to control for the offering method, since no rights issues are included in the sample.

estimation. This problem calls for a slightly different approach: I compute one regression for the complete sample and use differential intercepts (DUM_j) along with differential slope coefficients (DSC_j) for the different samples j to test whether the implications of the signaling-hypothesis are supported by the data. Regression results are shown in table V.9.

Regression 1 includes differential intercepts for MCF and OCF concurrent offerings, as well as for the convertible bond sample but excludes differential slope coefficients. Equity issues are the benchmark category and their mean effect is captured by the constant. The regression is designed to confirm that the differences of cumulative average abnormal returns across transaction-type samples are not due to common variation in other variables. Consistent with the findings of the univariate analysis, however, I find the constant to be significantly negative. So are the differential intercepts, DUM_{OCF} and DUM_{CBS}.

To understand why announcement returns for OCF concurrent offerings are highly adverse, I analyze whether firm management wants to send a positive signal about the level of future cash flows to the market, but erroneously uses a transaction structure that actually conveys negative information about the discount rate. Alternatively, OCF firms have been overvalued prior to the transaction, which is revealed when the transaction is announced. Further insights on this matter may be gained from an analysis of the determinants of abnormal returns. The signaling-hypothesis for OCF firms predicts that differential slope coefficients (DSC_{OCF}) are negative for *RISK* (column 2) and positive for *MTB* and *RUNUP* (columns 3 and 4). Especially the latter two coefficients enhance my ability to test the signaling-hypothesis, because it implies that the signs of the coefficients should be positive. If OCF firms are overvalued, the coefficients should be negative.

Table V.9: The cross-section of cumulative abnormal returns

This table shows regression results from OLS-regressions where the dependent variable is a firm's cumulative abnormal return for the event window [-1;+1] and the independent variables are the same as in the multinomial logistic regression plus the inverse Mill's ratio. I include those variables that are of interest to test the implications of the signaling-hypothesis in the form of differential slope coefficients, *DSC()*. Here, I multiply a dummy variable indicating the transaction type (MCF, OCF or CBS) with the corresponding covariate. To allow for a variation in the constant for my different samples, I also include transaction-type dummies, denominated *DUM()*. Equity issues are defined as the benchmark category. Regression 1 only includes differential intercepts. In regression 2 to 7, I include *RISK, MTB, RUNUP, DISTRESS, BR* and *SURPRISE* as differential slope coefficients, as shown in the top row of the table. The explanatory variables are: *SIZE* is computed as the natural logarithm of the market value of equity measured one month prior to the offering announcement. *RISK* is the standard deviation of stock returns during the year preceding the issue. *DISTRESS* is defined as the average of long-term debt plus short-term debt divided by total assets minus the value of this ratio that would prevail, if the firm issued debt. *MTB* is the industry-adjusted market-to-book ratio. *RUNUP* is the market-adjusted cumulative excess return during the year preceding the issue. *FCF* is the free cash flow proxy defined as cash flow minus capital expenditures plus common and preferred dividends standardized by the sales level. *AC* is computed as fixed assets divided by total assets. *TIMEQU* and *TIMCON* are forecast variables for the equity and convertible bond market, respectively, in terms of number of issues. *PROF* is measured as net income scaled by total assets. *TAX* are tax payments scaled by total assets. *RIS* are total proceeds from the issue scaled by the market value of the firm. *SURPRISE* is the inverse Mill's ratio. *BR* is Altman's bankruptcy risk variable. *PU* is a dummy variable that takes the value one, if the issuer's SIC code starts with 481 or 491 to 494. Industry dummy variables are included in the regression, but omitted in the table. ***, ** and * indicate a significance level of 1%, 5% and 10%, respectively. I use the White (1980) procedure to obtain efficient least-squares estimates. Concurrent offerings where an ordinary convertible security is issued alongside common stock are denominated as OCF, while concurrent offerings of common stocks and mandatory convertibles are denominated as MCF. CBS is the abbreviation for the convertible bond sample.

	1	2	3	4	5	6	7
		DSC = RISK	DSC = MTB	DSC = RUNUP	DSC = DISTRESS	DSC = BR	DSC = SURPRISE
Constant	-0.08 **	-0.08 **	-0.08 **	-0.07 **	-0.07 *	-0.08 **	-0.06
DUM_{MCF}	-0.01	-0.02	0.00	-0.01	-0.01	-0.01	-0.03
DUM_{OCF}	-0.05 **	0.06	-0.03	-0.08 ***	-0.05 ***	-0.03	0.02
DUM_{CBS}	-0.02 ***	-0.02	-0.03 ***	-0.02 ***	-0.03 ***	-0.02 ***	0.02
DSC_{MCF}		0.69	-0.01	0.01	-0.01	0.00	-0.03
DSC_{OCF}		-2.17 **	-0.01 ***	0.06 ***	-0.11 **	0.00	0.08
DSC_{CBS}		-0.07	0.00	0.00	-0.05	0.00	0.07
SIZE	0.01 **	0.01 **	0.01 **	0.01 **	0.01 **	0.01 *	0.00
RISK	-0.23	-0.13	-0.24	-0.23	-0.18	-0.28	-0.27
DISTRESS	0.02	0.02	0.02	0.02	0.05 *	0.02	0.00
MTB	0.00	0.00	0.00	0.00	0.00 *	0.00	0.00
RUNUP	0.01	0.01 *	0.00	0.01	0.01 *	0.01	0.00
FCF	0.00	0.00	0.01 *	0.00	0.00	0.00	0.01
AC	0.00	0.00	0.00	0.00	0.00	0.00	0.00
TIMEQU	0.00	0.00	0.00	0.00	0.00	0.00	0.00
TIMCON	0.00	0.00	0.00	0.00	0.00	0.00	0.00
PROF	0.01	0.01	0.01	0.01	0.01	0.02	0.01
TAX	0.06	0.08	0.05	0.06	0.06	0.14	0.07
RIS	0.01	0.01	0.01	0.01	0.01	0.01	0.01
SURPRISE	0.01	0.01	0.01	0.01	0.02	0.00	-0.02
BR						0.00	
PU	0.01	0.02 *	0.01	0.01	0.01	0.01	0.01
Adjusted R^2	3.3%	3.3%	3.5%	3.4%	3.5%	2.9%	3.2%
F-Test	[1.72] **	[1.61] **	[1.64] **	[1.67] **	[1.70] **	[1.51] **	[1.53] **

I start with *RISK* and find (with the exception of the benchmark category) that the differential intercepts cease to be significant. Instead, the differential slope coefficient for OCF firms is highly negative (-2.17) and significant at the 5%-level. This indicates that for this sample adverse stock price reactions towards the issue announcement are more sensitive to *RISK* than for the other samples. This is consistent with the notion that negative private information is conveyed through an OCF concurrent offering, which has adverse consequences for a transaction's valuation impact. Regression 3 includes differential slope coefficients for the market-to-book ratio. I find that cumulative abnormal returns for OCF firms show a negative relation to *MTB*, which is inconsistent with the signaling-hypothesis. It would rather be expected when *MTB* captures the degree of overvaluation of a firm. However, the coefficient of *RUNUP*, my second measure of the availability of valuable investment opportunities, is positive and significant. This supports the signaling-hypothesis and contradicts a timing-explanation.

In columns 5 and 6, I test the predictions of the signaling-hypothesis for MCF concurrent offerings. To do so, I include differential slope coefficients for *DISTRESS* and *BR*. The signaling-hypothesis postulates that stock price reactions should be more negative for MCF firms with higher incremental financial distress costs (*DISTRESS*) and higher bankruptcy risk (*BR*). Therefore, the differential slope coefficient (DSC_{MCF}) should be significant and positive for *DISTRESS* and *BR*, which are both negatively related to the magnitude of incremental financial distress costs and bankruptcy risk, respectively. However, the coefficients are not significant.

Finally, in regression 7, I examine the role of anticipation of an issue by including differential slope coefficients for *SURPRISE*, the inverse Mill's ratio, which I obtain from the multinomial logistic regression. If investors do not anticipate OCF concurrent offerings, one explanation for the highly negative announcement return is that they are disappointed by the transaction.[256] I do not find this notion supported by the data.[257]

The magnitude of investor reactions to the transaction announcements supports the signaling-hypothesis for MCF concurrent offerings. OCF concurrent offerings, however, are puzzling. Perhaps OCF firms are firms with valuable investment opportunities that experience significantly more negative announcement effects than all other firms in the sample because of an inappropriate transaction structure. This explanation receives support from the security choice model. Furthermore, according to Stein (1992), one should expect that OCF concurrent offerings *cannot* constitute a positive signal about firm value: signals must come at a cost. For

[256] Bayless/Chaplinsky (1991), p. 195 ff. show that expectations of a security type and the magnitude of abnormal returns are related.

[257] A general finding from table V.9 is that my regressions have overall little explanatory power for the cross-sectional variation of cumulative abnormal returns for the event window [-1;+1]. Adjusted R^2 values are low and the F-test statistics are only significant at the 5%-level. It appears likely that the poor explanatory power of the model is due to the fact that I regress cumulative abnormal returns on ex-ante observable firm characteristics, which are public information prior to the event and are therefore largely unrelated to announcement effects.

convertible bonds, these costs are those related to financial distress in case of non-conversion of the bond.[258] A concurrent offering alleviates financial distress costs and may rather communicate firm insiders' negative private information about the firms' riskiness to investors. Evidence consistent with this notion is that announcement returns are negatively related to risk (*RISK*). An alternative explanation for the adverse valuation impact is that OCF firms have been substantially overvalued prior to the transaction, which the offering conveys to the capital market. The cross-sectional analysis of *CARs* provides mixed evidence in this regard, since the coefficients of *MTB* and *RUNUP* have opposite signs. Hence, I explore the overvaluation-argument further in the next section.

6 *Long-run abnormal returns*

Event studies, such as the one in the previous section, generally focus on returns in a short event window to measure the investor reaction to the information arrival and assume a semi-strong form of market efficiency. In this context, a 'successful' signal could be interpreted as one, which fully reveals the value of a firm to the capital market immediately.[259]

However, some researchers argue that investors underreact to the informational content of financing events and hence, stock prices adjust slowly to new information. In particular firms that issue securities when they are overvalued have been found to perform poorly during the post-issue period.[260] To this end, a test of long-run performance enhances the understanding of OCF concurrent offerings. If OCF firms possess valuable investment opportunities, no negative abnormal performance should be detected. If OCF firms do not possess valuable investment opportunities but are overvalued, investors may underreact to the informational content of the offering and one can expect that the post-issue stock price performance will be poor. Therefore, despite some methodological issues in long-run return computation,[261] the analysis of long-run post-issue returns is useful to further test the signaling-hypothesis for OCF concurrent offerings.

---

[258] An interesting result in column 5 of table V.9 are the negative and significant differential slope coefficients for the OCF and CBS sample (DSC_{OCF} and DSC_{CBS}): they indicate that stock price reactions are higher for OCF and CBS firms with higher incremental costs of financial distress. This reinforces the notion that incremental costs of financial distress are a necessary condition for the signal to be credible.

[259] See Fama/Fisher/Jensen/Roll (1969), p. 1 ff.; Brav/Gompers (1997), p. 1794; Fama (1998), p. 283 f.

[260] See for example Spiess/Affleck-Graves (1995), p. 243 ff.; Loughran/Ritter (1995), p. 23 ff.; Loughran/Ritter (1997), p. 1823 ff.; McLaughlin/Safieddine/Vasudevan (1998), p. 373 ff.; Spiess/Affleck-Graves (1999), p. 45 ff.

[261] See for example Barber/Lyon (1997), p. 361 ff., Kothari/Warner (1997), p. 301 ff., Fama (1998), p. 284, Lyon/Barber/Tsai (1999), p. 165 ff., Loughran/Ritter (2000), p. 361 ff. and Mitchell/Stafford (2000), p. 287 ff.

6.1 Buy-and-hold abnormal returns

As in chapter III, the buy-and-hold abnormal return approach follows Lyon/Barber/Tsai (1999).[262] Equal-weighted buy-and-hold abnormal returns are computed for six, twelve and eighteen months following the event.[263]

Corresponding results are shown in table V.10.[264] The average raw return of OCF firms amounts to –43.22% over an 18-month post-issue period, while the average raw return of the respective reference portfolio is only –9.01%. This yields an average (median) *BHAR* of approximately –34.21% (–41.78%). Firms that lose more than a third of their market value during an 18-month period compared to the benchmark do not seem to possess valuable investment projects. It stands out that not only *BHARs* are highly negative in the OCF concurrent offerings sample, but also the percentage of delistings is very high: eight out of 26 firms (30.8%) cease to be traded independently. In contrast, MCF firms do not show abnormal post-issue stock price performance and only two firms are delisted in this sample.[265]

How do these results reconcile with the signaling-hypothesis? Obviously, MCF concurrent offerings can be completely explained by this hypothesis and announcement returns as well as long-run stock returns are as expected.

---

[262] See Lyon/Barber/Tsai (1999), p. 165 ff. The approach has been described in section 5.1.1 of chapter III.

[263] I do not report value-weighted returns since I am more interested in the managerial implications of post-issue performance of the firm. Equal-weighted returns draw a better picture of a firm's stock price performance independent of firm size. However, examining value-weighted returns does not materially change my conclusions.

[264] Due to multiple issuance activity during an 18-month post-issue period, a number of transactions drop out of the analysis. For the OCF sample, one transaction has to be deleted, while six transactions are deleted for the MCF sample. 48 transactions drop out of the convertible bond sample and seventeen transactions drop out of the equity sample.

[265] In the convertible bond and equity samples, respectively, 24 out of 242 (9.9%) and nineteen out of 225 (14.2%) firms cease to be traded independently.

Table V.10: Buy-and-hold abnormal returns

This table contains mean and median equal-weighted buy-and-hold abnormal returns for issuers in the different transaction-type samples for six months in panel A, twelve months in panel B and eighteen months in panel C. Buy-and-hold abnormal returns are calculated following Lyon/Barber/Tsai (1999). The benchmark returns are buy-and-hold returns for 70 portfolios formed on the basis of size and book-to-market ratio. Jarque-Bera tests for normality are contained in the column denoted JB. Since *BHARs* in some of the samples are skewed, I use bootstrapped skewness-adjusted test statistics calculated from 1,000 random resamples containing 25% of all observations in a sample. To test for significant differences in the mean and median abnormal returns between the different samples, I use standard t-tests as well as a non-parametric Wilcoxon signed-rank tests and report the values of the test statistics in parentheses. Concurrent offerings where an ordinary convertible security is issued alongside common stock are denominated as OCF, while concurrent offerings of common stocks and mandatory convertibles are denominated as MCF. CBS is the abbreviation for the convertible bond sample and SEO for the equity sample. ***, ** and * indicate a significance level of 1%, 5% and 10%, respectively. Tests of equality are one-sided tests.

Panel A: 6-month buy-and-hold abnormal returns

Sample	Mean	Median	JB	Mean test of equality					Median test of equality				
Complete sample	-10.36% ***	-7.20% ***	195.94 ***		MCF	OCF	CBS	SEO		MCF	OCF	CBS	SEO
Ordinary conversion feature (OCF)	-17.35% *	-15.13% *	0.31	MCF	0				MCF	0			
Mandatory conversion feature (MCF)	-5.73%	-3.81%	2.60	OCF	[1.01]	0			OCF	[1.42]	0		
Convertible bond sample (CBS)	-9.39% ***	-8.38% ***	425.89 ***	CBS	[0.35]	[0.92]	0		CBS	[0.49]	[0.58]	0	
Equity sample (SEO)	-10.78% ***	-3.73% ***	10.72 ***	SEO	[0.41]	[0.74]	[0.28]	0	SEO	[0.12]	[0.79]	[0.31]	0

Panel B: 12-month buy-and-hold abnormal returns

Sample	Mean	Median	JB	Mean test of equality					Median test of equality				
Complete sample	-16.94% ***	-17.41% ***	4.89 *		MCF	OCF	CBS	SEO		MCF	OCF	CBS	SEO
Ordinary conversion feature (OCF)	-22.65% *	-36.10% *	0.90	MCF	0				MCF	0			
Mandatory conversion feature (MCF)	-8.87%	-6.40%	0.88	OCF	[1.11]	0			OCF	[1.08]	0		
Convertible bond sample (CBS)	-16.77% ***	-18.49% ***	1.57	CBS	[0.66]	[1.00]	0		CBS	[0.90]	[0.94]	0	
Equity sample (SEO)	-16.95% ***	-17.36% ***	5.45 *	SEO	[0.61]	[0.93]	[0.01]	0	SEO	[0.48]	[1.02]	[0.08]	0

Panel C: 18-month buy-and-hold abnormal returns

Sample	Mean	Median	JB	Mean test of equality					Median test of equality				
Complete sample	-21.87% ***	-23.56% ***	48.45 ***		MCF	OCF	CBS	SEO		MCF	OCF	CBS	SEO
Ordinary conversion feature (OCF)	-34.21% **	-41.78% **	1.28	MCF	0				MCF	0			
Mandatory conversion feature (MCF)	-6.95%	-9.89%	2.29	OCF	[1.51] *	0			OCF	[1.68] *	0		
Convertible bond sample (CBS)	-22.25% ***	-24.05% ***	93.01 ***	CBS	[1.09]	[1.05]	0		CBS	[1.78] *	[0.97]	0	
Equity sample (SEO)	-21.28% ***	-22.41% ***	4.16	SEO	[0.95]	[1.04]	[0.18]	0	SEO	[1.27]	[0.99]	[0.03]	0

The case is different for OCF concurrent offerings. For these firms, investors are not able to infer the true firm value from the transaction announcement. Yet already around this date, the market value of equity of OCF firms is reduced by 6.95% on average. After the announcement, underperformance increases over time: OCF firms underperform their benchmark portfolios by 17.35% after six months, by 22.65% after twelve months and by 34.21% after eighteen months.

The continuation of negative abnormal performance from the announcement period into the post-issue period shows that investors underreact to the information conveyed through the announcement, which suggests that they have severe difficulties in evaluating the prospects of OCF firms. This is consistent with the findings of Loughran/Ritter (1995, 1997), who document poor post-issue performance of firms that have previously conducted seasoned equity offerings in order to exploit transitory mispricings of their stock.[266]

However, overvaluation cannot explain the high delisting rate for the OCF sample. Also the magnitude of underperformance appears more pronounced than reported by earlier studies.[267] To this end, overvaluation cannot be more than part of the answer. Before turning to a deeper discussion, I examine whether the results are robust in alternative computation methods.

6.2 Tests of robustness

Given the intense discussion with regard to long-run return computation methodology, I perform a number of robustness checks. These are illustrated for 18-month returns in table V.11.

Even though buy-and-hold returns are said to magnify abnormal performance, my results appear very low at first glance. As in Fama/French (1992, 1993) and Mitchell/Stafford (2000), I use 25 portfolios formed on size and book-to-market quintiles, created on the basis of NYSE breakpoint intersections, as benchmark returns.[268] I find the same pattern of underperformance with regard to the different samples as above, however, abnormal returns are slightly higher.[269]

---

[266] See Loughran/Ritter (1995), p. 23 ff.; Loughran/Ritter (1997), p. 1823 ff.

[267] Other studies document yearly abnormal returns ranging between –6% and –8% for convertible debt and equity issuers. See Loughran/Ritter (1995), p. 46; Spiess/Affleck-Graves (1995), p. 254; Loughran/Ritter (1997), p. 1840; Spiess/Affleck-Graves (1999), p. 55; Lewis/Rogalski/Seward (2001), p. 459.

[268] See Fama/French (1992), p. 427 ff.; Fama/French (1993), p. 3 ff.; Mitchell/Stafford (2000), p. 294.

[269] Analyzing the source of this deviation, it turns out that the breakpoints for firm allocation into BE/ME quintiles are different. While Lyon/Barber/Tsai (1999) create breakpoints within size portfolios and using all firms, the Fama/French (1992, 1993) portfolios use NYSE breakpoints that are independent of size

Deleting public utilities from the event firms does not alter the results very much. Only performance for the MCF sample increases, since public utilities in this sample have a worse post-issue stock price development than industrial firms.

Table V.11: Tests of robustness

This table contains robustness tests of *BHARs*, where different parameters of the abnormal return computation approach are altered. Apart from the Lyon/Barber/Tsai (1999) approach, I use 25 portfolios as in Fama/French (1992, 1993) based on size and BE/ME NYSE breakpoints. Also, I recompute benchmark returns for the 70 Lyon/Barber/Tsai (1999) portfolios using NYSE breakpoints to form BE/ME portfolios and delete public utilities from the sample of event firms. For calendar-time median monthly returns, I calculate monthly returns of a portfolio containing all sample firms that participated in an event, that is the issue of convertible bonds, seasoned equity or a combination of the two, during the previous eighteen months. Portfolios are formed monthly from July 2001 to December 2003 to add companies that have offered securities during the previous eighteen months and drop companies that offered securities more than eighteen months ago. From this return series, I subtract the returns of the equal-weighted CRSP index. Since the time series of monthly abnormal returns is skewed, I report medians and use Wilcoxon signed-rank tests to assess statistical significance. Concurrent offerings where an ordinary convertible security is issued alongside common stock are denominated as OCF, while concurrent offerings of common stocks and mandatory convertibles are denominated as MCF. CBS is the abbreviation for the convertible bond sample and SEO for the seasoned equity offerings sample. ***, ** and * indicate a significance level of 1%, 5% and 10%, respectively.

Sample	25 Fama/French Portfolios	70 Portfolios (NYSE breakpoints)	70 Portfolios (without public utilitities)	Median monthly abnormal returns
Complete sample	-15.45% ***	-13.65% ***	-19.72% ***	-3.09% **
Ordinary conversion feature (OCF)	-22.24% **	-24.74% *	-24.24% *	-5.89% **
Mandatory conversion feature (MCF)	-14.47%	-9.03%	8.26%	-0.44%
Convertible bond sample (CBS)	-15.15% ***	-12.59% ***	-21.07% ***	-2.01% *
Equity sample (SEO)	-15.35% ***	-13.51% ***	-18.93% ***	-2.05% **

In another robustness check, I use calendar-time methodology to compute abnormal returns.[270] To calculate median monthly abnormal calendar-time returns, I form portfolios containing all sample firms that participated in an event, that is the issuance of convertible bonds, seasoned equity or a combination of the two, during the previous eighteen months. Portfolios are formed monthly to add companies that have issued securities during the previous eighteen months and drop companies that offered securities more than eighteen months ago. From this time series of monthly portfolio returns, I subtract returns of the equal-weighted CRSP index. Because the distribution of monthly abnormal returns is significantly skewed, I report medians and use Wilcoxon signed-rank tests to assess statistical significance.

portfolios. Since in the Lyon/Barber/Tsai (1999) portfolios size-BE/ME portfolio breakpoints are lower than the Fama/French (1992, 1993) NYSE breakpoints, there is an increased likelihood that event firms are sorted into a higher BE/ME portfolio. This in turn increases the probability that the benchmark return is larger and hence, underperformance using the Lyon/Barber/Tsai (1999) approach is greater. Using NYSE breakpoints in the Lyon/Barber/Tsai (1999) yields less negative abnormal performance.

270 For a discussion of the calendar-time method compare section 5.2.1 of chapter III.

I find the results of the event-time analysis confirmed: OCF concurrent offering firms have a median monthly abnormal performance of –5.89%, while the median monthly abnormal calendar-time return for MCF firms is insignificant.

6.3 Discussion

The results for MCF concurrent offerings are consistent with the signaling-hypothesis with regard to pre-issue characteristics, announcement returns and long-run stock returns. In contrast, the findings for OCF concurrent offerings are much more puzzling.

OCF firms appear to have valuable investment opportunities prior to the offering. The median (mean) industry-adjusted market-to-book ratio is 1.09 (2.69) and the average pre-issue share price runup during the year preceding the announcement is 53%. Furthermore, OCF firms are risky. This evidence is consistent with the signaling-hypothesis. However, successful signaling implies that stock price reactions to the transaction announcement should on average be more favourable than announcement returns for equity issues, which is not the case. The valuation impact of OCF transaction announcements amounts to –6.95%, which is significantly more negative than the announcement return of –1.97% for stock-warrant issues reported by Byoun/Moore (2003).[271] Yet, this is not necessarily inconsistent with signaling, because firm insiders may convey negative information about firm risk rather than positive information about profitable investment opportunities by using an OCF concurrent offering, which appears to be an inappropriate vehicle to transport a positive signal about the expected level of future cash flows. The multivariate analysis of announcement returns supports this interpretation.

To further test the signaling-hypothesis, the financial performance during an 18-month post-issue period is examined. OCF firms on average underperform their reference portfolios by 34%, which is in obvious contradiction to the signaling-hypothesis. One explanation for this finding is that the risk associated with the firms' investment programs causes projects to fail for some firms, which negatively impacts performance. Most OCF firms are in the high-tech, telecom or health care business. In these industries, uncertainty is high and an elevated failure rate of investment projects might be reasonable. But given the magnitude of *BHARs*, risk is unlikely to be more than a partial explanation for the documented patterns.

---

[271] See Byoun/Moore (2003), p. 582.

An alternative interpretation for the findings could be that OCF firms do not primarily want to signal information.[272] Rather, they are overvalued around the time of the transaction and use this window of opportunity to obtain external capital. Loughran/Ritter (1995, 1997) relate the poor post-issue financial performance of equity issuers to the fact that these firms exploit their overvaluation to issue stock.[273] However, if a firm is overvalued, a concurrent offering does not appear to be an optimal strategy to maximize issue proceeds. If an overvalued firm issues convertible bonds, these are unlikely to be converted and have to be repaid. Yet, this might even be the intention of issuers: expecting that the equity option attached to the bond will expire out-of-the-money, it will nevertheless achieve a high valuation, which reduces interest costs compared to straight debt issues.[274] However, this explanation leaves several aspects open as well. First, equity issuers exploit periods of overvaluation, too. But I am not aware of any study that reports stock price reactions in the range of –6.95% around equity issue announcements. In my sample, equity is issued by firms with an industry-adjusted market-to-book ratio comparable to those of OCF firms and even higher pre-issue share price runups (58% on average). Yet the *CAAR* for these firms is only -3.09%. And also the *BHAR* for equity issuers is higher during the eighteen months following the offering (-21.28%). Second, in the multivariate analysis of announcement returns, I find a positive relation with the pre-issue share price runup, which is inconsistent with the overvaluation-explanation.[275] Third, overvaluation does not explain the high percentage of delistings of 31% during the post-issue period. In sum, these arguments indicate that OCF firms are overvalued, but overvaluation alone cannot explain the use of this type of concurrent offerings.

Especially the delisting rate and the magnitude of *BHARs* suggest an alternative interpretation. Suppose that for some reason OCF firms are distressed firms that cannot cover their financing needs in the market for seasoned equity. A concurrent offering might be a firm's last alternative to survive, because an issuing firm that is partially rationed out of the equity

---

[272] An explanation for the use of concurrent offerings based on free cash flow, similar to the one forwarded by Schultz (1993), p. 199 ff. for the use of unit IPOs and Mayers (1998), p. 83 ff. for convertible debt, has been rejected in an earlier version of this analysis. Mandatory convertibles are inappropriate instruments to mitigate free cash flow problems, since they convert automatically into common stock. OCF concurrent offerings would theoretically be prone to mitigate costs of free cash flow. However, the corresponding argument is shaky in theory and, more importantly, it is not supported by the data. A firm that really wants to mitigate costs of free cash flow and economize on transaction costs should issue convertible debt only: firms conducting concurrent offerings pay an average underwriting fee of 2.88%, while convertible debt issuers pay 2.65%. Transaction costs for convertible debt offerings are lower, although these are smaller transactions, which benefit less from economies of scale. See Lee/Lochhead/Ritter/Zhao (1996), p. 62 f.

[273] See Loughran/Ritter (1995), p. 23 ff.; Loughran/Ritter (1997), p. 1823 ff.

[274] In this case, a concurrent offering may be used to raise a given amount of external capital while adjusting the debt ratio towards a target.

[275] See for example Graham/Harvey (2001), p. 216.

market may turn to the equity-linked market to obtain the remainder of funds it requires.[276] Here, convertible investors may be willing to provide more capital, since they have a downside protection (the bond) during a screening phase until the bond can be converted and are therefore less exposed to asymmetric information.

Rationing has the potential to explain the post-issue stock price performance and high delisting rates of OCF firms. However, it has an important shortcoming. Stiglitz/Weiss (1981) provide a model of rationing in credit markets, where credit rationing is in the discretion of banks.[277] They show that some firms do not receive credits when adverse selection costs are high, regardless which interest rate a firm is willing to pay. Hence, loan applicants are either rationed out of the credit market or not. In this context, a concurrent offering would constitute the case of partial rationing: the decision to provide equity funds to a firm is distributed over various investor groups. Some investors are willing to provide a firm with equity funds, while others are not. This differential behaviour implies that beliefs about the issuing firm's value are strongly heterogeneous. To explain this heterogeneity, some investors will hardly act rationally. On the one hand, there would have to exist a first investor group that keeps buying shares of OCF firms prior to the transaction, causing their share price to appreciate on average 53% during the year preceding the transaction. When the concurrent offering is announced, some investors from this first group realize that the firm is significantly overvalued. They consequently sell their stock, which leads to a negative announcement effect of –6.95%. Despite the actions of these investors, there are other investors from the first group who are still convinced that the firm is a good investment and increase their stake in the company. In addition, some outside investors may invest in the firm. Yet, these investors do not provide enough funds for the firm to meet its financing requirement. Therefore, the firm turns to a second group of outside investors that is willing to invest in convertible debt and obtains the remainder of funds in the convertible market. After the offering, all investors gradually realize that the firm performs poorly and sell their stock, which causes the stock price to decline significantly.

A first problem with this explanation is that it is difficult to identify the reasons why beliefs across investors are so much apart. Assuming investors have equal access to corporate information, the differences in the investors' assessment of a firm's future earnings or cost of

[276] See Lewis/Rogalski/Seward (2001), p. 447 ff., Lewis/Rogalski/Seward (2002), p. 67 ff. and the discussions in chapter III and IV for the rationale of investor rationing in convertible debt issues. This interpretation appears especially promising, given that five out of eight delisted companies filed for chapter 11 in the OCF sample up to 2003.

[277] See Stiglitz/Weiss (1981), p. 393 ff.

capital or in their degree of risk-aversion would have to be considerably large to explain the documented performance patterns.

A second problem is that the source of value for convertible security investors is unknown. Either the investors are uncertain about the prospects of issuing firms and require time to screen issuers until conversion may occur, or they have the possibility to make some form of arbitrage profit, which may have an impact on a firm's stock price as well.[278] Since my analysis offers no direct evidence in this regard, this is a subject for further research.

A third problem with the rationing-argument is that OCF firms do not conduct an MCF offering. Since the mandatory is automatically converted into stock, the issuing firm would be guaranteed more equity capital, which should be in a distressed firm's best interest.

7 *Conclusion*

In this paper, I investigated concurrent offerings of common stock and convertible securities that were conducted during the years 2000 through 2002.

I examine a signaling-hypothesis to explain the use and valuation impact of concurrent offerings and find this hypothesis supported for concurrent offerings where common stock is issued alongside *mandatory convertibles*.

Concurrent offerings where *ordinary convertibles* are combined with common stock issues (OCF concurrent offerings) are puzzling. I only find partial evidence in favour of the signaling-hypothesis. My first test, a model of security choice based on firms' pre-issue characteristics, suggests that OCF concurrent offerings are conducted by firms possessing valuable investment opportunities that want to reduce adverse selection costs. My second test, the analysis of announcement returns, is inconsistent with successful signaling, given that OCF firms have highly negative abnormal returns (–6.95%) around the transaction announcement. Yet, this finding can be explained by the fact that a concurrent offering may

[278] In a related analysis of so-called 'death spiral' convertibles, Hillion/Vermaelen (2004), p. 391 examine a rationing-hypothesis for the use of floating-priced convertibles and document poor post-issue returns as well. In floating-priced convertibles, the conversion price is set at a discount from an average of past stock prices determined in a look-back period. The rationing-argument of Hillion/Vermaelen (2004), too, assumes that beliefs differ across investors groups: current stockholders believe the stock to be fairly valued but cannot or do not want to buy more stock. Outside investors believe the shares to be overvalued and do not want to buy stock. Floating-priced convertibles may be attractive for these outside investors, because the conversion price may be set at a lower level than the current share price. The authors find support for the rationing-argument, but acknowledge that short sales can have adverse consequences on a firm's stock price. A similar conclusion is drawn by Bechmann (2004), p. 421 ff.

convey negative information about the risk of a firm rather than positive information about the expected level of future cash flows. A cross-sectional analysis of abnormal returns supports this interpretation. In a third test, I examine the post-issue financial performance and find OCF firms to underperform significantly. These firms lose almost half of their pre-issue market value during the eighteen months following the offering and 31% of OCF firms are delisted. This finding is inconsistent with the signaling-hypothesis.

I discuss other explanations for the use and valuation impact of concurrent offerings, but always find some inconsistency of the argument with empirical results. Market timing may explain OCF concurrent offerings. In this case, firms should issue equity only to maximize issue proceeds. If a firm issued equity in combination with convertible debt, firm insiders might use a convertible to reduce interest costs compared to straight debt issues, knowing the bond will probably not be converted. However, the overvaluation-explanation is inconsistent with results from the cross-sectional analysis of announcement returns, the magnitude of post-issue stock price returns and in particular with the high post-issue delisting rate.

An explanation based on demand-side constraints also receives partial support only. Firstly, partial rationing would have to occur in the equity market, which appears inconsistent with rational investors. Secondly, the average pre-issue share price runup for OCF firms is 53% in the year prior to the offering. If firms are distressed and need capital to survive, why would the market's assessment of a company's value systematically and greatly increase during the pre-issue period and change dramatically at the announcement of the transaction that some market participants refuse to provide a firm with equity capital, while others still consider the firm to be a good investment?

No matter which argument one believes in, there is always an inconsistency with the data and moreover, each argument implies that either some market participants or firm managers act irrationally. Therefore, OCF concurrent offerings remain a puzzle and further research is in order to explain the documented patterns.

VI Divestment of equity stakes – An analysis of exchangeable debt

Exchangeable debt bears structural resemblance to convertible debt. However, it is not converted into common stock of the issuer, but exchanged into stock of a third firm.

The trend to issue exchangeable debt has become increasingly pervasive in Germany and Western Europe during the last couple of years. Although the market for hybrid securities is larger in the US than in Western Europe (figure VI.1), exchangeable debt has been more commonly issued by Western European firms during recent years (figure VI.2).[279]

Figure VI.1: Size of the US and Western European hybrid security markets

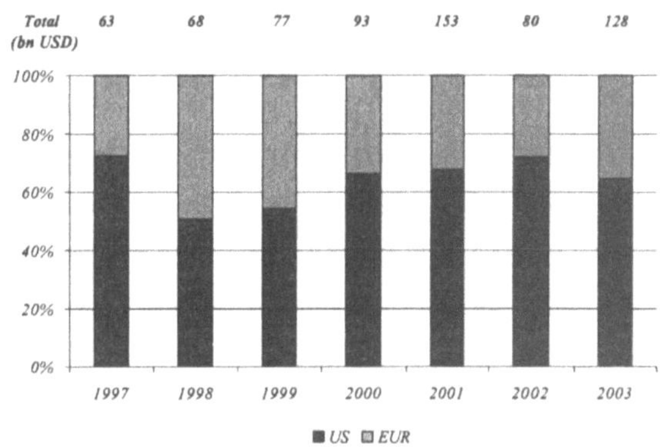

Figure VI.2: Size of the US and Western European exchangeable debt markets

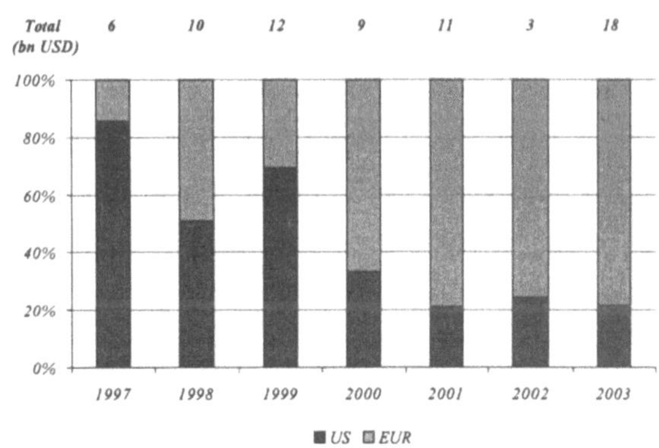

279 Issuance volumes were obtained from Thomson One Banker deals and Danielova/Smart/Boquist (2004), p. 26. Currency translation uses year-end exchange rates.

1 Introduction

An example of a transaction, which has caught the public's attention due to its size, is German Kreditanstalt für Wiederaufbau's (KfW) exchangeable bond offering. With a volume of 5 billion Euro, this exchangeable bond has been the largest issue of a hybrid security worldwide so far. KfW used the transaction to sell 50% of its 12% share block in Deutsche Telekom AG in an effort to gradually divest its stake.

A natural question is why firms issue exchangeable debt. Ghosh/Varma/Woolridge (1990) and Barber (1993) argue that US firms use this type of hybrid security to divest equity stakes they hold in other corporations. Exchangeable debt may be an attractive divestment strategy, because underwriting fees and valuation effects associated with it are substantially less pronounced than those associated with other forms of secondary distributions that disperse concentrated share blocks.[280]

However, recent empirical evidence of Danielova (2003) and Danielova/Smart/Boquist (2004) contrasts this perception.[281] These studies argue that US firms use exchangeable debt to 'sweeten' straight debt issues and not to sell equity stakes. The term 'sweeten' refers to the fact that managers tend to view conversion features as devices to lower coupon rates:[282] financial managers exploit periods during which they perceive a stock in their portfolio to be overvalued to reduce costs of external debt finance. In situations where the capital market considers the exchange stock to be fairly valued, managers of issuing firms can use their private information to sell an overvalued exchange option to investors, which allows them to reduce interest payments below the level payable in straight debt issues.

Given the controversial evidence on its use, it is the objective of this study to examine why Western European firms issue exchangeable debt. To achieve it, it conducts a press research to examine the stated issuer motives and the circumstances surrounding exchangeable bond issues in a first step. Second, it analyzes the magnitude of announcement returns and examines their cross-section to find out which factors determine the capital market's reaction towards the issue announcement. Third, it calculates the exchange company's stock returns

---

280 See Ghosh/Varma/Woolridge (1990), p. 259; Barber (1993), p. 49. The term 'secondary distribution' refers to the sale of a block of previously issued shares that is dispersed through the offering. A 'block trade' is a transaction where the share block is sold to a different investor as a package.

281 See Danielova (2003), p. 1 ff.; Danielova/Smart/Boquist (2004), p. 1 ff.

282 See Billingsley/Smith (1996), p. 93 ff.

prior and following the issue to assess whether these firms may have been overvalued around the time of the transaction.

The results based on a sample of 57 Western European exchangeable debt offerings that occur between 1997 and 2003 are as follows: in press statements, issuers indicate their intention to divest an equity stake contained in their portfolio. The stock price reaction to this announcement is on average –1.57% for the exchange firm, which is higher than the valuation impact of other forms of secondary distributions that disperse concentrated share blocks.[283] Hence, the use of exchangeable debt by Western European firms may be justified by the fact that it is a cost-efficient strategy to restructure a firm's assets. Consistent with the stated issue motive, the analysis of the cross-section of announcement returns suggests that the offer's potential to decrease the ownership concentration of the exchange firm causes announcement returns to be negative. If a large stockholder increases the efficacy of the monitoring of the exchange firm's management, an exchangeable debt offer signals the termination of his effort. Accordingly, the firm value will decline, if the remaining stockholders do not believe that the exchange company's management maximizes value, because they incur higher costs arising from agency conflicts themselves.[284]

In this sense, my conclusions contradict those of Ammann/Fehr/Seitz (2004) for Germany and Switzerland and of Danielova (2003) for the US who suggest that adverse announcement returns are caused by price pressure or asymmetric information.[285] Although some issuers may use exchangeable debt to sell overvalued equity, the typical issuer intends to divest a share block. The fact that neither large share price appreciations prior to the offering nor poor long-run stock returns after the issue can be observed supports this notion.

The remainder of this chapter is organized as follows: section 2 briefly illustrates motives for exchangeable debt issuance, presents existing empirical evidence and develops hypotheses with regard to the sign and magnitude of stock price reactions. Section 3 describes the data and methodology. Section 4 presents empirical results. Section 5 concludes.

---

[283] Mikkelson/Partch (1985), p. 175 calculate an average announcement return of –1.97% for unregistered and of –2.87% for registered secondary distributions.

[284] See Jensen/Meckling (1976), p. 323 ff. This notion is also confirmed by Ghosh/Varma/Woolridge (1990), p. 251 ff.

[285] See Danielova (2003), p. 35; Ammann/Fehr/Seiz (2004), p. 8.

2 *Theoretical background*

2.1 Motives for exchangeable debt issuance

Explanations for the use of exchangeable debt emphasize a favourable tax treatment and lower transaction costs. Before I illustrate these characteristics of exchangeable debt, I briefly outline its structure and provide a comparison to alternative forms of secondary offerings.

Exchangeable debt is similar to convertible debt: the investor receives periodic coupon payments and an option to exchange the bond into a certain number of shares during a pre-specified time period. While a convertible bond is converted into shares of the issuing firm, an exchangeable bond is exchanged into shares of a third firm, which will be referred to as target or exchange firm in the following.

Although convertible and exchangeable bonds bear structural resemblance, the objectives issuers pursue with these two types of securities may be very different: convertible debt is a substitute for common stock or straight debt.[286] According to Ghosh/Varma/Woolridge (1990) and Barber (1993), exchangeable debt is primarily used to restructure a firm's assets by disposing of share blocks contained in an issuer's portfolio.[287] A question that follows from this interpretation is why firms prefer exchangeable debt to other forms of secondary offerings, which are presented in table VI.1.

Although the choice of an appropriate divestment strategy depends on a variety of parameters, a generic advantage often put forward for the use of exchangeable debt is its favourable tax treatment. On the one hand, proceeds from the sale of the share block are not taxed immediately, but when they are realized at a future point in time. Hence, issuers may benefit from a tax deferral effect.[288] On the other hand, coupon payments on the bond are tax deductible, while dividends accrue to the issuing firm until the bond is exchanged, which allows the issuer to (partly) refinance interest payments by using the dividend stream from the exchange company.[289]

---

[286] See Green (1984), p. 115 ff.; Brennan/Schwartz (1988), p. 55 ff.; Stein (1992), p. 3 ff.; Mayers (1998), p. 83 ff.

[287] See Ghosh/Varma/Woolridge (1990), p. 257; Barber (1993), p. 48.

[288] This argument is not valid for German issues after the year 2002, since proceeds from the sale of equity holdings have been tax-free since then. See Bundesministerium der Finanzen (2000) and paragraph 8 (2) of the German corporation tax law. According to Barber (1993), p. 49 f., taxes are no predominant motive for exchangeable debt issues of US firms either.

[289] See Barber (1993), p. 55 and 57. While being a positive side effect, he does not find dividend-stripping to be a dominant motive for exchangeable debt issuance.

Table VI.1: Overview of alternative forms of secondary offerings[290]

	Block trade	Secondary distribution	Options	Exchangeables
Structure	• Private transaction • Direct sale to one or few selected investors without involvement of a stock exchange • Individual negotiation about price	• Public transaction • Comparable to IPO • Seller indicates price range and investors bid • Different structures with regard to speed of execution exist	• Sale of stock using options ('covered call writing') • With or without involvement of stock exchange	• Exchange contingent upon stock price performance of exchange company • Issued as debt exchangeable into stock of a third company
Advantages (issuer perspective)	• Immediate financing effect • High probability of divestment • No involvement of stock exchange • Transaction can be executed without much public attention	• Immediate financing effect • High probability of divestment • Large stakes can be divested • Active marketing • Bookbuilding is likely to yield a fair and clearing offer price	• Exchange stock can be sold at a premium • Option premium is generated as direct income • Sale of stock volatility • Tax deferral effect	• Immediate financing effect • Option premium lowers coupon payments compared to straight debt issues • Tax treatment of coupon payments • Tax deferral effect • Exchange stock can be sold at a premium • Sale of stock volatility • Usually high investor demand
Disadvantages (issuer perspective)	• Often involves sale at a discount • Searching costs for buyer(s) • Immediate taxation	• High underwriting costs • Price heavily dependent on stock market environment • High public attention • Time-consuming, if marketed actively • Immediate taxation	• Uncertainty about exercise of option • No immediate financing effect	• Uncertainty about exchange of the bond • Increase in leverage may be unattractive for some firms

Apart from tax considerations, existing research emphasizes that exchangeable debt is cheaper than other forms of secondary offerings. Direct transaction costs, in particular underwriting fees for investment banks, amount to 1.95% of issue proceeds in my data set. Other studies of exchangeable debt issuance report similar fees ranging from 1.56% to 2.80%, which is significantly less than 4.70% that have to be paid on average in direct registered secondary distributions.[291]

Indirect transaction costs are not immediately cash relevant, but affect the market price of exchangeable bonds at issuance.[292] US studies document that negative valuation effects are less pronounced around exchangeable debt issues (-1.64% on the average of studies cited in

[290] This table is adapted from Mikkelson/Partch (1985), p. 165 ff., Wruck (1989), p. 3 ff., Ghosh/Varma/ Woolridge (1990), p. 251 ff., Barber (1993), p. 48 ff. and Schäfer (2002), p. 514 ff. It does not provide a complete characterization of alternative forms of secondary offerings, but highlights some important features relevant in the context of this analysis.

[291] See Mikkelson/Partch (1985), p. 188; Barber (1993), p. 56; Gentry/Schizer (2002), p. 25.

[292] See Gentry/Schizer (2002), p. 28.

this chapter) than for other forms of secondary distributions (-2.87% for registered secondary distributions).[293] If the analysis confirms that announcement returns are lower for Western European issues as well, a significant cost advantage of exchangeable debt may justify its use.

Recent findings show that some firms do not use exchangeable debt as a divestment vehicle. In fact, managers of issuing firms take advantage of transitory windows of opportunity when they consider the underlying stock to be overvalued.[294] Such a market timing-behaviour may be driven by the mispricing of the exchange option, which is attached to a bond, and which reduces coupon rates below rates payable in straight debt issues. As long as the price of the exchange stock reverts to a normal level, poor stock returns during the post-issue period reduce the probability of exchange.

2.2 Existing empirical evidence for exchangeable debt issuance

Event studies represent a large fraction of the corporate finance literature. Yet, none of them has dealt with issues of exchangeable debt by Western European firms.[295]

Studies of exchangeable debt issuance listed in table VI.2 document significantly negative announcement returns for exchange companies. However, the magnitude of market responses to new issue announcements in the US market varies considerably between –1.03% and –2.85%.

This heterogeneity of stock price reactions may follow a systematic pattern: generally, studies that conclude that exchangeable debt is used to divest equity stakes calculate higher announcement returns.

---

[293] See Mikkelson/Partch (1985), p. 175; Asquith/Mullins (1986), p. 71. It has to be taken into account that there may be only limited comparability between stock price reactions towards US and Western European security offerings, since some studies calculate announcement returns that have different signs for Western European transactions than for US transactions. Examples are Gebhardt/Entrup (1993), p. 1 ff. for warrants or De Roon (1998), p. 1481 ff. for convertible debt. However, Banerjee/Leleux/Vermaelen (1997), p. 25 show that block purchases by French holding companies generate positive abnormal returns of 6.2% on average for the target firm. This finding suggests that block transactions are control-relevant in Western European countries as well, which corresponds to evidence provided by Wruck (1989), p. 3 ff. for the US. To this end, it seems reasonable to use US evidence as a benchmark for Western European exchangeable debt offerings.

[294] See Danielova (2003), p. 35.

[295] The study by Ammann/Fehr/Seiz (2004), p. 1 ff. only covers Germany and Switzerland.

Table VI.2: Existing empirical evidence for exchangeable debt issuance

Author(s)	Year	Sample period	Market	N	Event window	*CAAR* IC	*CAAR* EC
Exchangeable bonds							
Ghosh/Varma/Woolridge	1990	1969-1987	US	36	[-1;0]	+0.04%	-1,11%**
Barber	1993	1970-1987	US	37	[0;+1]	-0.17%	-1.10%**
Gentry/Schizer	2002	1992-2000	US	62	[0]	+0.36%	-1.03%**
Danielova	2003	1981-2001	US	104	[-1;+2]	-0.25%	-2.85%***
Ammann/Fehr/Seiz	2004	1996-2003	CH/GER	28	[0;+1]	-	-2.09%***
Secondary offerings							
Mikkelson/Partch[296]	1985	1972-1981	US	146	[-1;0]	-	-2.87%***
Mikkelson/Partch[297]	1985	1972-1981	US	321	[0;+1]	-	-1.96%***
Asquith/Mullins	1986	1963-1981	US	85	[-1;0]	-	-2.00%***
Barclay/Holderness	1991	1978-1982	US	106	[-1;0]	-	+5.10%***
Convertible bonds							
Dann/Mikkelson	1984	1970-1979	US	129	[-1;0]	-2.31%***	-
Mikkelson/Partch	1986	1972-1982	US	25	[-1;0]	-1.97%***	-
Eckbo	1986	1964-1981	US	75	[-1;0]	-1.25%***	-
Gebhardt/Entrup[298]	1993	1979-1989	GER	69	[-1;0]	+0.53%	-
Lewis/Rogalski/Seward	2003	1978-1992	US	588	[0;+1]	-1.09%[301]	-
Ammann/Fehr/Seiz	2004	1996-2003	CH/GER	55	[0;+1]	-1.36%**	-
Dutordoir/Van de Gucht	2004	1990-2002	West. Europe	222	[-1;0]	-1.18%***	-
Bonds							
Dann/Mikkelson	1981	1970-1979	US	150	[0;+1]	-0.37%*	-
Mikkelson/Partch	1986	1972-1982	US	147	[-1;0]	-0.23%	-
Eckbo	1986	1964-1981	US	459	[-1;0]	-0.06%	-
Entrup	1995	1970-1991	GER	78	[-1;0]	+0.06%	-
Divestments							
Wheatley/Brown/Johnson (Spin-Offs)	1997	1980-1993	US	112	[-1;+5]	+3.10%***	-
Slovin/Sushka/Ferraro (Sell-Offs)	1995	1980-1991	US	179	[-1;0]	+1.70%***	-
Kaiser/Stouraitis (Sell-Offs)	2001	1984-1994	various[299]	34	[-1;+1]	+0.46%	-
Vijh (Carve-Outs)	2002	1980-1997	US	336	[-1;+1]	+1.93%***	-
Veld/Veld-Markoulova (Spin-Offs)	2004	1987-2000	various[300]	156	[-1;+1]	+2.62%***	-

***, **, * denotes a significance level of 1%, 5% and 10%

In particular, Ghosh/Varma/Woolridge (1990) find the valuation impact of exchangeable debt announcements to be −1.11% on average.[302] They argue that the offer's potential to decrease the ownership concentration of the exchange firm leads to higher costs arising from agency conflicts for the remaining stockholders, which reduces the value of their claim and causes announcement returns to be negative. Barber (1993) calculates an average stock price reaction of −1.10% and relates this announcement return to the repurchase guarantee implicit within

[296] This result concerns registered secondary distributions.
[297] This result concerns unregistered secondary distributions.
[298] The study is on warrants.
[299] Included countries are Germany, Italy, the Netherlands, Norway, Portugal, Spain, Sweden and Switzerland.
[300] Countries of the European Union, Norway and Switzerland.
[301] No significance level was indicated by the authors.
[302] See Ghosh/Varma/Woolridge (1990), p. 259.

exchangeable debt: if the exchange firm does not perform well, the issuer returns the principal to the investor in cash.[303]

A more recent study by Danielova (2003) concludes that negative information conveyed by exchangeable debt causes the average valuation impact to be –2.85%.[304] If exchangeable debt is issued to sell equity, which the issuer perceives to be overvalued, less-informed investors may interpret the signal correctly and infer negative information from the announcement, which leads to a more adverse stock price reaction.

The general picture drawn by this literature suggests that a relation between the issuance motive and the magnitude of announcement returns exists. Studies documenting a divestment motive in exchangeable debt issues calculate higher announcement returns than studies that reject the divestment motive.

To explain the valuation impact of exchangeable debt by Western European firms, it is necessary to find out which, if any, of the two mutually exclusive explanations for its use applies. A press research, an analysis of announcement returns and of pre- and post-issue stock returns of the exchange company are employed to draw conclusions about the objectives Western European issuers pursue with the offering.

2.3 The magnitude of announcement returns

Two hypotheses explain negative announcement returns of exchangeable debt issues: signaling-models (information-hypothesis) suggest that financing decisions convey firm insiders' private information to outside investors in a market characterized by asymmetric information. The agency-hypothesis postulates that stockholders can, depending on the size of their stake, increase the efficacy of monitoring of a firm's management.[305]

---

303 See Barber (1993), p. 49. Direct secondary offerings do not have this guarantee and hence, abnormal returns are lower.

304 See Danielova (2003), p. 22. Ammann/Fehr/Seiz (2004), p. 8 also explain abnormal returns with adverse selection. Moreover, they suggest that price pressure causes abnormal returns to be negative.

305 Finally, short sales by institutional investors may cause returns around issuance or announcement of exchangeable debt issues to be abnormally poor. I come back to this aspect in section 3.2.2.3 of this chapter.

2.3.1 *Exchange firms*

2.3.1.1 *Information-hypothesis*

Signaling-models argue that financing decisions convey an insider's private information about the value of a firm to the capital market. Myers/Majluf (1984) show that managers of firms facing high costs of adverse selection choose to issue equity when it is overpriced.[306] Since the management is likely to know more about the value of the firm than investors, and investors are aware of their relative ignorance, they will interpret signals sent by financing decisions accordingly and adjust their view on the firm's value, which results in a negative (average) stock price effect for firms issuing equity.[307]

Stein (1992) suggests that convertible debt can mitigate the costs of adverse selection.[308] A convertible bond can be regarded as a form of 'backdoor' equity capital, which sends a positive signal about the management's confidence in the firm's future stock price performance to outside investors. This reduces the adverse informational consequences equity transactions have on the stock price when they are announced.[309]

Unfortunately, the signaling-models of Myers/Majluf (1984) and Stein (1992) do not readily extend to situations where firms sell the stock of a third company, unless the issuer possesses inside information about the exchange firm's prospects around the time of the issue. If this is the case, there are three possible scenarios: first, a manager who wants to divest a stock contained in his firm's portfolio and who perceives the stock to be overvalued will choose a type of secondary offering where shares are sold directly, because this enables him to maximize issue proceeds. Second, a manager who does not consider restructuring the firm's assets may issue exchangeable debt to reduce the interest costs of external debt finance by attaching an overvalued exchange option to the bond. As long as the overly high valuation level of the exchange stock is of transitory nature, the offering is unlikely to result in a change of the firm's asset composition.[310] Third, a manager who wants to divest an equity stake and does not consider the target stock to be overvalued may use an exchangeable bond.

Hence, a similar argument to Stein's (1992) for the use of convertible debt is that the structure of exchangeable debt contradicts the notion that negative information is conveyed by these

---

306 See Myers/Majluf (1984), p. 187 ff.
307 See Myers/Majluf (1984), p. 220.
308 See Stein (1992), p. 3 ff.
309 See Eckbo/Masulis (1995), p. 1042 f. for a survey of event study results that confirms this notion.
310 See Danielova (2003), p. 1 ff. and Danielova/Smart/Boquist (2004), p. 1 ff. for related analyses.

securities, because the divestment is contingent upon target firm performance.[311] If divestment is not the issue motive, exchangeable bonds may be used to exploit temporary overvaluations of an exchange stock, which is bad news for outside investors.

2.3.1.2 Agency-hypothesis

Negative announcement returns can also be explained by an agency-hypothesis, which assumes that managerial objectives do not always coincide with those of stockholders. Jensen/Meckling (1976) and Jensen (1986) show that conflicts of interest entail suboptimal investment policies when managers invest to increase the resources under their control rather than stockholder value.[312] Stockholders have to take actions to mitigate these inefficiencies. An important tool at their disposition is monitoring, i.e. actions to control distortionary incentives of managers and to align diverging interests.[313] Holderness/Sheehan (1985, 1987) show that concentrated ownership can enhance the efficacy of monitoring.[314] Higher concentrations of dividend claims and especially of voting rights can enable large stockholders to control the management of the exchange firm more effectively than when voting stock is widely dispersed. A large shareholder may even be able to actively participate in the decision making-process of a company, which reduces the monitoring costs for other shareholders.[315]

Exchangeable debt issues, which are commonly used to divest larger share blocks (in my sample on average 12.2% of the market value of the exchange firm), may signal a reduction in the ownership concentration of the exchange company, which reduces the capacity and/or the incentive of the issuing firm to monitor the management of the target firm.[316] In situations where the remaining stockholders believe that the management of the exchange company does not maximize value, the elimination of a blockholder decreases the efficacy of monitoring, which reduces firm value because increased monitoring costs have to be borne by remaining stockholders. Moreover, residual losses from agency-conflicts are likely to increase, since the monitoring is less effective when voting rights are widely dispersed.[317]

---

311 See Stein (1992), p. 3 ff. Ghosh/Varma/Woolridge (1990), p. 261 forward a similar argument.

312 See Jensen/Meckling (1976), p. 305 ff.; Jensen (1986), p. 323 ff.

313 Monitoring methods include for example auditing, formal control systems, budget restrictions or the establishment of incentive compensation systems. Costs of monitoring have to be borne by stockholders and reduce the value of their claim. See Jensen/Meckling (1976), p. 323 ff.

314 See Holderness/Sheehan (1985), p. 555 ff.; Holderness/Sheehan (1987), p. 317 ff.

315 See Mikkelson/Ruback (1991), p. 545.

316 See Ghosh/Varma/Woolridge (1990), p. 262; Burkart/Gromb/Panunzi (2000), p. 647 and 649.

317 See Ghosh/Varma/Woolridge (1990), p. 261 f. Residual losses are losses that arise due to an imperfect resolution of agency conflicts through monitoring and other control activities. See Müller-Trimbusch (1999), p. 99.

Pound (1988) and Wruck (1989) show that increases in the ownership concentration are accompanied by positive abnormal stock returns.[318] In turn, exchangeable debt offerings, which have the potential to decrease the ownership concentration, are likely to result in negative announcement returns.

Exchangeable debt issues have the potential to eliminate another positive effect of the existence of large stockholders: as argued by Sheifer/Vishny (1986), blockholders may make it easier to effect changes in corporate control.[319] This may increase firm value even if the blockholder is not capable of effective monitoring, because the threat of replacement in a takeover scenario will provide an incentive for the management to maximize shareholder value.

A prediction of the market response to exchangeable debt issue announcements has to take into consideration that the ownership concentration of the exchange firm will only decrease when the bond is exchanged at a future point in time. Hence, the adverse announcement effect will mirror the market's expectation of whether or not exchange occurs.[320] This leads to the following hypothesis:

Hypothesis 1: Abnormal returns for the exchange firm will be negative at the announcement of the exchangeable bond issue.

2.3.2 Issuing firms

The market response to an exchangeable debt offering for the issuing firm depends on two effects:[321] first, the asset composition of the issuer may change, which is likely to positively affect firm value. Firms that divest (non-core) stakes tend to gain in value, since a

[318] See Pound (1988), p. 237 ff.; Wruck (1989), p. 3 ff. A controlling stockholder can also have a negative influence on firm value, if he acts opportunistically on the costs of other stockholders, thereby abusing his dominant position. However, Dyck/Zingales (2004), p. 537 show that such private benefits of control tend to be low in countries contained in the data set. Because capital markets are mature and regulation authorities monitor them closely, misuse of a dominant stockholder position is rather the exception than the rule. Consequently, Burkart/Gromb/Panunzi (2000), p. 649 conclude that often the abuse of private benefits of control tends to be lower than the potential gain in firm value from more effective monitoring.

[319] See Shleifer/Vishny (1986), p. 462 and 464.

[320] A possibility to measure this expectation is the exchange probability that will be discussed in section 2.4.1.2 of this chapter.

[321] See Ghosh/Varma/Woolridge (1990), p. 252.

diversification can be replicated cheaper by investors and firm resources can be allocated to the core business, where issuing firms may use them more effectively.[322]

Second, firms raise external debt capital. On the one hand, this represents a leverage-increasing event that is usually accompanied by positive abnormal returns.[323] On the other hand, debt issues are external financing events, for which signaling-models from Myers/Majluf (1984) and Miller/Rock (1985) predict a negative announcement effect.[324] Event studies listed in table VI.2, which measure the combined impact of these effects, document slightly negative announcement returns for external debt issues.

In sum, it appears likely that the negative impact of the debt issue and the positive impact of the divestment cancel each other out.

<u>Hypothesis 2:</u> *Abnormal returns for the issuing firm will be insignificant at the announcement of the exchangeable bond issue.*

2.4 The cross-section of announcement returns

Announcement returns for exchange companies will be negative on average. However, the cross-section of abnormal returns is likely to display a certain degree of variation that can be analyzed to test whether information effects or agency conflicts explain abnormal returns. In this test, I address different parameters in transaction and security design as well as the timing of exchangeable debt issues.

2.4.1 Transaction and security structure

2.4.1.1 Relative issue size

The models of Myers/Majluf (1984) and Miller/Rock (1985) ascribe the relative issue size an important informational role as to the degree of overvaluation of a firm's securities or the extent of a firm's internal cash flow shortage in seasoned equity or convertible debt issues.[325]

---

322 Corresponding empirical evidence is listed in table VI.2. For a more extensive literature overview see Stienemann (2003), p. 131 ff.

323 See Masulis (1980), p. 139 ff.; Ross (1977), p. 23 ff.; Shyam-Sunder/Myers (1999), p. 219 ff.

324 In Myers/Majluf (1984), p. 187 ff., issuers sell overpriced securities, albeit this effect is less pronounced in debt than in equity issues. Miller/Rock (1985), p. 1031 ff. argue that firms, which raise external capital signal a shortage of internally available funds that will be accompanied by negative announcement returns, if the financing event has not been anticipated by the market.

325 See Myers/Majluf (1984), p. 219; Miller/Rock (1985), p. 1038.

Hence, as argued by Krasker (1986), the relative issue size should be negatively related to the magnitude of announcement returns.[326]

One has to be careful when transferring this rationale to exchangeable debt: in these transactions, the size of the issue is restricted by the size of the equity stake to be divested or may be determined by strategic or financial considerations.[327] To this end, the relative issue size should have no informational content that is relevant for the investors' valuation of the exchange firm. The relation between the relative issue size and abnormal returns should therefore be insignificant.[328]

In contrast, the agency-hypothesis implies a negative relation between the magnitude of abnormal returns and the relative issue size: according to Holderness/Sheehan (1985, 1987), ownership concentration and firm value are positively related.[329] As a consequence, the dispersal of a larger share block implies a higher reduction of the ownership concentration of the exchange firm. This should lead to more adverse announcement returns, since the efficacy of monitoring declines and the remaining stockholders have to increase their monitoring expenditures significantly. Moreover, they may incur larger residual losses, which reduces the value of their claim.

In sum, an analysis of the relation between the relative issue size and the magnitude of abnormal returns allows to discriminate between the agency- and the information-hypothesis as an explanation for abnormal returns.

> Hypothesis 3: *The larger the relative issue size, the lower is the abnormal return for the exchange firm at the announcement of the exchangeable bond issue.*

The relative issue size (*RIS*) is defined as the ratio of total issue proceeds to the market value of the common stock of the exchange company measured one month prior to the offering.

2.4.1.2 Exchange probability

Apart from the size of the transaction, the variety of parameters that characterizes an exchangeable bond may be relevant for the evaluation of new issues from an investor's point-

326 See Krasker (1986), p. 93 ff.
327 See Mikkelson/Ruback (1985), p. 523 ff.; Schipper/Smith (1986), p. 3 ff.; Mikkelson/Ruback (1991), p. 544 ff.
328 This argument assumes a divestment motive. If this motive cannot be detected, it is possible that the size of the transaction has negative informational content.
329 See Holderness/Sheehan (1985), p. 555 ff.; Holderness/Sheehan (1987), p. 317 ff.

of-view. A measure that encompasses different design features of exchangeable debt, such as the exchange premium or the maturity, is the exchange probability.[330] Formally, it represents the ex-ante probability that the bond is exchanged at maturity measured on the issue day. This metric is useful in this analysis, since investors may take the structural parameters of an exchangeable bond and the characteristics of the underlying stock into consideration to form expectations about the likelihood that the bond is exchanged and the ownership concentration is reduced. The lower this probability, the less likely becomes the dispersal of the issuer's share block that would cause monitoring costs to rise for remaining stockholders.

Hypothesis 4: The lower the exchange probability, the higher is the abnormal return for the exchange firm at the announcement of the exchangeable bond issue.

Formally, the exchange probability is defined as in formula VI.1[331]

Formula VI.1
$$d_2 = \frac{\ln(S/X) + (R_{ft} - Div - \sigma^2/2)T}{\sigma\sqrt{T}}$$

The average exchange probability in my sample is 64.5%, which hints to divestment as motive for exchangeable debt issues.[332]

2.4.1.3 Convertible arbitrage

Kang/Lee (1996) and Ammann/Kind/Wilde (2003) document that convertible and exchangeable bonds issued in the US and France are underpriced.[333] Although investment bankers who underwrite issues of hybrid securities are sophisticated, the valuation of call and other provisions commonly encountered in exchangeable debt issues is involved and

---

330 A relation between the magnitude of abnormal returns and the exchange probability can only be examined when the announcement and issue day are identical. This is the case for 53 out of 57 transactions in my data set.

331 The exchange probability is $N(d_2)$, where $N()$ is the cumulative probability under a standard normal distribution function. It underlies general Black/Scholes assumptions. S is the stock price at issuance, X is the exchange price, R_{ft} is the yield of a 10-year government security at the issue date, Div is the dividend yield of the issuer at fiscal year-end prior the year of issuance, T is the number of years to maturity of the exchangeable bond and σ^2 is the variance of the continuously compounded return of the exchange firm's stock price estimated over [-200;-11]. See Black/Scholes (1973), p. 644; Lewis/Rogalski/Seward (2003), p. 160.

332 Lewis/Rogalski/Seward (2003), p. 160 argue that a conversion probability above 60% correspond to equity-like securities, which are used by issuers that want the bond to be converted.

333 See Kang/Lee (1996), p. 231 ff.; Ammann/Kind/Wilde (2003), p. 635 ff. Some of the exchangeable bonds studied by Ammann/Kind/Wilde (2003) are also contained in my dataset.

introduces uncertainty about the market price of a new issue.[334] To ensure that all securities can be sold, the offering price may be set at a level lower than the theoretical value. This underpricing may also compensate investors for increased liquidity risk, since liquity in exchangeable bond markets is typically lower than the liquidity of the underlying stock.[335]

Hedge funds exploit underpricing to make arbitrage profits.[336] They take a long position in the hybrid security and simultaneously short the underlying stock, which they are able to obtain cheaper through the mispriced exchange option than in the stock's secondary market. High transaction volumes encountered in Western European exchangeable debt issues suggest that short sales can have a significant impact on the underlyings' stock prices.[337] Bechmann (2004) empirically confirms this notion for calls of convertible bonds.[338] Hence, abnormal returns can be caused by price pressure absent from information- or agency-problems, which has to be considered in the analysis.

Hypothesis 5: *The higher the volume of short sales, the lower is the abnormal return for the exchange firm at the announcement of the exchangeable bond issue.*

Since short interest data were unavailable, I use the abnormal trading volume to measure short sales. As the issuer does not sell securities around the announcement day, increasing short sale activity should according to Gentry/Shizer (2002) lead to higher trading volumes.[339] It has to be noted, however, that the trading volume provides ambiguous evidence on hedge fund activity: it will be determined by trades of other parties as well, such as investment banks, which support the price level of the exchange stock during the transaction phase. To this end, the abnormal trading volume cannot be more than a rough and biased estimate for hedge fund activity.[340]

2.4.2 Market timing

When managers of issuing firms time the market, they sell equity securities during windows of opportunity when they achieve higher prices. This strategy can reduce costs of external

---

334 See for example Bühler/Koziol (2002), p. 302 ff. for a model of convertible bond valuation.
335 See Ammann/Kind/Wilde (2003), p. 651.
336 See Gentry/Schizer (2002), p. 38.
337 The average issue size in the data set is 682 million Euro.
338 See Bechmann (2004), p. 421 ff.
339 See Gentry/Schizer (2002), p. 43.
340 To calculate the abnormal trading volume (*AV*), I compute the average trading volume (*DV*) during [-200;-11] and then calculate the ratio of observed to average trading volume and subtract one.

equity finance and plays an important role in security issue decisions.[341] The analysis of market timing in exchangeable debt issues is closely related to the role of informational asymmetry and its relation to abnormal returns.

2.4.2.1 Time-varying costs of adverse selection

Two types of market timing can be distinguished. A first version goes back to Myers/Majluf (1984) and their dynamic asymmetric information model, in which costs of adverse selection vary across time. According to this model, there are windows of opportunity where information costs are on a comparatively low level. If a company issues a type of security whose value is sensitive to information, it is optimal to use these windows of opportunity to reduce information costs. Bayless/Chaplinski (1996) and Mann/Moore/Ramanlal (1999) show that a lot of firms issuing equity and convertible debt follow this recommendation. As a consequence, 'hot issue' markets for these securities exist, which are characterized by a high activity in the new issue market and during which issuers experience announcement returns that are less negative than those of otherwise comparable firms that issue in 'cold' markets.[342] According to Choe/Masulis/Nanda (1993) and Korajczyk/Lucas/McDonald (1991, 1992), windows of opportunity open during times where macroeconomic conditions are favourable or after many firms release credible information, such as earnings figures.[343]

If issuers of exchangeable debt are concerned about the mispricing of their securities in the capital market due to asymmetric information, one should observe that exchangeable bonds issued during periods of reduced adverse selection entail a less adverse market response than exchangeable bonds issued during periods of higher adverse selection.

Hypothesis 6: The lower the degree of adverse selection costs, the higher is the abnormal return for the exchange firm at the announcement of the exchangeable bond issue.

---

[341] That market timing is an important determinant in security issue decisions is shown by studies of actual financing decisions, analyses of the post-issue stock price performance, survey evidence and research on firms' capital structures. See for example Marsh (1982), p. 121 ff.; Loughran/Ritter (1995), p. 23 ff.; Spiess/Affleck-Graves (1995), p. 243 ff.; Loughran/Ritter (1997), p. 1823 ff.; Spiess/Affleck-Graves (1999), p. 45 ff.; Graham/Harvey (2001), p. 187 ff.; Baker/Wurgler (2002), p. 1 ff.

[342] See Bayless/Chaplinsky (1996), p. 253 ff.; Mann/Moore/Ramanlal (1999), p. 101 ff.

[343] See Korajczyk/Lucas/McDonald (1991), p. 685 ff.; Korajczyk/Lucas/ McDonald (1992), p. 397 ff.; Choe/ Masulis/Nanda (1993), p. 3 ff.

Bayless/Chaplinski (1996) and Marsh (1982) use the aggregated equity issuance volume to proxy for time-varying costs of adverse selection. I measure expected issuance volumes in a given quarter using the framework suggested by Marsh (1982):[344]

Formula VI.2 $$ISSUES_t = \gamma_{0t} + \gamma_{1t} I_{t-1} + \gamma_{2t} R_{M\,t-1} + \gamma_{3t} R_{M\,t-2} + \gamma_{4t} r_{t-1} + \gamma_{5t} r_{t-2} + \varepsilon_t$$

Formula VI.2 shows a forecast model of the number of security issues in a given quarter. *ISSUES* is the expected level of security issues, where t is the quarter of the security issue. I is the issuance volume during the quarters $t-1$ and $t-2$.[345] R_M is the return on the equity market in quarter $t-1$ and $t-2$ and r is the yield of a medium-term government security in these quarters.[346] I include r to account for the fact that exchangeable bond issuers are likely to consider the interest rate environment in their issue decision. If the signaling-hypothesis applies, stock price reactions should be higher for higher values of *ISSUES*.

2.4.2.2 *Valuation level*

A second version of market timing assumes that managers attempt to issue securities at high prices.[347] A market timing-argument for exchangeable debt issuance suggests that a firm issues securities during periods when a manager perceives the exchange stock to be overvalued in order to achieve a high price of the exchange option. The information disparity will lead to a differential assessment of the exchange option's value between firm insiders and outside investors: unlike the market, firm insiders expect that the exchange firm's stock high valuation level is transitory, resulting in a poor post-issue performance when prices revert to their fair value.[348] The combination of a bond and an overvalued exchange option, which represents a part of the investor's compensation, reduces interest costs below a firm's rate in straight debt issues. Danielova/Smart/Boquist (2004) document that market timing is an

---

[344] See Marsh (1982), p. 133.

[345] Issuance volumes were obtained from Thomson One Banker Deals. They are aggregated over all countries represented in the data set and measured as number of equity and equity-linked issues per quarter. The model is estimated for five years of pre-issue data.

[346] The market return is the return of a country index in a given quarter. For Germany I use the DAX 30, for France the CAC 40, for the Netherlands the AEX, for Great Britain the FTSE 100, for Austria the ATX, for Switzerland the SPI Total Return and for Italy the MIB 30.

[347] See Baker/Wurgler (2002), p. 1.

[348] See Danielova/Smart/Boquist (2004), p. 3.

important consideration in the decision to issue exchangeable debt of for a lot of firms in the US.[349]

Obviously, firms that issue exchangeable debt to sell overvalued equity pursue objectives other than divesting the underlying stock. If divestment is not the principal motive for issues in my data set, it is possible that the transactions convey negative information about the valuation level of the exchange stock. This implies a negative relation of the valuation level and abnormal returns.

The agency-hypothesis, in contrast, suggests a positive relation: if an exchange stock is overvalued at issuance, there is an increased likelihood that stock returns are poor during a post-issue period of up to five years.[350] This reduces the ex-ante probability that exchange occurs significantly for the typical issue. From an investors' point-of-view, this is good news because it becomes less likely that costs arising from agency conflicts increase when the concentrated share block is dispersed. If the potential increase in agency costs in case of a reduction in the exchange firm's ownership concentration dominates the negative information effect associated with the offering of an overvalued exchangeable bond, one should observe that the valuation level and announcement returns are positively related.

> Hypothesis 7: *The higher the valuation level of the exchange stock, the higher is the abnormal return for the exchange firm at the announcement of the exchangeable bond issue.*

Proxy variables commonly used to measure the valuation level of a stock are the market-to-book (*MTB*) and price-earnings ratios (*PE*).[351] A problem of these variables is their interpretation. In a lot of empirical examinations, market-to-book and price-earnings are used as indicators for investment opportunities.[352] Hence, they may not only reflect the manager's perception of misvaluation, as argued above, but also the market's perception of the quality of a firm's future investment opportunities. If this latter interpretation is correct, the expected sign of the coefficients of *MTB* and *PE*, respectively, changes from negative to positive for

---

349 See Danielova/Smart/Boquist (2004), p. 1 ff. A similar argument for convertible debt was put forward in chapter III of this thesis.

350 See for example Spiess/Affleck-Graves (1999), p. 45 ff.

351 The market-to-book and price-earnings ratios are obtained from Thomson Financial Datastream. The market-to-book ratio is defined as market value of common stock divided by the balance sheet value of common stock. The price-earnings ratio is defined as stock price divided by earnings per share.

352 See for example Jung/Kim/Stulz (1996), p. 170; Baker/Wurgler (2002), p. 4;

the information-hypothesis, because higher ratios imply positive future returns, and from positive to negative for the agency-hypothesis, because expected agency costs for stockholders increase.

To accommodate this interpretation problem, I include an exchange firm's share price increase (*RUNUP*) during the year preceding the issue. Survey evidence by Graham/Harvey (2001) shows that managers equate high pre-issue share price runups with high achievable prices, which is consistent with an 'overvaluation'-interpretation of pre-issue returns.[353] Furthermore, I calculate the long-run post-issue stock price performance of exchange firms. If exchange stocks underperform during the post-issue period, it appears likely that they have been overvalued at issuance. These conclusions have been drawn by a wide array of studies of security issuers' post-issue stock price performance.[354]

I calculate long-run returns for the year preceding, the year following and the three years following the transaction as in Barber/Lyon (1997) according to formula VI.3.[355]

Formula VI.3 $$BHAR_{iT} = \prod_{t=1}^{T}[1 + R_{it}] - \prod_{t=1}^{T}[1 + E(R_{it})]$$

To model expected returns, I use returns of large national market indices as well as of control firms matched on industry affiliation and size.[356]

---

353 See Graham/Harvey (2001), p. 216.

354 See for example Loughran/Ritter (1995), p. 23 ff.; Spiess/Affleck-Graves (1995), p. 243 ff.; Loughran/Ritter (1997), p. 1823 ff.; Spiess/Affleck-Graves (1999), p. 45 ff.

355 See Barber/Lyon (1997), p. 341 ff. The corresponding time frames are [-250;-6], [+6;+250] and [+6;+750].

356 Relevant indices are the DAX 30 for Germany, the CAC 40 for France, the AEX for the Netherlands, the FTSE 100 for the United Kingdom, the ATX for Austria, the SPI Total Return for Switzerland and the MIB 30 for Italy. Industry affiliation is determined relying on the Datastream industry classification system. From firms in the range of 25% and 200% of the market value of the exchange firm measured one month prior to the transaction announcement, the firm with the closest market value is selected as the control firm. Spiess/Affleck-Graves (1995), p. 243 ff. use firms matched on the basis of size and industry affiliation to calculate long-run abnormal returns as well.

3 *Data and methodology*

3.1 Data

3.1.1 Sample selection procedure

The data set comprises 57 Western European exchangeable bond issues and is selected on the basis of the following criteria:

1. Issuance occurs between January 1, 1997 and December 31, 2003.
2. The issuer is based in Austria, France, Germany, Great Britain, Italy, the Netherlands or Switzerland.[357]
3. The SDC Platinum Global New Issues Database lists the transaction as "Exchangeable" deal.
4. An announcement date can be identified using the press research engine "Factiva".
5. The transaction announcement does not coincide with the announcement of other relevant news about the issuing or exchange firm.
6. Stock prices can be obtained from Thomson Financial Datastream.[358]

I compute abnormal returns for 57 exchange firms as well as 31 issuers.[359]

3.1.2 Data summary information

Table VI.3 shows that the average issue volume, 682 million EUR, is rather high. The mean relative issue size is 12.2% and underlines that exchangeable bonds are used to sell larger share blocks. Exchangeable debt typically carries coupon rates below market levels for interest rates, because investors are (partly) compensated by the exchange option. The average maturity of exchangeable bonds in the sample is 4.45 years. During this time horizon, prices of exchange stocks have on average to rise by 28.77% for the exchange option to be at-the-money.

---

[357] Spanish or Portuguese exchangeable debt issues were not contained in the SDC database.

[358] I require the issuing and exchange firms to have stock price data for the year preceding the issue. Stock prices are total return index levels, which assume a reinvestment of (cash) dividends and are adjusted for capital actions.

[359] Since not all issuers are publicly traded companies, I only have 31 observations for issuing firms. The sample includes three cases, where mandatory exchangeables have been issued. In contrast to ordinary exchangeable bonds, these securities grant investors no conversion right, but exchange occurs automatically according to pre-specified terms. I discuss these securities further in section 4.3 of this chapter.

Table VI.3: Data summary information

Descriptive Measure	*Mean*	*Median*	*Max*	*Min*	*St. Dev.*
Issuance volume (mio. EUR)	682	450	5,000	40	794
Relative issue size	12.18%	7.33%	65.88%	0.12%	13.67%
Coupon	2.69%	2.00%	9.00%	0.00%	2.19%
Maturity (years)	4.45	4.80	10.00	1.00	1.70
Exchange premium	28.77%	27.07%	65.00%	15.00%	8.84%

An analysis of the geographical distribution of exchangeable debt issues in table VI.4 shows that the inner-German market (i.e. issuing and exchange company are German firms) dominates other markets, given a total transaction volume of more than 10 billion Euros. The proportion of German exchange companies is the largest in the sample. The relatively high volume of transactions between Germany and the Netherlands is due to the prominent use of Dutch financing vehicles employed by German corporations.[360]

Table VI.4: Geographical distribution of issuance volumes

This table shows the geographical distribution of issuance volumes. Country abbreviations are as follows: A is Austria, CH is Switzerland, F is France, GER is Germany, I is Italy, L is Luxembourg, NL are the Netherlands and UK is the United Kingdom. Figures are in million EUR.

Country issuer	Country exchange company								
	A	*CH*	*GER*	*F*	*I*	*L*	*NL*	*UK*	***Total***
A	770								770
CH									0
F			768	8,390			4,599	660	14,417
GER		2,176	10,213	375					12,764
I					1,200				1,200
L			270	800					1,070
NL			6,126	100					6,226
UK		362		222	77		850	909	2,420
Total	770	2,538	17,377	9,887	1,277	0	5,449	1,569	***38,867***

Figure VI.3 shows an industry overview of issuing firms based on issuance volumes. It documents that the industry composition of issuing firms is heterogeneous. 36% of the Euro amount of exchangeable debt is issued in transactions initiated by financial firms. Especially

[360] In my data set, German corporations Allianz AG, Siemens AG and HypoVereinsbank have issued exchangeable bonds via a foreign financing vehicle in order to benefit from a better tax environment and facilitated administration. Apart from this aspect, the German capital gains tax makes the exchangeable bond unattractive for international investors, which can be evaded with a foreign financing vehicle as well. See Schäfer (2002), p. 515 f.

the German KfW has divested formerly public companies in the course of privatization programs that primarily involved the divestment of shares in Deutsche Post and Deutsche Telekom. With regard to the industry affiliation of exchange companies, it is apparent from figure VI.4 that most transactions involved technology and telecommunication companies.

Figure VI.3: Industry overview issuing firms

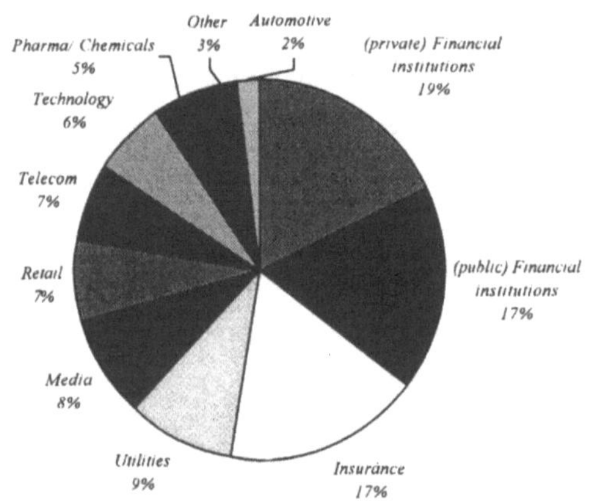

Figure VI.4: Industry overview exchange firms

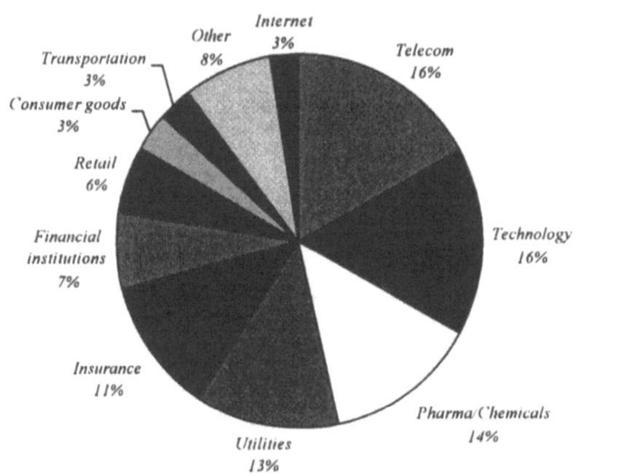

3.1.3 *Circumstances surrounding exchangeable debt issues*

The primary objective of this paper is to examine why Western European firms choose to issue exchangeable debt and explain the market's response to this decision. Whether exchangeable debt is issued to divest an equity stake or to exploit a window of opportunity to sell overvalued equity to an ignorant investor largely shapes the informational consequences of exchangeable debt issues.

I obtain preliminary evidence on the issue motive following Ghosh/Varma/Woolridge (1990) and Barber (1993) who conduct a press research to analyze filings distributed by issuers to announce the transaction. The main result of this analysis can be summarized as follows: issuers indicate their intention to divest an equity stake contained in their portfolio. The relationships with the exchange firm suggest that issuers have access to insider information and are capable of effective monitoring. Whether the capital market shares this interpretation is analyzed in section 5, where I calculate announcement returns.

Table VI.5 shows the circumstances surrounding exchangeable debt issues in my sample. I classify the transactions according to a number of different categories.[361]

Table VI.5: Circumstances surrounding exchangeable debt issues

Category	Description	N	%
Investment	The issuer has a financial interest in the exchange company.	22	38.6%
Affiliated	The issuer is the parent company of the exchange company or vice versa.	8	14.0%
Merger acquisition	The exchange company has been the target of an acquisition or merger that has not been completed or the exchange company is sold in the course of a merger or an acquisition.	5	8.8%
Alliance partnership	The issuer and the exchange company engaged in a partnership that involved cross-shareholdings.	5	8.8%
Privatization	Public institutions use exchangeable bonds to privatize formerly public firms.	4	7.0%
Other	Re-issue of treasury stock for tax reasons.	1	1.8%
Unknown	No information is available.	12	21.1%
Total		***57***	***100.0%***

The most important category in my sample is 'Investment', which contains almost 40% of all transactions. It includes offerings, where institutional investors, in particular insurance companies or banks, hold stakes in other corporations, which they would like to sell. For such

[361] The classification follows my own judgement. To this end, it has only illustrative character and is not the basis for further statistical analyses.

firms, asset management is a core activity, which indicates a high degree of sophistication. These investors certainly do not only have a strong incentive but also the capability to maximize the value of their stake by monitoring the exchange firm's management. It is also highly likely that they have superior access to corporate information. An example illustrates how issuing firms may interact with exchange firms: a number of exchangeable bonds in the sample have been issued by Allianz Group in order to reduce or completely divest equity holdings. Underlying firms of these exchangeables include E.ON, BASF and RWE. As a manifestation of their interest, executives of Allianz are members of the supervisory board of each company: the CEO of Allianz Leben is a member of the supervisory board of E.ON, the CEO of Allianz Group of BASF and the CFO of Allianz Group of RWE.

Similar relationships can be found in the category privatization (7.0%): the CEO of KfW is a member of the supervisory board of Deutsche Post and Deutsche Telekom, both target firms in exchangeable debt issues by KfW.

The second-largest category is 'Affiliated' (14.0%). It contains all sales of stakes issuers have in affiliated firms and identifies a close relationship between issuing and exchange company. Given that financial statements are likely to be consolidated and that division managers report to a headquarter, it is almost certain that the issuer has access to all insider information and is able to control the activities of the exchange firms' managers.

Hence, for 60% of all transactions contained in the categories 'Investment', 'Affiliated' and 'Privatization', it appears highly likely that the issuer plays an important role in the governance process of the exchange firm that grants him access to inside information.

The remaining categories 'Merger/acquisition' and 'Alliance/partnership' (each contain 8.8% of all observations) are more difficult to evaluate. 'Merger/acquisition' (M&A) comprises transactions where the issuer has acquired a stake in another company, which shall be disposed via the exchangeable bond. Also M&A transactions where the exchange company was not an integral part of the new entity and shall therefore be divested are included. In the course of a merger or acquisition, the issuer will be able to obtain detailed information about the value of the exchange company. However, whether an aborted M&A transaction is due to negative information about the exchange firm is difficult to determine. The termination of a takeover attempt can also be due to a new strategic focus or a revised assessment of the synergy potential between the two firms. However, if any acquisition premium is contained in the stock price, it is likely to disappear when the exchangeable bond is announced.[362] The category 'Alliance/partnership' contains stakes issuers had in (former) partner companies. How much information an issuer will have and how important it was for the exchange companies depends on the nature of the alliance and is difficult to determine ex-post.

3.2 Methodology

3.2.1 Computation of announcement returns

When issuing an exchangeable bond, the issuer has a major interest that the valuation level of the exchange stock is favourable when the transaction is priced. The announcement return of the exchange company's stock will directly impact the costs the exchangeable bond issuer incurs. To analyze this aspect, I use an event study approach that allows to identify the abnormal return caused by an event. I examine stock price reactions primarily for the event window [-1;0], where 0 is the announcement day.[363]

To compute abnormal returns, I rely on the market model, which provides a basis to calculate normal firm returns and has proven to be the dominant approach in short-horizon event studies. It is shown in a general form in formula VI.4.[364]

Formula VI.4 $R_{it} = \alpha_i + \beta_i R_{Mt} + \varepsilon_i$

Formula VI.5 $AR_{it} = R_{it} - E(R_{it})$ with $E(R_{it}) = \hat{\alpha}_i + \hat{\beta}_i R_{Mt}$

Formula VI.5 shows how abnormal returns are computed. AR_{it} denotes the abnormal return of security i on day t, R_{it} is the real return and $E(R_{it})$ is the expected return computed from the market model. R_{Mt} is defined as the return of a large national index on day t.[365] Estimates of the market model parameters, $\hat{\alpha}$ and $\hat{\beta}$ are obtained in OLS-regressions for an estimation period of [-200;-11].

---

362 See Barber (1993), p. 54.

363 To assess the robustness of my results and to eliminate biases introduced by uncertainty about the true information arrival date, I examine different event windows.

364 See Brown/Warner (1980), p. 207 ff. The advantage of the market model is that it allows to adjust for risk of event firm returns and to increase the power of tests of abnormal returns, which makes it the model most commonly used in event studies. I test for the robustness of results using the mean- and market-adjusted model. See Dyckman/Philbrick/Stephan (1984), p. 4 ff.; Strong (1992), p. 537; Armitage (1995), p. 27 ff.; Campbell/Lo/MacKinlay (1997), p. 155 and 163.

365 For Germany I use the DAX 30, for France the CAC 40, for the Netherlands the AEX, for the United Kingdom the FTSE 100, for Austria the ATX, for Switzerland the SPI Total Return and for Italy the MIB 30.

The market model requires the regression residuals to be independently identically distributed. This assumption may be violated in my investigation, since some transactions cluster in calendar-time: SwissLife Finance issued a multi-tranche bond exchangeable in stock of four different companies. Furthermore, Allianz issued a so-called MILES-exchangeable, which can be exchanged into one of three different stocks.[366] These transactions cluster in calendar-time and might be cross-sectionally dependent, which may lead to biases in the inference process.[367]

Several possibilities allow for a solution of this problem: Binder (1985) suggests the application of a seemingly unrelated regressions-model.[368] This approach has the disadvantage that test statistics tend to have low power and have distributional properties that hold only asymptotically.[369] Given the low number of observations in this analysis and the low number of cases, where the independence assumption is potentially violated, this approach appears not to be optimal. Brown/Warner (1985) develop specific tests that use a variance estimator from the time series of stock returns and that do not suffer from problems induced by cross-sectional dependence.[370] Most studies choose this approach. However, it does not control for event-induced variance.[371] It neither solves the cross-sectional dependence problem in the multivariate regression analysis of cumulative abnormal returns. To accommodate these problems, I employ a portfolio-approach, where all possibly dependent observations are treated as one data point.[372] Abnormal returns are aggregated according to formulae VI.6 to VI.8.

Formula VI.6 $$AAR_t = \frac{1}{N}\sum_{i=1}^{N} AR_{it}$$

Formula VI.7 $$CAR_i(t_1, t_2) = \sum_{t=t_1}^{t_2} AR_{it}$$

Formula VI.8 $$CAAR(t_1, t_2) = \frac{1}{N}\sum_{i=1}^{N} CAR_i(t_1, t_2)$$

366 A MILES (market index-linked equity securities) exchangeable can be exchanged into one out of three exchange stocks (E.ON AG, BASF AG or Munich Re). In addition, the bond pays a premium, which depends on the performance of the DAX 30. Since three firms are concerned, I test stock price reactions for all three.

367 See Bernard (1987), p. 1 ff.

368 See Binder (1985), p. 370 ff.

369 See MacKinlay (1997), p. 27; Bernard (1987), p. 4 f.

370 See Brown/Warner (1985), p. 7 f.

371 See Boehmer/Musumeci/Poulsen (1991), p. 253 ff.

372 See MacKinlay (1997), p. 27.

AAR_t denotes the average abnormal return on day t, CAR_i denotes the cumulative abnormal return of security i for the event window $[t_1;t_2]$ and $CAAR$ denotes the cumulative average abnormal return for the event window $[t_1;t_2]$.

3.2.2 *Inference and cross-sectional analysis of announcement returns*

To test the null hypothesis that (cumulative) average abnormal returns are zero, I use two statistical tests.[373] On the one hand, I employ a parametric test as in Boehmer/Musumeci/ Poulsen (1991).[374] Under the assumption that abnormal returns are not cross-sectionally correlated, which is fulfilled using the portfolio-approach, this test does not suffer from biases arising from event-induced variance.

Since abnormal returns in my analysis are not always normally distributed, as required by the parametric test, there is an increased probability of falsely rejecting the null hypothesis.[375] For this reason, I also use a non-parametric Wilcoxon signed-rank test, which does not require abnormal returns to be distributed normally. By ranking abnormal returns, the distribution is normalized, which makes the median test less susceptible to outliers and reduces the probability of type I errors.[376]

I analyze the cross-section of abnormal returns on a univariate basis first, and examine the joint effect of proxy variables on abnormal returns in a multivariate framework in a second step. Univariate tests are median tests of equality as well as univariate regression models.

The multivariate analysis uses an OLS-regression model. Its assumptions are examined separately. With regard to the cross-sectional dependence problem discussed above, the regression is estimated with all observations first and then the analysis is repeated using the portfolio approach. If significant deviations in the results exist, both sets of regressions are reported.

---

373 See Campbell/Lo/MacKinlay (1997), p. 168; Brown/Warner (1985), p. 7.

374 See Boehmer/Musumeci/Poulsen (1991), p. 269 f.

375 See Brown/Warner (1980), p. 217.

376 I also calculate a non-parametric test as in Corrado (1989), p. 385 ff. The use of this test statistic does not qualitively affect my conclusions.

4 *Presentation and interpretation of results*

4.1 The magnitude of announcement returns

Table VI.6 shows *AARs* for issuing and exchange firms calculated on the basis of the mean-, the market-adjusted and the market model. Table VI.7 presents *CAARs* for different event windows for the market model.

On average, exchange stocks respond significantly negative to the announcement of an exchangeable debt issue on day 0. The *AAR* is –1.57% for the market model. *AARs* for the mean- and market-adjusted models are slightly higher.

During the event window [-1;0], 68% of all *CARs* are negative and the *CAAR* is –1.52%, which confirms hypothesis 1. Announcement returns for a sample of Western European transactions are in a similar range to those documented by US studies of Ghosh/Varma/ Woolridge (1990) and Barber (1993). They are less negative than stock price reactions computed by Mikkelson/Partch (1985) of –1.96% for unregistered and of –2.87% for registered secondary distributions.[377] Hence, the use of exchangeable debt by Western European firms may be justified by the fact that it is a cost-efficient divestment strategy.

The negative average announcement return has three possible explanations. First, negative information may be conveyed by exchangeable debt issues. On the basis of the results of the press research, this appears rather unlikely. Second, it is possible that the capital market ascribes the issuers an important role in the monitoring process of the exchange companies and expects that the issuers will be unable or unwilling to adopt this role after the bonds may have been exchanged. Third, price pressure induced by short sales could cause abnormal returns to be negative.

Before I turn to the question of which explanation applies in the next section, it should be noted that *CAARs* for issuing firms are not significantly different from zero. The distribution of positive and negative abnormal returns on the announcement day is roughly equal (57% and 43%) and the average stock price reaction is +0,38% for [-1;0], which confirms the results of previous event studies of debt issue announcements and supports hypothesis 2: the positive effects from restructuring the issuer's assets and the negative effects from raising external debt capital neutralize.

---

[377] See Mikkelson/Partch (1985), p. 175.

Table VI.6: ***AARs*** **of exchange and issuing firms**

This table shows average abnormal returns for exchange firms in panel A and for issuing firms in panel B from day −10 to day +10, where 0 is the announcement day. In columns 1 and 4, I show results for a mean-adjusted event study-model. Columns 2 and 5 contain results for a market-adjusted model and columns 3 and 6 for a market model. For the market-adjusted and the market model, market indices are the largest national indices of a given country. The estimation period for event study-model parameters is [-200;-11]. t-statistics follow Boehmer/Musumeci/Poulsen (1991) for the market model and are standard t-tests for the mean- and market-adjusted model. z-statistics are Wilcoxon signed-rank tests. Test statistics are shown in parentheses. ***, **, * denote a significance-level of 1%, 5% and 10%, respectively.

Panel A: Average abnormal exchange firm returns										Panel B: Average abnormal issuing firm returns									
	1			2			3				4			5			6		
	Mean-adjusted			Market-adjusted			Market model				Mean-adjusted			Market-adjusted			Market model		
Day	*AAR*	*t-statistic*	*z-statistic*	*AAR*	*t-statistic*	*z-statistic*	*AAR*	*t-statistic*	*z-statistic*	*Day*	*AAR*	*t-statistic*	*z-statistic*	*AAR*	*t-statistic*	*z-statistic*	*AAR*	*t-statistic*	*z-statistic*
-10	-0.05%	[-0.12]	[0.68]	0.16%	[0.51]	[0.15]	0.34%	[0.78]	[0.81]	*-10*	-0.32%	[-0.55]	[0.73]	-0.03%	[-0.06]	[0.34]	0.18%	[-0.09]	[0.19]
-9	0.34%	[0.86]	[1.12]	-0.02%	[-0.06]	[0.18]	0.03%	[-1.57]	[1.52]	*-9*	1.36%	[2.34] **	[2.56] **	0.96%	[2.16] **	[2.13] **	1.07%	[1.55]	[2.05] **
-8	-0.26%	[-0.65]	[0.69]	-0.36%	[-1.15]	[1.59]	-0.36%	[-1.31]	[1.60]	*-8*	0.15%	[0.26]	[0.36]	-0.27%	[-0.61]	[0.54]	-0.23%	[-0.43]	[0.75]
-7	-0.11%	[-0.28]	[0.05]	-0.26%	[-0.82]	[0.76]	-0.37%	[2.71] **	[0.26]	*-7*	0.41%	[0.71]	[0.89]	0.16%	[0.35]	[0.30]	0.13%	[0.07]	[0.03]
-6	-0.02%	[-0.05]	[0.05]	-0.42%	[-1.35]	[1.80] *	-0.25%	[0.51]	[0.19]	*-6*	0.66%	[1.15]	[1.28]	0.03%	[0.08]	[0.54]	0.14%	[0.10]	[0.68]
-5	-0.15%	[-0.38]	[0.20]	0.14%	[0.46]	[1.13]	0.06%	[-0.82]	[1.26]	*-5*	0.19%	[0.34]	[0.21]	0.38%	[0.85]	[0.48]	0.25%	[0.61]	[0.66]
-4	0.44%	[1.11]	[0.83]	0.08%	[0.26]	[0.70]	0.09%	[0.26]	[0.72]	*-4*	-0.05%	[-0.08]	[0.32]	-0.18%	[-0.40]	[0.60]	-0.06%	[-0.23]	[0.62]
-3	-0.60%	[-1.51]	[1.95] *	-0.33%	[-1.04]	[1.13]	-0.29%	[-1.33]	[1.27]	*-3*	0.29%	[0.50]	[0.60]	0.17%	[0.38]	[0.85]	0.18%	[0.88]	[0.34]
-2	0.41%	[1.04]	[0.93]	0.15%	[0.48]	[0.28]	0.21%	[0.19]	[0.25]	*-2*	0.31%	[0.53]	[0.52]	-0.04%	[-0.10]	[0.34]	-0.22%	[-0.60]	[0.46]
-1	0.28%	[0.71]	[0.28]	0.13%	[0.40]	[0.12]	0.05%	[1.02]	[0.03]	*-1*	0.03%	[0.06]	[0.05]	0.11%	[0.25]	[0.19]	0.09%	[0.20]	[0.03]
0	**-1.26%**	**[-3.18] *****	**[3.27] *****	**-1.42%**	**[-4.54] *****	**[3.92] *****	**-1.57%**	**[-5.75] *****	**[3.92] *****	***0***	**0.61%**	**[1.05]**	**[0.60]**	**0.42%**	**[0.94]**	**[0.95]**	**0.29%**	**[0.90]**	**[0.73]**
1	-0.40%	[-1.00]	[1.64]	-0.11%	[-0.35]	[0.77]	-0.31%	[-0.4]	[0.91]	*1*	-0.03%	[-0.04]	[0.21]	0.46%	[1.03]	[1.26]	0.41%	[0.83]	[0.58]
2	0.14%	[0.36]	[0.66]	0.39%	[1.25]	[1.64] *	0.30%	[0.54]	[0.40]	*2*	0.48%	[0.82]	[0.44]	0.26%	[0.58]	[0.54]	0.15%	[0.52]	[0.23]
3	-0.39%	[-0.99]	[1.76] *	-0.20%	[-0.62]	[1.32]	-0.20%	[-1.25]	[1.67] *	*3*	0.02%	[0.03]	[0.46]	0.18%	[0.41]	[0.15]	0.47%	[0.41]	[0.36]
4	0.28%	[0.71]	[0.76]	0.38%	[1.21]	[1.44]	0.19%	[-1.05]	[0.94]	*4*	-0.45%	[-0.78]	[0.95]	-0.74%	[-2.12] **	[1.83] *	-0.67%	[-1.34]	[1.97] **
5	-0.14%	[-0.35]	[0.14]	0.13%	[0.41]	[0.21]	-0.03%	[0.47]	[0.54]	*5*	0.36%	[0.62]	[0.91]	0.25%	[0.56]	[0.95]	0.12%	[0.45]	[0.13]
6	0.21%	[0.53]	[0.39]	-0.23%	[-0.74]	[0.71]	-0.10%	[0.69]	[0.25]	*6*	0.66%	[1.14]	[0.93]	0.12%	[0.27]	[0.01]	-0.04%	[0.21]	[0.58]
7	0.33%	[0.84]	[0.52]	0.62%	[1.98] **	[1.59]	0.44%	[1.82] *	[0.96]	*7*	0.38%	[0.65]	[1.05]	0.62%	[1.39]	[1.22]	0.49%	[1.20]	[0.81]
8	-0.12%	[-0.29]	[0.37]	-0.10%	[-0.32]	[0.11]	-0.35%	[0.07]	[1.04]	*8*	0.89%	[1.54]	[2.03] **	0.36%	[0.82]	[1.24]	0.33%	[0.71]	[1.11]
9	0.15%	[0.38]	[0.09]	0.16%	[0.50]	[0.39]	0.09%	[0.26]	[0.78]	*9*	-0.16%	[-0.28]	[0.58]	-0.36%	[-0.81]	[1.56]	-0.41%	[-0.26]	[1.71] *
10	0.44%	[1.10]	[1.50]	0.37%	[1.17]	[1.99] *	0.50%	[0.85]	[1.63]	*10*	-0.20%	[-0.34]	[0.73]	-0.08%	[-0.17]	[0.75]	-0.05%	[-0.09]	[1.03]

Table VI.7: *CAARs* of exchange and issuing firms

This table shows cumulative average abnormal returns for exchange firms in panel A and for issuing firms in panel B for different event windows. *CAARs* are calculated on the basis of the market model. Market indices are the largest national indices of a given country. The estimation period of market model parameters is [-200;-11]. t-statistics follow Boehmer/Musumeci/Poulsen (1991) and z-statistics are Wilcoxon signed-rank tests. Test statistics are shown in parentheses. ***, **, * denote a significance-level of 1%, 5% and 10%, respectively.

Panel A: *CAARs* for exchange firms

Event window	*Mean*	*t-statistic*	*Median*	*z-statistic*	*CAR < 0*
[-10;0]	-2.07%	[-1.29]	-3.26%	[2.15] **	67%
[-5;0]	-1.46%	[-1.89] **	-2.45%	[1.74] *	68%
[-1;0]	-1.52%	[-3.21] ***	-1.32%	[3.57] ***	68%
[0]	-1.57%	[-5.75] ***	-1.08%	[3.92] ***	75%
[0;+1]	-1.87%	[-4.35] ***	-1.98%	[3.73] ***	72%
[0;+5]	-1.61%	[-2.54] ***	-0.89%	[2.12] **	58%
[0;+10]	-1.02%	[-1.15]	-1.61%	[1.74] *	62%
[-1;+1]	-1.82%	[-2.69] ***	-2.10%	[3.01] ***	67%
[-5;+5]	-1.50%	[-2.43] **	-2.07%	[2.42] **	61%
[-10;+10]	-1.52%	[-0.63]	-1.85%	[1.32]	60%

Panel B: *CAARs* for issuing firms

Event window	*Mean*	*t-statistic*	*Median*	*z-statistic*	*CAR < 0*
[-10;0]	1.82%	[1.12]	0.80%	[0.93]	43%
[-5;0]	0.53%	[0.45]	0.34%	[0.30]	43%
[-1;0]	0.38%	[0.04]	1.03%	[0.68]	40%
[0]	0.29%	[0.87]	0.57%	[0.73]	47%
[0;+1]	0.70%	[1.23]	0.05%	[0.40]	47%
[0;+5]	0.78%	[0.56]	0.40%	[0.95]	32%
[0;+10]	1.10%	[0.97]	0.71%	[1.01]	32%
[-1;+1]	0.79%	[0.51]	0.14%	[0.36]	43%
[-5;+5]	1.02%	[0.65]	0.91%	[1.05]	40%
[-10;+10]	2.63%	[1.04]	1.61%	[1.56]	33%

4.2 The cross-section of announcement returns

4.2.1 Transaction and security structure

4.2.1.1 Relative issue size

To identify whether the relative issue size is related to the magnitude of abnormal returns, I divide the data set in two and three subsamples, respectively, and test the median *CAR* of the subsamples against each other for different event windows.

In panel A of table VI.8, the sample is split based on the relative issue size. The median *CAR* of the group with lower *RIS* values (below median *RIS*) is tested against the median *CAR* of the group with higher *RIS* values (above median *RIS*) using a Wilcoxon signed-rank test of equality. In the table, I indicate the difference in median *CARs* of the two groups as well as the significance level of the test statistic: for example, for the event window [-1;0], transactions in the below median-group have a median *CAR* that is 1.36% higher than the median *CAR* of the group with *RIS* values above the median. This difference is significant at the 5%-level. The row denoted 'Low tercile – high tercile' contains a similar analysis for a division of the sample in terciles. Panel B shows coefficients and adjusted R^2 values from univariate regression analyses where *CAR* is the dependent and *RIS* is the independent variable.

Hypothesis 3 argues that the relative issue size is useful to discriminate between the information- and agency-hypothesis for negative announcement returns. According to the information-hypothesis, the relation between *RIS* and *CAR* should be insignificant, while the agency-hypothesis postulates a negative relation.

It becomes obvious from the table that there is statistical evidence supporting the agency-hypothesis: the negative announcement return indicates that higher ownership concentrations increase a firm's market value of equity. The more the ownership concentration is reduced, the more adverse are stock price reactions to the announcement of the exchangeable bond. This observation corresponds to Wruck (1989) who finds that an increase in ownership concentration increases shareholder value.[378] In addition, Barclay/Holderness (1991) show that also the specific capabilities of a large stockholder for effective monitoring are related to firm value.[379] To this end, the negative announcement return and its negative relation to the

[378] See Wruck (1989), p. 3. She analyzes private placements of share blocks sold to private equity firms, which are accompanied by an average abnormal return of +4,5%.

[379] See Barclay/Holderness (1991), p. 861 ff.

relative issue size suggest that the issuer plays an important role in the governance process of the exchange firm from the capital market's point-of-view.[380]

Table VI.8: Univariate analysis of relative issue size

This table contains a univariate analysis of cumulative abnormal returns for different event windows. Panel A calculates differences in medians. I rank the sample in ascending order according to a transaction's relative issue size. I then form two subsamples, where the first subsample has values of *RIS* below the median *RIS* and the second subsample above the median *RIS*. I conduct a Wilcoxon signed-rank test of equality of median *CARs* of the two subsamples in the row denominated 'Below median-above median'. In the row 'Low tercile-high tercile' I conduct a similar test, but I divide the sample into terciles. The numbers shown in panel A are differences of the median *CARs* of the two subsamples and low minus high terciles, respectively. In panel B, I show coefficients and adjusted R^2 values for a univariate regression, where the dependent variable is the cumulative abnormal return of a firm for different event windows and the independent variable is the relative issue size. ***, **, * denote a significance-level of 1%, 5% and 10%, respectively.

Panel A: Differences in medians

Event window	*[-1;0]*	*[0;+1]*	*[-1;+1]*
Below median - above median	1.36% **	1.94%	1.14% *
Low tercile - high tercile	1.02% **	1.75% *	1.16% *

Panel B: Univariate regression

Event window	*[-1;0]*	*[0;+1]*	*[-1;+1]*
Coefficient	-0.09 ***	-0.04	-0.06 *
Adjusted R^2	14.3%	1.4%	4.1%

4.2.1.2 Exchange probability

Apart from the size of the transaction, the structure of the exchangeable bond itself may have an influence on abnormal returns.

Table VI.9 shows results from an analysis comparable to the one in the previous section. It illustrates that the exchange probability, which may serve as an operator for the market's expectation that the bond is exchanged and the ownership concentration of the exchange firm is reduced, is not significantly related to the magnitude of abnormal returns on the announcement day. This is inconsistent with hypothesis 4 and suggests that either the capital market correctly anticipates the probability that the share block is dispersed. Or the risk-

380 It should be noted that the negative relation of abnormal returns and relative issue size is also consistent with a price pressure-explanation. The higher the relative issue size, the more stocks will be shorted, all else equal, which causes abnormal returns to be more negative. I further analyze this aspect in section 4.2.1.3 of this chapter.

neutral probability calculated from the Black/Scholes formula is not a relevant measure for investor expectations in the 'risky' world.[381]

Table VI.9: Univariate analysis of exchange probability

This table contains a univariate analysis of cumulative abnormal returns for different event windows. Panel A calculates differences in medians. I rank the sample in ascending order according to a transaction's exchange probability. I then form two subsamples, where the first subsample has values of *EXPROB* below the median *EXPROB* and the second subsample above the median *EXPROB*. I conduct a Wilcoxon signed-rank test of equality of median *CARs* of the two subsamples in the row denominated 'Below median-above median'. In the row 'Low tercile-high tercile' I conduct a similar test, but I divide the sample into terciles. The numbers shown in panel A are differences of the median *CARs* of the two subsamples and low minus high terciles, respectively. In panel B, I show coefficients and adjusted R^2 values for a univariate regression, where the dependent variable is the cumulative abnormal return of a firm for different event windows and the independent variable is the exchange probability. ***, **, * denote a significance-level of 1%, 5% and 10%, respectively.

Panel A: Differences in medians

Event window	*[-1;0]*	*[0;+1]*	*[-1;+1]*
Below median - above median	0.20%	1.11%	-0.80%
Low tercile - high tercile	1.07%	0.08%	-0.23%

Panel B: Univariate regression

Event window	*[-1;0]*	*[0;+1]*	*[-1;+1]*
Coefficient	-0.05	-0.08	-0.01
Adjusted R^2	-4.0%	-2.0%	-4.0%

4.2.1.3 Convertible arbitrage

Adverse announcement effects may arise from short sales of hedge fund investors, which exploit mispricings of exchangeable bonds by taking a long position in the bond and a short position in the exchange stock to make an arbitrage profit. This activity may put significant pressure on the share price of the exchange stock. To measure short sales, I use the abnormal trading volume (*AV*) in the exchange stock. I am aware of the fact that this proxy cannot be more than a rough estimate of hedge fund activity, but given that hedge funds are primary investor groups for exchangeable bonds and that the issuer does not sell securities on the announcement day, it would be plausible if their orders dominated the trading in the stock.

Figure VI.5 documents significantly positive abnormal trading volumes in the exchange stock. When the transaction is announced (day 0), the trading volume increases more than two-fold compared to the average pre-announcement trading volume.

[381] Despite this disadvantage, the conversion probability is commonly used in the literature. See for example Lewis/Rogalski/Seward (2003), p. 160; Ammann/Fehr/Seiz (2004), p. 10.

Figure VI.5: Abnormal trading volume exchange firms

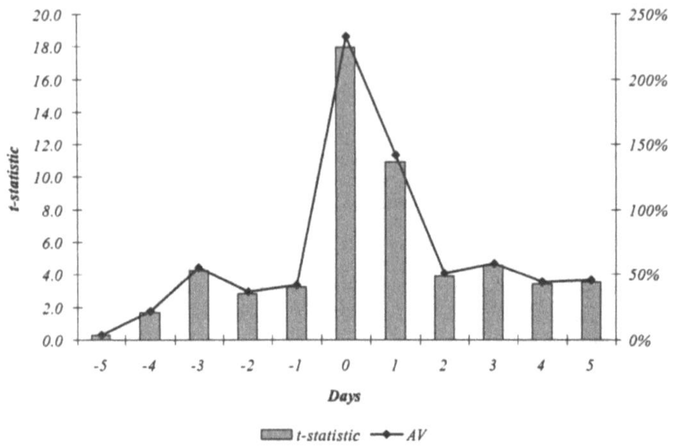

Also the days following the announcement are characterized by significant abnormal trading volume of up to five days. However, table VI.10 illustrates that abnormal trading volume and announcement returns are not related, which is inconsistent with hypothesis 5.

Exchangeable debt issues are underwritten transactions where investment banks buy the new securities from the issuer and sell them to investors. Hence, banks have an interest to stabilize the price of the exchange stock to facilitate the sale of the bond and lock in a high price, which also allows them to increase their fee income. They will generate a certain demand for the exchange stock.[382] One might reason that this demand absorbs the price pressure induced by short sales. As long as the banks resell their positions in the exchange stock during the days following the issue, the abnormal trading volume during this period is explained as well.[383]

---

[382] See Gentry/Schizer (2002), p. 38.

[383] A further indication that price pressure does not cause abnormal returns to be negative is that *CAARs* have a permanent character in table VI.7 and persist up to ten days after the offering. Price pressure often has temporary effects on an issuer's stock price. See Bechmann (2004), p. 421. Given that short sales do not appear to cause abnormal returns to be negative, it becomes obvious that the negative relation of the relative issue size and abnormal returns hints to the agency-hypothesis as an explanation for negative announcement returns.

Table VI.10: Univariate analysis of abnormal trading volume

This table contains a univariate analysis of cumulative abnormal returns for different event windows. Panel A calculates differences in medians. I rank the sample in ascending order according to a transaction's abnormal trading volume. I then form two subsamples, where the first subsample has values of *AV* below the median *AV* and the second subsample above the median *AV*. I conduct a Wilcoxon signed-rank test of equality of median *CARs* of the two subsamples in the row denominated 'Below median-above median'. In the row 'Low tercile-high tercile' I conduct a similar test, but I divide the sample into terciles. The numbers shown in panel A are differences of the median *CARs* of the two subsamples and low minus high terciles, respectively. In panel B, I show coefficients and adjusted R^2 values for a univariate regression, where the dependent variable is the cumulative abnormal return of a firm for different event windows and the independent variable is the abnormal trading volume. ***, **, * denote a significance-level of 1%, 5% and 10%, respectively.

Panel A: Differences in medians

Event window	*[-1;0]*	*[0;+1]*	*[-1;+1]*
Below median - above median	0.49%	0.45%	0.23%
Low tercile - high tercile	0.96%	2.05% **	-0.35%

Panel B: Univariate regression

Event window	*[-1;0]*	*[0;+1]*	*[-1;+1]*
Coefficient	0.00	-3.77	0.00
Adjusted R^2	-2.0%	-2.0%	-2.0%

4.2.2 *Market timing*

4.2.2.1 Time-varying costs of adverse selection

This section contains further tests that characterize the role of asymmetric information in exchangeable debt issues. First, time-varying costs of adverse selection are examined. Bayless/Chaplinski (1996) show that announcement returns are less negative during periods of reduced adverse selection costs, for example after many firms release earnings figures.[384] The issue activity is measured by a forecast model for the number of security offerings in a given quarter.

The results of this analysis are shown in table VI.11. No relation between abnormal returns and the degree of adverse selection costs can be detected. Hypothesis 6 postulates a negative relationship and has to be rejected. If managers of issuing firms do not care to issue exchangeable bonds during periods of reduced adverse selection, it is likely that they do not consider information costs to be material in the offering. This, in turn, supports the notion that managers do not issue securities when they consider them to be overvalued, which suggests that negative information is not the primary reason for the market's adverse response. This points to the agency-hypothesis to explain abnormal returns.

[384] See Bayless/Chaplinsky (1996), p. 253 ff.

Table VI.11: Univariate analysis of time-varying adverse selection costs

This table contains a univariate analysis of cumulative abnormal returns for different event windows. Panel A calculates differences in medians. I rank the sample in ascending order according to a transaction's *ISSUES* value. I then form two subsamples, where the first subsample has values of *ISSUES* below the median *ISSUES* and the second subsample above the median *ISSUES*. I conduct a Wilcoxon signed-rank test of equality of median *CARs* of the two subsamples in the row denominated 'Below median-above median'. In the row 'Low tercile-high tercile' I conduct a similar test, but I divide the sample into terciles. The numbers shown in panel A are differences of the median *CARs* of the two subsamples and low minus high terciles, respectively. In panel B, I show coefficients and adjusted R^2 values for a univariate regression, where the dependent variable is the cumulative abnormal return of a firm for different event windows and the independent variable is *ISSUES*. ***, **, * denote a significance-level of 1%, 5% and 10%, respectively.

Panel A: Differences in medians

Event window	*[-1;0]*	*[0;+1]*	*[-1;+1]*
Below median - above median	0.91%	0.34%	2.02%
Low tercile - high tercile	1.16%	-0.68%	0.80%

Panel B: Univariate regression

Event window	*[-1;0]*	*[0;+1]*	*[-1;+1]*
Coefficient	0.00	0.00	0.00
Adjusted R^2	-2.0%	0.0%	-1.0%

4.2.2.2 Valuation level

Market timing implies that securities are issued when they achieve high prices. This strategy has been found to have a major impact on the managerial decision to issue equity and equity-linked securities in the US.[385] However, whether this form of market timing is important in Western European exchangeable debt issues depends on the issue motive: if a manager decides to issue an exchangeable bond during a phase where the exchange stock is overvalued, the newly issued securities will achieve higher prices. When the stock price reverts to its fair value during the post-issue period, exchange becomes unlikely. To this end, issuing exchangeable debt during a period where the underlying stock is overvalued means issuing debt 'sweetened' with an exchange option.

A preliminary analysis on the basis of press statements distributed to announce the transaction shows that managers of issuing firms appear to pursue the divestment of a stock contained in their portfolio.

Further evidence on the issue motive is provided by an analysis that aims to determine whether exchange stocks are overvalued at issuance. Studies of market timing calculate pre- and post-issue abnormal stock returns to assess whether overvaluation may motivate security

[385] See Loughran/Ritter (1995), p. 23 ff., Loughran/Ritter (1997), p. 1823 ff., Danielova (2003), p. 1 ff., Danielova/Smart/Boquist (2004), p. 1 ff. and the discussion in chapter III.

issues. If so, these studies document significantly positive abnormal returns prior to the offering and significantly negative abnormal returns during a post-issue period of up to five years.[386]

Table VI.12: Pre- and post-issue abnormal returns

This table shows pre- and post-issue abnormal stock returns for exchange companies. *RUNUP* is the net-of-the-market buy-and-hold return for the year preceding the issue. 1-year *BHAR* is an abnormal buy-and-hold return for the year following and 3-year *BHAR* for the three years following the issue. Market adjustments are conducted using the largest national indices. Matching firms are drawn from a universe of firms in the same industry and within a market value range of 25% to 200% of the exchange firm's size. From this universe, the firm with the closest market value to the exchange firm's market value is the matching firm. Test statistics are skewness-adjusted t-tests as described in section 5.1.1 of chapter IV. ***, **, * denote a significance-level of 1%, 5% and 10%, respectively.

	Market-adjusted		**Matching firm-adjusted**	
Event window	***Mean***	***Median***	***Mean***	***Median***
RUNUP	13.47% ***	7.74% ***	1.83%	-3.03%
1-year BHAR	-0.04%	-3.16%	-2.45%	2.43%
3-year BHAR	0.01%	-3.61%	2.59%	3.41%

Table VI.12 shows that mean and median buy-and-hold market-adjusted returns preceding the issue (*RUNUP*) are significantly positive. However, an average pre-issue share price runup of 13.47% is relatively low compared to other studies, which document average share price appreciations of 93.1% during the year preceding equity offerings and of 55.8% preceding convertible debt issues.[387] When the matching firm-adjusted returns are considered, no abnormal returns can be detected at all.

According to the market timing-hypothesis, issuing a security after marginally positive share price increases would be a very uncommon behaviour. In fact, exchangeable debt issues appear not to be timed with periods of high valuation. This notion is supported by 1- and 3-year post-issue stock returns that are not abnormally low, which indicates that the exchange stocks are not overvalued at issuance: Danielova/Smart/Boquist (2004) document an average market-adjusted return of –32% for the year following the offering whereas mine is –0.04%.[388]

---

[386] See Loughran/Ritter (1995), p. 23 ff.; Spiess/Affleck-Graves (1995), p. 243 ff.; Loughran/Ritter (1997), p. 1823 ff.; Spiess/Affleck-Graves (1999), p. 45 ff.

[387] See Loughran/Ritter (1997), p. 1840; Lewis/Rogalski/Seward (2001), p. 460.

[388] See Danielova/Smart/Boquist (2004), p. 22. I lose twenty observations when computing 3-year *BHARs* due to the unavailability of stock price data for more recent transactions.

Table VI.13 examines the relationship between *RUNUP* and announcement returns. If, as I argue, exchangeable debt issues are not timed with periods of high valuation levels, it is unlikely that investor reactions show systematic patterns according to the pre-issue share price runup.

Table VI.13: Univariate analysis of pre-issue share price runup

This table contains a univariate analysis of cumulative abnormal returns for different event windows. Panel A calculates differences in medians. I rank the sample in ascending order according to a transaction's pre-issue share price runup. I then form two subsamples, where the first subsample has values of *RUNUP* below the median *RUNUP* and the second subsample above the median *RUNUP*. I conduct a Wilcoxon signed-rank test of equality of median *CARs* of the two subsamples in the row denominated 'Below median-above median'. In the row 'Low tercile-high tercile' I conduct a similar test, but I divide the sample into terciles. The numbers shown in panel A are differences of the median *CARs* of the two subsamples and low minus high terciles, respectively. In panel B, I show coefficients and adjusted R^2 values for a univariate regression, where the dependent variable is the cumulative abnormal return of a firm for different event windows and the independent variable is the pre-issue share price runup. ***, **, * denote a significance-level of 1%, 5% and 10%, respectively.

Panel A: Differences in medians

Event window	***[-1;0]***	***[0;+1]***	***[-1;+1]***
Below median - above median	0.00%	0.37%	-0.30%
Low tercile - high tercile	0.26%	0.48%	-0.51%

Panel B: Univariate regression

Event window	***[-1;0]***	***[0;+1]***	***[-1;+1]***
Coefficient	-0.01	-0.01	-0.01
Adjusted R^2	0.0%	-1.0%	-1.0%

This interpretation is confirmed in table VI.13, which shows no significant relation between *RUNUP* and *CARs*. It receives further support by table VI.14, which documents insignificant relationships between *MTB* and *PE*, respectively, and *CARs*. To this end, hypothesis 7 has to be rejected. That market timing is not a determinant in the decision to issue exchangeable bonds in Europe appears consistent with the previous arguments and results.

Table VI.14: Univariate analysis of valuation level

This table contains a univariate analysis of cumulative abnormal returns for different event windows. Panel A calculates differences in medians. I rank the sample in ascending order according to a transaction's market-to-book ratio. I then form two subsamples, where the first subsample has values of *MTB* below the median *MTB* and the second subsample above the median *MTB*. I conduct a Wilcoxon signed-rank test of equality of median *CARs* of the two subsamples in the row denominated 'Below median-above median'. In the row 'Low tercile-high tercile' I conduct a similar test, but I divide the sample into terciles. The numbers shown in panel A are differences of the median *CARs* of the two subsamples and low minus high terciles, respectively. In panel B, I show coefficients and adjusted R^2 values for a univariate regression, where the dependent variable is the cumulative abnormal return of a firm for different event windows and the independent variable is the market-to-book ratio. Panel C and D repeat the analysis for the price-earnings ratio (*PE*). ***, **, * denote a significance-level of 1%, 5% and 10% respectively.

Panel A: Differences in medians (*MTB*)

Event window	*[-1;0]*	*[0;+1]*	*[-1;+1]*
Below median - above median	-0.19%	0.19%	-0.22%
Low tercile - high tercile	-0.16%	-0.33%	-0.42%

Panel B: Univariate regression (*MTB*)

Event window	*[-1;0]*	*[0;+1]*	*[-1;+1]*
Coefficient	0.00	0.00	0.00
Adjusted R^2	-1.0%	0.0%	-1.0%

Panel C: Differences in medians (*PE*)

Event window	*[-1;0]*	*[0;+1]*	*[-1;+1]*
Below median - above median	-0.53%	-0.87%	-0.37%
Low tercile - high tercile	0.58%	-1.08%	1.37%

Panel D: Univariate regression (*PE*)

Event window	*[-1;0]*	*[0;+1]*	*[-1;+1]*
Coefficient	0.00	0.00	0.00
Adjusted R^2	-2.0%	-2.0%	0.0%

4.2.3 Multivariate analysis of announcement returns

The evidence provided by the univariate analysis of announcement returns of Western European exchangeable bond issues suggests that these securities are used by firms to divest equity holdings. To assess whether this result holds in a multivariate context, I use an OLS-regression model to examine the joint effect of proxy variables on *CARs* for the event window [-1;0].[389] The results of different model specifications are shown in table VI.15.[390]

---

[389] The variable *EXPROB*, the exchange probability, is not included in the analysis, since data items for a lot of observations were unavailable.

[390] Here, I also control for the liquidity of the exchange stock to ensure that I do not detect significant coefficients for the abnormal trading volume due to illiquidity of exchange stocks, which may overstate the

Generally, I find the conclusions of the univariate analysis confirmed in a multivariate context, where I also control for country-specific effects. The relative issue size is significant across all model specifications. Its negative relation to cumulative abnormal returns points to the agency-hypothesis as the explanation for negative announcement returns.

Dummy variables, which are used to capture country-specific effects are partly significant and positive. The dummy *FINANCE* takes the value one, if the issuer is a financial institution. In particular, it allows to capture the effect of transactions, which are motivated financially.[391]

Regression 1 shows a model that includes the proxy for time-varying costs of adverse selection (*ISSUES*). It confirms that *ISSUES* is not related to announcement returns, which is inconsistent with the information-hypothesis. Regression 2 drops *ISSUES* and includes *RUNUP*, the pre-issue stock price runup of the exchange firm. The regression model appears misspecified, given a low adjusted R^2 value and F-test statistic. In contrast, adjusted R^2 values are unusually high in regressions 1, 3 and 4. These values are largely driven by *RIS*, which is strongly correlated with abnormal returns (the Pearson coefficient is -0.40). If regression models 1, 3 and 4 are estimated without *RIS*, adjusted R^2 values drop by 50%.

Regression 3 and 4 include the market-to-book ratio and the price-earnings ratio. Their coefficients are both negative and significant at the 5%-level. This result is unexpected, since neither *MTB* nor *PE* have shown a significant relation to abnormal returns in the univariate analysis. The coefficients only become significant when country-specific effects are controlled for. The previous evidence suggests that these ratios should rather be interpreted as measures for the quality of a firm's investment opportunity set in the context of this analysis, since exchange stocks do not appear to be overvalued at issuance of the bonds. In this case, the negative coefficients would be consistent with the agency-hypothesis: higher valuation levels may imply positive expected future returns, when valuable investment projects pay off. This increases the probability that bonds are exchanged, which dilutes the ownership concentration of the target firms and may cause announcement returns to be negative.

abnormal trading volume around the announcement of an exchangeable bond issue. The negative coefficient of *LIQU*, however, suggests that stocks that are traded more prior to the transaction have lower returns.

391 Danielova/Smart/Boquist (2004), p. 1 ff. show that issuers that sell overvalued equity call options in combination with bonds often have several equity stakes in their portfolios. They tend to write the call options on the particular stake that appears to be most overvalued around the time of the issue. Since financial firms typically possess larger portfolios including various equity stakes, they may be more likely to follow a market timing-strategy for exchangeable debt issuance than industrial firms. However, since the dummy *FINANCE* is not significant, this notion is not supported by the data.

Table VI.15: Multivariate analysis of announcement returns

This table shows results of an OLS-regression analysis. The dependent variable are *CARs* for [-1;0]. The independent variables are: *RIS* is the relative issue size. *RUNUP* is the cumulative market-adjusted return during [-250;-6]. *MTB* is the market-to-book ratio. *PE* is the price-earnings ratio. *ISSUES* is a measure for time-varying adverse selection costs. *AV* is the abnormal trading volume measured as ratio from observed trading volume and average trading volume over during [-200;-11]. *LIQU* is used to control for the liquidity of the exchange stock. It is measured as the natural logarithm of the average trading volume during [-200;-11]. Dummy variables capture country-specific effects. *F* denotes France, *GER* Germany, *I* Italy, *A* Austria, *CH* Switzerland and *UK* the United Kingdom. The dummy *FINANCE* takes the value one when the issuer is a financial institution. The last four rows contain statistics to control for the validity and explanatory power of the regression model. In this table, I show regression results for the complete sample. I recompute the regressions using the portfolio-approach and find the results largely unchanged. ***, **, * denote a significance-level of 1%, 5% and 10%, respectively.

	1	2	3	4
Constant	0.01	0.01	0.02	0.03
RIS	-0.13 ***	-0.10 *	-0.13 ***	-0.14 ***
RUNUP		-0.02		
MTB [a)]			-0.03 **	
PE [a)]				-0.02 **
ISSUES	0.00			
AV [a)]	0.07	-0.01	0.01	-0.01
LIQU	-0.01 *	-0.01 *	-0.01 **	-0.01 **
Dum F	0.03 *	0.03 *	0.03 *	0.04 **
Dum GER	0.00	0.01	0.00	0.00
Dum I	0.04	0.06 *	0.05 **	0.04
Dum A	0.02	0.03	0.02	0.02
Dum CH	0.03	0.03	0.03	0.04 *
Dum UK	0.05 **	0.05 **	0.07 ***	0.05 **
Dum FINANCE	0.01	0.01	0.01	0.00
Adj. R^2	25.6%	10.9%	35.8%	33.9%
F-Test	[2.25] **	[1.42]	[3.03] ***	[2.87] **
White (p-Wert)	0.58	0.75	0.32	0.42
JB Residuen	0.71	0.32	0.54	0.24

[a)] The coefficients are multiplied with 100.

The White-test controls for homoskedasticity of regression residuals. Jarque-Bera tests are included to control for the distributional properties of the residuals. Both tests do not indicate a violation of the assumptions of the OLS-regression model. To control for cross-sectional dependence, all regressions have been re-computed using the portfolio approach. The results are unaltered.

The multivariate analysis supports the agency-hypothesis as an explanation for negative announcement effects: the *RIS* variable is the single-most influential variable in the multivariate analysis and explains a significant portion of the cross-sectional variation in *CARs*. I find that the typical exchange stock is on average not overvalued, given that the pre-issue return is only marginally significant and it does not underperform in a three-year period that follows the transaction. While each indication for itself leaves room for several interpretations, the complete picture provided by the analyses favours the agency-hypothesis to explain adverse announcement returns: stock price reactions to the announcement of exchangeable bond issues are more negative, the more important the role of the issuing firm is in the governance process of the exchange firm and the more the capital market expects that the issuer will not be able to play this role in future.

4.3 Mandatory exchangeables

It appears likely that the valuation impact of direct secondary distributions examined by Mikkelson/Partch (1995) is a manifestation of two effects: on the one hand, the ownership concentration of the target firm is reduced. On the other hand, negative information is conveyed by the offering. Announcement returns to exchangeable debt issues may be less negative, because adverse information effects are hardly pronounced for this divestment strategy.

If this interpretation is correct, mandatory exchangeables, which essentially represent forward sales of the exchange stock, have interesting implications for the role of informational asymmetries: an ordinary exchangeable bond will be exchanged when the price of the target stock exceeds the exchange price. If a firm wants to divest an equity stake it has in a third firm, exchangeable bonds do not appear to be the best exit strategy, if the issuer expects the future performance of the exchange firm to be poor. In this case, the issuer would be better-off to directly sell its stake. Or it issues a mandatory exchangeable, where exchange is not contingent upon the exchange stock's post-issue performance, but occurs automatically.

Consistent with the notion that mandatory exchangeables convey negative information, table VI.16 illustrates that stock price reactions to the three mandatory exchangeable bond issues are lower than for ordinary exchangeable bonds: the average announcement return is –4.47%. While this is no conclusive statistical evidence, this highly adverse return suggests that investors not only infer a reduction of the ownership concentration from the announcement of mandatory exchangeable, but also an issuer's negative information about the prospects of the exchange firm.

Table VI.16: Mandatory exchangeables

	Mandatory exchangeables (N = 3)		Ordinary exchangeables (N = 54)	
Variable	*Mean*	*Median*	*Mean*	*Median*
CAR [-1;0]	-4.47%	-4.55%	-1.35%	-1.25%
CAR [0;+1]	-3.97%	-3.76%	-1.75%	-1.94%
CAR [-1;+1]	-4.64%	-3.33%	-1.67%	-1.93%
Coupon	5.75%	6.00%	2.19%	1.75%
Exchange premium	31.00%	31.00%	29.10%	27.10%
RIS	15.67%	16.60%	12.18%	7.33%
RUNUP	-16.90%	-11.63%	10.55%	4.75%
MTB	3.30	3.30	3.97	2.72
PE	30.21	23.13	65.23	47.51

The low values of *RUNUP*, *MTB* and *PE* may serve as indicators that the exchange firms' prospects are evaluated pessimistically by investors already prior to the offering. A similar argument is put forward by Kleidt/Schiereck (2004) in a study of Western European mandatory convertibles, which have a highly adverse valuation impact due to their negative informational content as well.[392]

5 *Conclusion*

The primary objective of this paper was to examine why Western European firms decide to issue exchangeable debt and explain the market response to this decision.

For a sample of 57 Western European exchangeable bond issues that occurred during 1997 and 2003, I conduct a press research to assess the issuers' transaction motives, analyze the magnitude and cross-sectional variation of announcement returns and calculate pre- and post-issue stock returns for exchange companies.

The analyses show that exchangeable debt issued by Western European firms is used to divest equity stakes. Exchangeable debt appears to be a more optimal divestment strategy, because transaction fees and adverse announcement returns are less pronounced (-1.57% on average on the announcement day) than those associated with other forms of secondary offerings that disperse concentrated share blocks.

[392] See Kleidt/Schiereck (2004), p. 18 ff. See also Koziol/Sauerbier (2003), p. 21 ff. for a discussion of mandatory convertibles.

The negative stock price effect can be explained by the offer's potential to reduce the ownership concentration of the exchange firm. A large blockholder increases the efficacy of monitoring and may facilitate changes in corporate control. When the block is dispersed, monitoring costs and residual losses from agency conflicts are likely to increase for the remaining stockholders, which reduces the value of their claim.

I do not find evidence that exchangeable bonds convey an issuer's negative information to outside investors as long as the exchangeable is used to divest an equity stake. If an issuer had concerns about the future stock price performance of an exchange firm, it would not make the divestment contingent upon its performance. Consistent with this interpretation, exchange stocks do not appear to be overvalued at issuance, since they do not underperform during a post-issue period of three years.

VII Conclusions and outlook

The purpose of this investigation was to explain the use and performance impact of hybrid securities issued by US and Western European firms. A contribution to existing literature was made for three forms of hybrid securities: convertible debt (*objective 1*), concurrent offerings of convertible securities and common stock (*objective 2*) and exchangeable debt (*objective 3*).

The results of this investigation can be summarized as follows:

Objective 1:

The central explanation put forward for the use of convertible debt consists in a market timing-hypothesis. It suggests that managers choose to issue convertible debt to benefit from temporary periods of overvaluation of their firm's common stock. The timing-hypothesis is tested using a sample of 437 convertible debt and equity transactions that occur during 2000 through 2002. It receives strong support by the data: convertible debt, as well as common stock, is issued after large share price increases by firms that have unusually high market-to-book ratios. After the issue, earnings and stock prices significantly decline. The decline is more pronounced for firms that have had stronger stock price appreciations prior to the offering. All in all, these findings suggest that the issuer's common stock is overvalued around the time of the transaction.

The implication of this interpretation is that convertible debt is used as a cheaper substitute for straight debt. The transitory mispricing of common stock spills over into a pricing gap of the conversion option, which allows managers to reduce interest costs below the levels that would be payable in straight debt issues. It is supported by the fact that issuing firms have unused debt capacity, whereas equity issuers have no room for further debt issues.

Apart from this sample-specific evidence, market timing appears to be a powerful explanation for the use of convertible debt in general. It is consistent with different lines of research, in particular with (i) survey evidence reporting that managers consider the valuation level to be an important consideration in convertible debt issues, (ii) research that documents increases in insider selling prior to convertible debt issues, and (iii) the observation that issuance volumes in convertible debt and equity markets are high at similar times. Hence, although a 'cheap debt'-argument for convertible debt issuance may be particularly relevant for transactions in times when overall market returns are lower, timing considerations appear to have some explanatory power for the convertible debt issue decision in general.

Apart from timing, the evidence is supportive for a rationing-hypothesis that argues that some firms may be foreclosed from participation in the market for seasoned equity due to uncertainty about their risk characteristics. If investors are risk averse or anticipate an adverse change in the cost of equity capital of an issuing firm that may not be adequately compensated with higher returns, they may be unwilling to provide a firm with equity funds. However, investors may grant a firm contingent access to external capital via convertible debt: the advantage of this security is that it allows investors to screen the issuer until conversion may occur. During the screening period, investors are protected from changes in firm risk, because the value of convertible debt is largely unaffected by an issuer's risk.

Objective 2:

Concurrent offerings, where firms issue convertible securities alongside common stock, have been used during the first years of this millennium by US corporations to raise well over 70 billion USD. To explain the use and valuation impact of concurrent offerings, I examine a signaling-hypothesis, which argues that issuing firms intend to trade off adverse selection against financial distress costs to reduce the mispricing of newly issued securities in the capital market.

I document important differences in firm characteristics and investor reactions for companies conducting concurrent offerings according to the nature of the conversion feature attached to the convertible security. Firms using mandatory convertibles alongside common stock are firms facing low adverse selection and high financial distress costs. These characteristics and abnormal return patterns around and after the transactions are consistent with the signaling-hypothesis for this form of concurrent offering. Firms using ordinary convertible securities alongside common stock (OCF concurrent offerings) are evaluated by the capital market like companies with attractive growth opportunities. Yet the valuation impact of the transaction announcement amounts to –7%. After the offering, one third of OCF firms are delisted and the market value is nearly halved for the survivors. Apart from a signaling-, I discuss a timing- and a rationing-hypotheses to explain the documented patterns, but the empirical observations remain a puzzle, which I lay in the hands of future research.

Objective 3:

Exchangeable debt bears structural resemblance to convertible debt, but can be exchanged into stock of a third firm. In Western European countries, the trend to issue exchangeable debt has become increasingly pervasive during the last couple of years. In fact, Western European markets for exchangeable debt are larger than the US market. However, research on the exchangeable debt issue decision is only available for US firms and provides controversial evidence on the use of this type of hybrid security. An analysis of 57 transactions that occurred from 1997 to 2003 shall therefore determine why Western European firms decide to issue exchangeable debt and how capital markets respond to this decision. The results show that exchangeable debt is a divestment strategy, which appears attractive due to lower transaction costs and higher announcement returns in comparison to other forms of secondary distributions that disperse concentrated share blocks. The negative valuation impact can be explained by the offer's potential to reduce the efficacy of the stockholders' ability to monitor the management of the exchange company. The evidence does not support the notion that Western European firms use exchangeable debt to sell an overvalued exchange option to investors allowing them to obtain cheap debt.

The results of this investigation yield new insights in the financing behaviour of firms. They contribute to the existing empirical finance literature that examines why and how firms use hybrid securities, how the use impacts the operating performance and how the market evaluates the issue decision.

Not surprisingly, the analyses also raise new questions and identify several aspects, which should be addressed by future research. First, the finding that market timing-strategies in security issues extend to a broader range of financing instruments than previously suspected has to be backed up by further research. This research should extent the scope of the analysis to longer and more recent time periods. In this analysis, it is important to determine how market timing in convertible debt issues affects firm performance across the business cycle. In particular, research should evaluate whether the sale of overvalued convertible debt can be used by issuers to obtain equity capital, when general market conditions are favourable. It should also evaluate whether timing-efforts of convertible debt issuers extend to the firms' pre-issue earnings performance.

Second, research is in order that further analyzes why and in what situations investors ration issuing firms out of the market for seasoned equity. Different performance patterns of firms prior and following the issue suggest that different investor groups have different beliefs about a firm's intrinsic value. Or they have different possibilities to generate positive returns from their investments. Therefore, future research should determine how risk aversion affects investment decisions in common stock issues. Especially, further research on concurrent offerings may be fruitful to examine how investors decide about the allocation of their funds. Moreover, convertible arbitrage strategies should be analyzed with regard to their potential to generate positive returns for the investor as well as to their potential to impact a firm's stock price performance in the shorter- and longer-run.

Third, evidence is needed to explain differences in the use of hybrid securities by Western European and US firms. While Western European firms use exchangeable debt to restructure their assets, a lot of US firms apparently regard it as a cheaper substitute for straight debt. Given this disparity, it is necessary to examine the market timing-behaviour of European firms in hybrid security issues in general. Recent survey evidence by Bancel/Mittoo (2004) indicates that European financial managers consider market timing an important consideration in convertible debt issues.[393] Dutordoir/Van de Gucht (2004) suggest that this market timing behaviour has a negative effect on stockholder reactions to convertible debt announcements.[394] The consequences this behaviour has on firm performance in the longer-run are yet to document.

In sum, this investigation shows that market timing, investor rationing, signaling and asset restructuring may motivate hybrid security issue decisions. Which explanation applies cannot be determined per se: different institutional settings make a one-dimensional explanation of hybrid security issues impossible. Hence, a very important insight is that the use of hybrid securities is as diverse as available structures for this class of financing instrument. Even if these structures bear resemblance, their use and valuation impact cannot be explained without specific reference to the issue motive as well as to transaction-, firm- and market-specific circumstances surrounding the offering.

---

393 See Bancel/Mittoo (2003), p. 350.

394 See Dutordoir/Van de Gucht (2004), p. 42.

Bibliography

Achleitner, Ann-Kristin (2001): Handbuch Investment Banking, 2nd edition, Gabler Verlag, Wiesbaden.

Ali, Ashiq (1997): Bias in Analysts' Earnings Forecasts as an Explanation for the Long-Run Underperformance of Stocks Following Equity Offerings, Working Paper, University of Arizona.

Altman, Edward I. (1968): Financial Ratios, Discriminant Analysis and the Prediction of Corporate Bankruptcy, in: Journal of Finance, Vol. 23, 589-609.

Amihud, Yakov/ Li, Kefei (2004): The Declining Information Content of Dividend Announcements and the Effects of Institutional Investors, Working Paper, New York University.

Ammann, Manuel/ Fehr, Martin/ Seiz, Ralf (2004): New Evidence on the Announcement Effect of Convertible and Exchangeable Bonds, Working Paper, University of St. Gallen.

Ammann, Manuel/ Kind, Axel/ Wilde, Christian (2003): Are Convertible Bonds Underpriced? An Analysis of the French Market, in: Journal of Banking and Finance, Vol. 27, 635-653.

Armitage, Seth (1995): Event Study Methods and Evidence on their Performance, in: Journal of Economic Surveys, Vol. 9, 25-52.

Arzac, Enrique R. (1997): PERCs, DECs, and Other Mandatory Convertibles, in: Journal of Applied Corporate Finance, Vol. 10, 54-63.

Asquith, Paul (1995): Convertible Bonds Are Not Called Late, in: Journal of Finance, Vol. 50, 1275-89.

Asquith, Paul/ Mullins, David W. Jr. (1986): Equity Issues and Offering Dilution, in: Journal of Financial Economics, Vol. 15, 61-89.

Baker, Malcolm/ Wurgler, Jeffrey (2002): Market Timing and Capital Structure, in: Journal of Finance, Vol. 57, 1-32.

Bancel, Franck/ Mittoo, Usha R. (2003): Why Do European Firms Issue Convertible Debt?, in: European Financial Management, Vol. 10, 339-373.

Banerjee, Saugata/ Leleux, Benoit/ Vermaelen, Theo (1997): Large Shareholdings and Corporate Control: An Analysis of Stake Purchases by French Holding Companies, in: European Financial Management, Vol. 3, 23-43.

Barber, Brad M. (1993): Exchangeable Debt, in: Financial Management, Vol. 22, 48-60.

Barber, Brad M./ Lyon, John (1996): Detecting Abnormal Operating Performance: The Empirical Power and Specification of Test Statistics, in: Journal of Financial Economics, Vol. 41, 359-399.

Barber, Brad M./ Lyon, John (1997): Detecting Long-Run Abnormal Stock Returns: The Empirical Power and Specifications of Test Statistics, in: Journal of Financial Economics, Vol. 43, 341-372.

Barclay, Michael J./ Holderness, Clifford G. (1991): Negotiated Block Trades and Corporate Control, in: Journal of Finance, Vol. 46, 861-878.

Bayless, Mark/ Chaplinsky, Susan (1991): Expectations of Security Type and the Information Content of Debt and Equity Offers, in: Journal of Financial Intermediation, Vol. 1, 195-214.

Bayless, Mark/ Chaplinsky, Susan (1996): Is There a Window of Opportunity for Seasoned Equity Issuance?, in: Journal of Finance, Vol. 51, 253-278.

Bechmann, Ken L. (2004): Short Sales, Price Pressure, and the Stock Price Response to Convertible Bond Calls, in: Journal of Financial Markets, Vol. 7, 421-451.

Bernard, Victor L. (1987): Cross-Sectional Dependence and Problems in Inference in Market-Based Accounting Research, in: Journal of Accounting Research, Vol. 25, 2-48.

Billingsley, Randall S./ Lamy, Robert E./ Thompson, Rodney G. (1988): The Choice Among Debt, Equity, and Convertible Bonds, in: Journal of Financial Research, Vol. 11, 43-55.

Billingsley, Randall S./ Smith, David M. (1996): Why Do Firms Issue Convertible Debt?, in: Financial Management, Vol. 25, 93-99.

Binder, John J. (1985): On the Use of the Multivariate Regression Model in Event Studies, in: Journal of Accounting Research, Vol. 23, 370-383.

Black, Fischer/ Scholes, Myron S. (1973): The Pricing of Options and Corporate Liabilities, in: Journal of Political Economy, Vol. 81, 637-654.

Boehmer, Ekkehart/ Musumeci, Jim/ Poulsen, Annette B. (1991): Event-Study Methodology under Conditions of Event-Induced Variance, in: Journal of Financial Economics, Vol. 30, 253-272.

Brav, Alon/ Geczy, Christopher/ Gompers, Paul A. (2000): Is the Abnormal Return Following Equity Issuances Anomalous?, in: Journal of Financial Economics, Vol. 56, 209-249.

Brav, Alon/ Gompers, Paul A. (1997): Myth or Reality? The Long-Run Underperformance of Initial Public Offerings: Evidence from Venture and Nonventure Capital-Backed Companies, in: Journal of Finance, Vol. 52, 1791-1821.

Brealey, Richard A./ Myers, Stewart C. (2000): Principles of Corporate Finance, 6th edition, McGraw-Hill, Boston.

Brennan, Michael J./ Kraus, Alan (1987): Efficient Financing under Asymmetric Information, in: Journal of Finance, Vol. 42, 1225-1243.

Brennan, Michael J./ Schwartz, Eduardo S. (1977): Convertible Bonds: Valuation and Optimal Strategies for Call and Conversion, in: Journal of Finance, Vol. 32, 1699-1715.

Brennan, Michael J./ Schwartz, Eduardo S. (1988): The Case for Convertibles, in: Journal of Applied Corporate Finance, Vol. 1, 55-64.

Brown, Stephen J./ Warner, Jerold B. (1980): Measuring Security Price Performance, in: Journal of Financial Economics, Vol. 8, 205-258.

Brown, Stephen J./ Warner, Jerold B. (1985): Using Daily Stock Returns: The Case of Event Studies, in: Journal of Financial Economics, Vol. 14, 3-31.

Bühler, Wolfgang/ Koziol, Christian (2002): Valuation of Convertible Bonds with Sequential Conversion, in: Schmalenbach Business Review, Vol. 54, 302-334.

Bundesministerium der Finanzen (2000): Steuerreform 2000: Steuerfreiheit von Dividenden und Beteiligungsveräußerungen bei Kapitalgesellschaften, <http://www.bundesfinanz-ministerium.de/Aktuelles/Neue/Weite-Veroeffentlichungen-.393.12228/PureHtml/.htm>, 15.01.2004.

Burkart, Mike/ Gromb, Denis/ Panunzi, Fausto (2000): Agency Conflicts in Public and Negotiated Transfers of Corporate Control, in: Journal of Finance, Vol. 55, 647-677.

Byoun, Soku/ Moore, William T. (2003): Stock vs. Stock-Warrant Units: Evidence from Seasoned Equity Offerings, in: Journal of Corporate Finance, Vol. 9, 575-590.

Calamos, John P. (1998): Convertible Securities: The Latest Instruments, Portfolio Strategies, and Valuation Analysis, Revised edition, McGraw-Hill, New York.

Campbell, John Y./ Lo, Andrew W./ MacKinlay, Craig A. (1997): The Econometrics of Financial Markets, Princeton University Press, Princeton.

Carhart, Mark M. (1997): On Persistence in Mutual Fund Performance, in: Journal of Finance, Vol. 52, 57-82.

Chemmanur, Thomas J./ Fulghieri, Paolo (1997): Why Include Warrants in New Equity Issues? A Theory of Unit IPOs, in: Journal of Financial and Quantitative Analysis, Vol. 32, 1-24.

Chemmanur, Thomas J./ Nandy, Debarashi K./ Yan, An (2003): Why Issue Mandatory Convertibles? Theory and Empirical Evidence, Working Paper, Boston College.

Choe, Hyuk/ Masulis, Ronald W./ Nanda, Vikram (1993): Common Stock Offerings Across the Business Cycle: Theory and Evidence, in: Journal of Empirical Finance, Vol.1, 3-31.

Constantinides, George M./ Grundy, Bruce D. (1989): Optimal Investment with Stock Repurchase and Financing as Signals, in: Review of Financial Studies, Vol. 2, 445-466.

Copeland, Thomas E./ Weston, Fred J. (1992): Financial Theory and Corporate Policy, 3rd edition, Addison-Wesley Publishing Company, Reading.

Corrado, Charles J. (1989): A Non-Parametric Test for Abnormal Security-Price Performance in Event Studies, in: Journal of Financial Economics, Vol. 23, 385-395.

Damodaran, Aswath (1996): Investment Valuation, John Wiley & Sons, New York.

Danielova, Anna (2003): When Do Firms Issue Exchangeable Debt?, Working Paper, Indiana University.

Danielova, Anna/ Smart, Scott B. / Boquist, John (2004): Deciphering the Motives for Exchangeable Debt Offerings, Working Paper, McMaster University.

Dann, Larry Y./ Mikkelson, Wayne H. (1984): Convertible Debt Issuance, Capital Structure Change and Financing-Related Information: Some New Evidence, in: Journal of Financial Economics, Vol. 13, 157-186.

De Bondt, W./ Thaler, Richard (1985): Does the Stock Market Overreact?, in: Journal of Finance, Vol. 40, 793-808.

De Bondt, W./ Thaler, Richard (1987): Further Evidence on Investor Overreaction and Stock Market Seasonality, in: Journal of Finance, Vol. 42, 557-581.

De Roon, Frans/ Veld, Chris (1998): Announcement Effects of Convertible Bond Loans and Warrant-Bond Loans: An Empirical Analysis for the Dutch Market, in: Journal of Banking and Finance, Vol. 22, 1481-1506.

Denis, David J./ Kadlec, Gregory B. (1994): Corporate Events, Trading Activity, and the Estimation of Systematic Risk: Evidence from Equity Offerings and Share Repurchases, in: Journal of Finance, Vol. 49, 1787-1811.

Dimson, Elroy (1979): Risk Measurement When Shares Are Subject To Infrequent Trading, in: Journal of Financial Economics, Vol. 7, 129-226.

D'Mello, Ranjan/ Ferris, Stephen P. (2000): The Information Effects of Analyst Activity at the Announcement of New Equity Issues, in: Financial Management, Vol. 29, 78-95.

Dutordoir, Marie/ Van de Gucht, Linda M. (2004): Determinants of Stockholder Reactions to Convertible Debt Offering Announcements: An Analysis of the Western European Market, Working Paper, K. U. Leuven.

Dyck, Alexander/ Zingales, Luigi (2004): Private Benefits of Control: An International Comparison, in: Journal of Finance, Vol. 59, 537-600.

Dyckman, Thomas/ Philbrick, Donna/ Stephan, Jens (1984): A Comparison of Event Study Methodologies Using Daily Stock Returns: A Simulation Approach, in: Journal of Accounting Research, Vol. 22, 1-29.

Eckbo, Espen B./ Masulis, Ronald W. (1995): Seasoned Equity Offerings: A Survey, in: Jarrow, R. et al. (Editors), Handbooks in Operations Research and Management Science, Finance, Elsevier Science, Amsterdam, 1017-1072.

Entrup, Ulrich (1995): Kapitalmarktreaktionen auf Optionsanleihen, Gabler Verlag, Wiesbaden.

Essig, Stuart M. (1992): Convertible Securities and Capital Structure Determinants, Unpublished Ph. D. Thesis, University of Chicago.

Fama, Eugene F. (1998): Market Efficiency, Long-Term Returns, and Behavioral Finance, in: Journal of Financial Economics, Vol. 49, 283-306.

Fama, Eugene F./ Fisher, Lawrence/ Jensen, Michael C./ Roll, Richard (1969): The Adjustment of Stock Prices to New Information, in: International Economic Review, Vol. 10, 1-21.

Fama, Eugene F./ French, Kenneth R. (1992): The Cross-Section of Expected Stock Returns, in: Journal of Finance, Vol. 47, 427-465.

Fama, Eugene F./ French, Kenneth R. (1993): Common Risk Factors in the Returns on Bonds and Stocks, in: Journal of Financial Economics, Vol. 33, 3-56.

Fama, Eugene F./ French, Kenneth R. (1995): Size and Book-to-Market Factors in Earnings and Returns, in: Journal of Finance, Vol. 50, 131-155.

Fowler, David J./ Rorke, Harvey C. (1983): Risk Measurement When Shares Are Subject To Infrequent Trading: Comment, in: Journal of Financial Economics, Vol. 12, 279-283.

Gajewski, Jean-Francois/ Ginglinger, Edith/ Lasfer, Ameziane M. (2003): Why Do Companies Include Warrants in SEOs: The Case of French Unit Offerings, Working Paper, Cass Business School.

Ganshaw, Trevor/ Dillon, Derek (2000): Convertible Securities: A Toolbox of Flexible Financial Instruments for Corporate Issuers, in: Journal of Applied Corporate Finance, Vol. 13, 22-30.

Gebhardt, Günther/ Entrup, Ulrich (1993): Kapitalmarktreaktionen auf Optionsanleihen, in: Zeitschrift für betriebswirtschaftliche Forschung, Special edition 31, 1-22.

Gentry, William/ Schizer, David (2002): Frictions and Tax-Motivated Hedging: An Empirical Exploration of Publicly-Traded Exchangeable Debt, in: Journal of Law and Policy, Vol. 13, 9-74.

Ghosh, Chinmoy/ Varma, Raj/ Woolridge, Randall J. (1990): An Analysis of Exchangeable Debt Offers, in: Journal of Financial Economics, Vol. 28, 251-263.

Gompers, Paul A./ Lerner, Josh (2003): The Really Long-Run Performance of Initial Public Offerings: The Pre-Nasdaq Evidence, in: Journal of Finance, Vol. 58, 1355-1392.

Graham, John R./ Harvey, Campbell R. (2001): The Theory and Practice of Corporate Finance: Evidence from the Field, in: Journal of Financial Economics, Vol. 60, 187-243.

Green, Richard C. (1984): Investment Incentives, Debt, and Warrants, in: Journal of Financial Economics, Vol. 13, 115-136.

Hansen, Robert S./ Crutchley, Claire (1990): Corporate Earnings and Financings: An Empirical Analysis, in: Journal of Business, Vol. 63, 347-371.

Harris, Milton/ Raviv, Artur (1991): The Theory of Capital Structure, in: Journal of Finance, Vol. 46, 297-355.

Healy, Paul M./ Palepu, Krishna G. (1990): Earnings and Risk Changes Surrounding Primary Stock Offers, in: Journal of Accounting Research, Vol. 28, 25-48.

Heckman, James J. (1979): Sample Selection Bias as a Specification Error, in: Econometrica, Vol. 47, 153-161.

Hillion, Pierre/ Vermaelen, Theo (2004): Death Spiral Convertibles, in: Journal of Financial Economics, Vol. 71, 381-415.

Holderness, Clifford G./ Sheehan, Dennis P. (1985): Raiders or Saviors: The Evidence on Six Controversial Investors, in: Journal of Financial Economics, Vol. 14, 555-579.

Holderness, Clifford G./ Sheehan, Dennis P. (1987): The Role of Majority Shareholders in Publicly Held Corporations: An Exploratory Analysis, in: Journal of Financial Economics, Vol. 20, 317-346.

Hovakimian, Armen/ Hovakimian, Gayané/ Theranian, Hassan (2004): Determinants of Target Capital Structure: The Case of Dual Debt and Equity Issues, in: Journal of Financial Economics, Vol. 71, 517-540.

Hovakimian, Armen/ Opler, Tim/ Titman, Sheridan (2001): The Debt-Equity Choice, in: Journal of Financial and Quantitative Analysis, Vol. 36, 1-24.

How, Janice C. Y./ Howe, John S. (2001): Warrants in Initial Public Offerings: Empirical Evidence, in: Journal of Business, Vol. 74, 433-457.

Ikenberry, David/ Lakonishok, Joseph/ Vermaelen, Theo (1995): Market Underreaction to Open Market Share Repurchases, in: Journal of Financial Economics, Vol. 39, 181-208.

Jensen, Michael C. (1986): Agency Costs of Free Cash Flow, Corporate Finance, and Takeovers, in: American Economic Review, Vol. 76, 323-329.

Jensen, Michael C./ Meckling, William (1976): Theory of the Firm: Managerial Behaviour, Agency Costs, and Capital Structure, in: Journal of Financial Economics, Vol. 3, 305-360.

Jung, Kooyul/ Kim, Yong-Cheol/ Stulz, Rene M. (1996): Timing, Investment Opportunities, Managerial Discretion, and the Security Issue Decision, in: Journal of Financial Economics, Vol. 42, 159-185.

Kahle, Kathleen M. (2000): Insider Trading and the Long-Run Performance of New Security Issues, in: Journal of Corporate Finance, Vol. 1, 25-53.

Kaiser, Kevin M./ Stouraitis, Aris (2001): Agency Costs and Strategic Considerations Behind Sell-Offs: The UK Evidence, in: European Financial Management, Vol. 7, 319-349.

Kang, Jun-Koo/ Lee, Yul W. (1996): The Pricing of Convertible Debt Offerings, in: Journal of Financial Economics, Vol. 41, 231-248.

Karpoff, Jonathan M./ Lee, Daniel (1991): Insider Trading Before New Issue Announcements, in: Financial Management, Vol. 20, 18-26.

Kleidt, Benjamin/ Scharmer, Eckhard/ Schiereck, Dirk (2005): Desinvestition von Aktienpaketen - Eine Analyse von Exchangeable Bonds, Working Paper, European Business School.

Kleidt, Benjamin/ Schiereck, Dirk (2004): Mandatory Convertibles, in: Zeitschrift für Bank- und Kapitalmarktrecht, Vol. 4, 18-21.

Kleidt, Benjamin/ Schiereck, Dirk (2005a): A Note on Risk Changes Around Convertible Debt Issues, Working Paper, European Business School.

Kleidt, Benjamin/ Schiereck, Dirk (2005b): Why Firms Issue Convertible Debt - Evidence on Market Timing and Investor Rationing, Working Paper, European Business School.

Kleidt, Benjamin/ Schiereck, Dirk/ Dziarski, Stefan (2005): The Concurrent Offerings Puzzle, Working Paper, European Business School.

Korajczyk, Robert A./ Lucas, Deborah J./ McDonald, Robert L. (1991): The Effect of Information Releases on the Pricing and Timing of Equity Issues, in: Review of Financial Studies, Vol. 4, 685-708.

Korajczyk, Robert A./ Lucas, Deborah J./ McDonald, Robert L. (1992): Equity Issues with Time-Varying Asymmetric Information, in: Journal of Financial and Quantitative Analysis, Vol. 27, 397-417.

Kothari, S. P./ Warner, Jerold B. (1997): Measuring Long-Horizon Security Price Performance, in: Journal of Financial Economics, Vol. 43, 301-339.

Koziol, Christian/ Sauerbier, Peter (2003): Pflichtwandelanleihen: Einsatzmotive, Aktienkursreaktion und Bewertung, in: Die Betriebswirtschaft, Vol. 65, 21-42.

Krasker, William (1986): Stock Price Movements in Response to Stock Issues Under Asymmetric Information, in: Journal of Finance, Vol. 41, 93-105.

Lee, Hei Wai/ Figlewicz, Raymond E. (1999): Characteristics of Firms that Issue Convertible Debt Versus Convertible Preferred Stock, in: Quarterly Review of Economics and Finance, Vol. 39, 547-563.

Lee, Inmoo (1997): Do Managers Knowingly Sell Overvalued Equity?, in: Journal of Finance, Vol. 50, 23-51.

Lee, Inmoo/ Lochhead, Scott/ Ritter, Jay R./ Zhao, Quanshui (1996): The Costs of Raising Capital, in: Journal of Financial Research, Vol. 19, 59-74.

Lee, Inmoo/ Loughran, Tim (1998): Performance Following Convertible Bond Issuance, in: Journal of Corporate Finance, Vol. 4, 185-207.

Lee, Lung-Fei (1983): Generalized Econometric Models With Selectivity, in: Econometrica, Vol. 51, 507-513.

Lee, Martin/ Lee, Philip/ Taylor, Stephen (2003): Unit Initial Public Offerings: Staged Equity or Signaling Mechanism?, in: Accounting and Finance, Vol. 43, 63-85.

Leland, Hayne E./ Pyle, David H. (1977): Informational Asymmetries, Financial Structure, and Financial Intermediation, in: Journal of Finance, Vol. 32, 371-387.

Lewis, Craig M./ Rogalski, Richard J./ Seward, James K. (1998): Agency Problems, Information Asymmetries, and Convertible Debt Security Design, in: Journal of Financial Intermediation, Vol. 7, 32-59.

Lewis, Craig M./ Rogalski, Richard J./ Seward, James K. (1999): Is Convertible Debt a Substitute for Straight Debt or for Common Equity?, in: Financial Management, Vol. 28, 5-27.

Lewis, Craig M./ Rogalski, Richard J./ Seward, James K. (2001): The Long-Run Performance of Firms That Issue Convertible Debt: An Empirical Analysis of Operating Characteristics and Analyst Forecasts, in: Journal of Corporate Finance, Vol. 7, 447-474.

Lewis, Craig M./ Rogalski, Richard J./ Seward, James K. (2002): Risk Changes Around Convertible Debt Offerings, in: Journal of Corporate Finance, Vol. 8, 67-80.

Lewis, Craig M./ Rogalski, Richard J./ Seward, James K. (2003): Industry Conditions, Growth Opportunities and Market Reactions to Convertible Debt Financing Decisions, in: Journal of Banking and Finance, Vol. 27, 153-181.

Loughran, Tim/ Ritter, Jay R. (1995): The New Issues Puzzle, in: Journal of Finance, Vol. 50, 23-51.

Loughran, Tim/ Ritter, Jay R. (1997): The Operating Performance of Firms Conducting Seasoned Equity Offerings, in: Journal of Finance, Vol. 52, 1823-1850.

Loughran, Tim/ Ritter, Jay R. (2000): Uniformly Least Powerful Tests of Market Efficiency, in: Journal of Financial Economics, Vol. 55, 361-389.

Lucas, Deborah J./ McDonald, Robert L. (1990): Equity Issues and Stock Price Dynamics, in: Journal of Finance, Vol. 45, 1019-1043.

Lyon, John D./ Barber, Brad M./ Tsai, Chih-Ling (1999): Improved Methods for Tests of Long-Run Abnormal Stock Returns, in: Journal of Finance, Vol. 54, 165-201.

MacKinlay, Craig A. (1997): Event Studies in Economics and Finance, in: Journal of Economic Literature, Vol. 35, 13-39.

Mann, Steven V./ Moore, William T./ Ramanlal, Pradipkumar (1999): Timing of Convertible Debt Issues, in: Journal of Business Research, Vol. 45, 101-105.

Marsh, Paul (1982): The Choice Between Equity and Debt: An Empirical Study, in: Journal of Finance, Vol. 37, 121-144.

Masulis, Ronald W. (1980): The Effects of Capital Structure Change on Security Prices: A Study of Exchange Offers, in: Journal of Financial Economics, Vol. 8, 139-177.

Mayers, David (1998): Why Firms Issue Convertible Bonds: The Matching of Financial and Real Investment Options, in: Journal of Financial Economics, Vol. 47, 83-102.

McLaughlin, Robyn M./ Safieddine, Assem/ Vasudevan, Gopala K. (1998): The Long-Run Performance of Convertible Debt Issuers, in: Journal of Financial Research, Vol. 21, 373-388.

McLaughlin, Robyn/ Safieddine, Assem/ Vasudevan, Gopala K. (1996): The Operating Performance of Seasoned Equity Issuers: Free Cash Flow and Post-Issue Performance, in: Financial Management, Vol. 25, 41-53.

Mikkelson, Wayne H./ Partch, Megan M. (1985): Stock Price Effects and Costs of Secondary Distributions, in: Journal of Financial Economics, Vol. 14, 165-194.

Mikkelson, Wayne H./ Partch, Megan M. (1986): Valuation Effects of Security Offerings and the Issuance Process, in: Journal of Financial Economics, Vol. 15, 31-60.

Mikkelson, Wayne H./ Ruback, Richard S. (1985): An Empirical Analysis of the Interfirm Equity Investment Process, in: Journal of Financial Economics, Vol. 14, 523-553.

Mikkelson, Wayne H./ Ruback, Richard S. (1991): Targeted Repurchases and Common Stock Returns, in: Rand Journal of Economics, Vol. 22, 544-562.

Miller, Merton H. (1988): The Modigliani-Miller Proposition After Thirty Years, in: Journal of Economic Perspectives, Vol. 2, 99-120.

Miller, Merton H./ Rock, Kevin (1985): Dividend Policy under Asymmetric Information, in: Journal of Finance, Vol. 40, 1031-1051.

Mitchell, Mark L./ Stafford, Erik (2000): Managerial Decisions and Long-Term Stock Price Performance, in: Journal of Business, Vol. 73, 287-329.

Modigliani, Franco (1988): MM - Past, Present, and Future, in: Journal of Economic Perspectives, Vol. 2, 149-158.

Modigliani, Franco/ Miller, Merton H. (1958): The Cost of Capital, Corporation Finance and the Theory of Investment, in: American Economic Review, Vol. 48, 261-297.

Müller-Trimbusch, Jobst (1999): High-Yield Anleihen – Perspektiven für die Risikofinanzierung deutscher Unternehmen, Deutscher Universitätsverlag, Wiesbaden.

Myers, Stewart C. (2001): Capital Structure, in: Journal of Economic Perspectives, Vol. 15, 81-102.

Myers, Stewart C./ Majluf, Nicholas S. (1984): Corporate Financing and Investment Decisions When Firms Have Information That Investors Do Not Have, in: Journal of Financial Economics, Vol. 13, 187-221.

Nagelkerke, N. J. D. (1991): A Note on a General Definition of the Coefficient of Determination, in: Biometrika, Vol. 78, 691-692.

Pinegar, Michael J./ Lease, Ronald C. (1986): The Impact of Preferred-for-Common Exchange Offers on Firm Value, in: Journal of Finance, Vol. 41, 795-814.

Pound, John (1988): Proxy Contests and the Efficiency of Shareholder Oversight, in: Journal of Financial Economics, Vol. 20, 237-265.

Purnanandam, Amiyatosh K./ Bhaskaran, Swaminathan (2004): Are IPOs Really Underpriced?, in: Review of Financial Studies, Vol. 17, 811-848.

Rangan, Srinivasan (1998): Earnings Management and the Performance of Seasoned Equity Offerings, in: Journal of Financial Economics, Vol. 50, 101-122.

Reilly, Frank K./ Brown, Keith C. (2003): Investment Analysis & Portfolio Management, 7th Edition, South-Western - Thomson Learning, Mason.

Ross, Stephen A. (1977): The Determination of Financial Structure: The Incentive-Signalling Approach, in: Bell Journal of Economics, Vol. 8, 23-40.

Ross, Stephen A./ Westerfield, Randolph W./ Jaffe, Jeffrey (2002): Corporate Finance, 6th edition, McGraw-Hill, New York.

Schäfer, Henry (2002): Renaissance der Wandelanleihen, in: Finanz-Betrieb, Vol. 9, 514-524.

Schipper, Katherine/ Smith, Abbie (1986): A Comparison of Equity Carve-Outs and Seasoned Equity Offerings: Share Price Effects and Corporate Restructuring, in: Journal of Financial Economics, Vol. 15, 3-29.

Schmid Klein, Linda/ O'Brien, Thomas J./ Peters, Stephen R. (2002): Debt vs. Equity and Asymmetric Information: A Review, in: Financial Review, Vol. 37, 317-350.

Scholes, Myron S./ Williams, Joseph (1977): Estimating Betas from Nonsynchronous Data, in: Journal of Financial Economics, Vol. 5, 309-327.

Schultz, Paul (1993): Unit Initial Public Offerings: A Form of Staged Financing, in: Journal of Financial Economics, Vol. 34, 199-229.

Schultz, Paul (2003): Pseudo Market Timing, and the Long-Run Underperformance of IPOs, in: Journal of Finance, Vol. 58, 483-518.

Shleifer, Andrei/ Vishny, Robert W. (1986): Large Shareholders and Corporate Control, in: Journal of Political Economy, Vol. 94, 461-488.

Shyam-Sunder, Lakshmi/ Myers, Stewart C. (1999): Testing Static Trade-Off against Pecking Order Models of Capital Structure, in: Journal of Financial Economics, Vol. 51, 219-244.

Slovin, Myron B./ Sushka, Marie E./ Ferraro, Steven R. (1995): A Comparison of the Information Conveyed by Equity Carve-Outs, Spin-Offs, and Asset Sell-Offs, in: Journal of Financial Economics, Vol. 37, 89-104.

Spiess, D. Katherine/ Affleck-Graves, John (1999): The Long-Run Performance of Stock Returns Following Debt Offerings, in: Journal of Financial Economics, Vol. 54, 45-73.

Spiess, Katherine D./ Affleck-Graves, John (1995): Underperformance in Long-Run Stock Returns Following Seasoned Equity Offerings, in: Journal of Financial Economics, Vol. 38, 243-267.

Stein, Jeremy C. (1992): Convertible Bonds as Backdoor Equity Financing, in: Journal of Financial Economics, Vol. 32, 3-21.

Stein, Jeremy C. (1996): Rational Capital Budgeting in an Irrational World, in: Journal of Business, Vol. 69, 429-455.

Stienemann, Marc (2003): Wertsteigerung durch Desinvestitionen bei großen deutschen Konzernen, Cuvillier Verlag, Göttingen.

Stiglitz, Joseph E./ Weiss, Andrew (1981): Credit Rationing in Markets with Imperfect Information, in: American Economic Review, Vol. 71, 393-410.

Strong, Norman (1992): Modelling Abnormal Returns: A Review Article, in: Journal of Business Finance and Accounting, Vol. 19, 533-553.

Teoh, Siew Hong/ Welch, Ivo/ Wong, T. J. (1998): Earnings Management and the Underperformance of Seasoned Equity Offerings, in: Journal of Financial Economics, Vol. 50, 63-99.

Veld, Chris/ Veld-Markoulova, Yulia V. (2004): Do Spin-Offs Really Create Value? The European Case, in: Journal of Banking and Finance, Vol. 28, 1111-1135.

Vijh, Anand M. (2002): The Positive Announcement-Period Returns of Equity Carve-Outs: Asymmetric Information or Divesture Gains?, in: Journal of Business, Vol. 75, 153-190.

Villalonga, Belén (2004): Does Diversification Cause the "Diversification Discount"?, in: Financial Management, Vol. 33, 5-27.

Wheatley, Clark M./ Brown, Robert M./ Johnson, George A. (1997): Accounting Disclosure and Valuation Revisions Around Voluntary Corporate Spin-Offs, Working Paper, Florida International University.

White, Halbert (1980): A Heteroskedasticity-Consistent Covariance Matrix and a Direct Test for Heteroskedasticity, in: Econometrica, Vol. 48, 817-838.

White Huckins, Nancy (1999): An Examination of Mandatorily Convertible Preferred Stock, in: Financial Review, Vol. 34, 89-108.

Woodson, Hart (2002): Global Convertible Investing - The Gabelli Way, John Wiley & Sons, New York.

Wruck, Karen Hopper (1989): Equity Ownership Concentration and Firm Value: Evidence from Private Equity Financings, in: Journal of Financial Economics, Vol. 23, 3-28.

MIX
Papier aus verantwortungsvollen Quellen
Paper from responsible sources
FSC® C105338

If you have any concerns about our products,
you can contact us on
ProductSafety@springernature.com

In case Publisher is established outside the EU,
the EU authorized representative is:
Springer Nature Customer Service Center GmbH
Europaplatz 3, 69115 Heidelberg, Germany

Printed by Libri Plureos GmbH
in Hamburg, Germany